Joel Cook

**A Holiday Tour in Europe**

Joel Cook

**A Holiday Tour in Europe**

ISBN/EAN: 9783337292249

Printed in Europe, USA, Canada, Australia, Japan

Cover: Foto ©Andreas Hilbeck / pixelio.de

More available books at **www.hansebooks.com**

# A HOLIDAY TOUR

# IN EUROPE.

JOEL COOK

NEW EDITION WITH ILLUSTRATIONS.

PHILADELPHIA:
DAVID McKAY, PUBLISHER,
23 South Ninth Street.
1889.

# INTRODUCTION.

WHEN the writer of this collected series of letters started on his "Holiday Tour," he had no thought of making a book, or of contributing any materials for a book. It happened, however, he being a trained journalist, with quickened faculty of observation, that, before passing out from the Capes of the Delaware, he had seen along the River and Bay that which he believed to be important to make publicly known in behalf of the material interests of the people of Philadelphia, and so the first letter of the series came to the *Public Ledger* office through the hands of the pilot. Next from Liverpool came the second letter, describing the voyage on the Ohio, one of the splendid steamships of the American Line, which ships the writer deemed to be worthy of every medium for more intimate introduction to the American public. Then began the three months of the European part of the "Holiday Tour," through England, Wales, Ireland, Scotland, France, Belgium, Rhenish Germany, Switzerland, and back through France, England, and Ireland, the letters prompting themselves as the writer passed along, until they expanded into the series now so familiar to the great constituency of the *Public Ledger*.

The collection and publication of the letters in book-form is the result of influences wholly outside of their author. While they were in course of publication, expressions of pleasure caused by the perusal of them were frequent and emphatic from readers of the *Public Ledger* in all stations in life,—not only from those who had never travelled in Europe, but from tourists who had gone over precisely the same ground, and who found a keen renewal of their satisfaction in the "Holiday Tour." This was natural, for the letters were far away removed from any hackneyed or conventional style, being sprightly, bright, and graphic descriptions of scenes, incidents, places, and other subjects of observation that had been seen by tens of thousands of other tourists, and written about by scores and hundreds, but which now had a fresh and attractive coloring thrown over them by these letters. Expressions of satisfaction were followed by numerous requests for back numbers, and when these could no longer be filled, there came requests for their publication in collected form. Hence the book.

The letters thus favorably received were written by Mr. Joel Cook, one of the editors of the *Public Ledger;* they are republished, with the concurrence of Mr. Childs, in compliance with the suggestions already mentioned, and the undersigned is glad of the opportunity to add his testimony as above written.

W. V. McKEAN, *Managing Editor.*

PUBLIC LEDGER OFFICE, PHILADELPHIA,

# CONTENTS.

| LETTER | | PAGE |
|---|---|---|
| I. | The Departure | 9 |
| II. | The Ocean Voyage—Neptune's Welcome | 9 |
| III. | The American Steamship Line | 14 |
| IV. | A Sunday at Sea—The British Squadron | 20 |
| V. | Ireland and Liverpool | 23 |
| VI. | The Ancient City of Chester | 29 |
| VII. | Chester to Holyhead | 32 |
| VIII. | Dublin—Brown Stout and the Phœnix | 37 |
| IX. | Crossing Boyne Water—Belfast—Linen | 42 |
| X. | The Giant's Causeway | 48 |
| XI. | The Clyde and Glasgow | 55 |
| XII. | The Highlands—The Pass of Glencoe | 60 |
| XIII. | Edinburgh and Rosslin | 66 |
| XIV. | Crossing the Border—York | 74 |
| XV. | Scarborough | 81 |
| XVI. | Haddon Hall and Chatsworth | 83 |
| XVII. | Warwick, Kenilworth, and Stratford-on-Avon | 89 |
| XVIII. | A Sunday in London—St. Paul's, and Westminster Abbey | 94 |
| XIX. | London—The Underground Railway | 100 |
| XX. | London Sketches—Cleopatra's Needle—The Bank of England—The Times Office | 105 |
| XXI. | London Taxation—The Old-Clothes Market | 113 |
| XXII. | London—The American Minister—Popular Recreation | 117 |
| XXIII. | Some English Impressions | 122 |
| XXIV. | Brighton — England's Great Watering-Place — The Brighton Aquarium | 129 |
| XXV. | Crossing the Channel | 134 |
| XXVI. | Some Parisian Impressions | 141 |
| XXVII. | A Sunday in Paris—Versailles | 147 |
| XXVIII. | Paris—A French Cemetery—Père la Chaise | 152 |

# LIST OF ILLUSTRATIONS.

|  | PAGE |
|---|---|
| DRACHENFELS | *Frontispiece.* |
| CHESTER CATHEDRAL AND CITY WALL | 31 |
| GIANTS' CAUSEWAY | 48 |
| GLASGOW | 58 |
| EDINBURGH CASTLE | 67 |
| HOLYROOD AND BURNS'S MONUMENT | 70 |
| DURHAM CATHEDRAL | 76 |
| HADDON HALL | 84 |
| CHATSWORTH | 88 |
| WESTMINSTER | 96 |
| LONDON BRIDGE | 101 |
| SOUTH KENSINGTON MUSEUM | 119 |
| PARIS AND THE SEVEN BRIDGES | 141 |
| PALAIS ROYAL GARDEN | 176 |
| RHEINFELS | 201 |
| SHATTERED TOWER OF HEIDELBERG | 205 |
| ST. THOMAS CHURCH, STRASSBURG | 216 |
| FALLS OF GEISBACH | 229 |
| FREIBURG CATHEDRAL | 240 |
| NOTRE DAME, WEST FRONT | 276 |
| CANTERBURY CATHEDRAL | 280 |

# A HOLIDAY TOUR.

## LETTER I.

#### THE DEPARTURE.

DELAWARE BREAKWATER, Friday, July 12.

The misfortunes that envelop an ocean voyage when fog prevails have come down like a pall over the company who sailed on the American line steamer Ohio from Philadelphia, on Thursday morning, July 11. Dense fog met us in Delaware Bay, and compelled anchorage during the night. With a steamer of the length and draught of the Ohio, navigation in a channel crowded with vessels like the path up and down the bay is extremely difficult at all times, and is dangerous, and, in fact, impossible, if safety is at all considered, during fog. What we should have met on the Banks of Newfoundland came to us below Newcastle. We passed the Cape May steamboat Republic, her passengers crowding every available spot for observation to give us a hearty send-off,—she going up to the city,—and then the fog came down over us and stopped the voyage. We have spent twenty-four hours in the bay. I do not write this, which, through the courtesy of the pilot, I am able to send you, as any matter of news, however, for fogs have enveloped our entire seaboard for weeks.

## LETTER II.

#### THE OCEAN VOYAGE.

ON BOARD AMERICAN LINE STEAMER OHIO, July 15.

The Five-Fathom Bank Light-ship off the entrance to Delaware Bay is one of the most important beacons on the coast. It is the earliest guide to the mariner seeking the

Delaware Breakwater, who comes across the ocean, and, in fact, is the beacon sought by the greater part of our Philadelphia foreign commerce. The dark ship, with its two huge globes, elevated on the masts, rocks up and down on the waves, and in thick weather the deep sound of the fog-siren, worked by steam-power, comes over the water, a warning to the shipmaster of the beacon he cannot see. The siren saluted the Ohio as she passed within a few hundred feet; the steamer answered; and thus we bade good-by to America and began the transatlantic journey. Cape May was too far off to see more than the dim outline of the light-house and the huge hotels, like little hazy specks along the shore; and in a few moments the land had all disappeared, as the steamer rapidly left it on her eastern journey.

## NEPTUNE'S WELCOME.

It is a curious physical fact, noticed by most landsmen who venture upon sea-voyages, that no matter how pleasantly the journey begins, or how keen the enjoyment, as land recedes the spirits sink and the interest wanes. The sea, which is at first charming as it rocks you in its cradle, gradually changes to an object of aversion, and then of disgust. There seems to be a difference of opinion arising between the ship and the traveller. One wants to be quiet and the other don't. The ship persists in a very bad habit of rolling about, and all the efforts of the traveller—his bracing up and holding on, and stretching out and doubling in—will not keep her quiet. At first there is an effort to keep the ship down, but it fails; and then there is an effort to keep the stomach down, and it fails. Then one loses all his reverence for the sea, and as he pays the inexorable tribute to Neptune he wishes that either he had never been born, or else had had good sense enough to stay home with his mother. Then comes a season of profound indifference to the beauties of the ocean and of positive hatred of victuals. Food is not only distasteful, but one does not want to see or smell it, or even have it talked about. In fact, one regards as his deadliest enemy the steward who will rattle the dishes and glasses, and thus from afar off recall the horrid idea of eating. Strange, what a metamorphosis. A few hours before, the first duty of the passenger was to get even with the steamship company by eating everything in the larder,—

but the steamship company has conquered. With shrewd business management, they had calculated all this when laying in supplies. Next comes the desire to hide away in corners, and to vanish from society; to cease shining as a social light and a conversational prince; in short, to go to bed,—and not to be particular about what bed, whether a sofa, berth, or even a plank. Then comes oblivion,—a period of self-abnegation and forgetfulness,—the only consciousness being of a very, very weak stomach. Thus pass hours, when the patient becomes aware of a vague returning interest in the world's affairs. He thinks that possibly he may at some time in the dim future become once more a useful citizen. Next is the stage of tea and toast, of gruel and good advice,—of gruel that will not stay in the stomach, and good advice that will not stay in the mind. Every one advises what is best to do or to take,—principally the latter. The prescriptions are as varied as they are numerous. In fact, you are told to take everything, from salt mackerel up or down the bill of fare, from soup at one end to toothpicks at the other; and to drink the entire wine list. Mankind are all born doctors when it comes to telling others how to cure their ills. The stage of advice over, the patient crawls out into the world again and appears on deck, surrounded by others who have been there, and a languid interest begins to be taken in what is going on—excepting the dinner-gong. Gradually this interest increases, until, amazing as it may seem, you actually muster up courage, in an unguarded moment, to look down a skylight at the table. Thus the Rubicon is passed, and as man is always progressing to higher and better and more complete knowledge, so in this case, the look creates the appetite, and the next thing is to boldly march to the task, snap fingers at old Neptune, and win the battle. Then rattle plates and glasses as you please, O steward, they have no more terrors for me. The stomach has become an aching void, a yawning chasm that the bill of fare is incompetent to fill. The solicitude is no longer lest food should come in sight: it is now to devise the most expeditious ways and means of putting it out of sight. The conflict with the steamship company recommences, and the pleasant labor of getting even with the larder begins with the rising of the sun, but by no means stops with the going down of the same. Then you poke fun at fellow-sufferers not so well advanced in convalescence; but if any one should ask, "Have you been sea-sick?" the answer will be, "Oh, my, no; never felt better in my life." How quickly we forget our ills!

## ON THE SEA.

It would be difficult to devise a method of obtaining more perfect rest than a sea-voyage. As the best rest is always to do just the opposite of what is the ordinary occupation, so the sea-voyage accomplishes this by being the complete antithesis of what happens on land. You cannot do anything if you would. There is no space to do it. Your abiding-place is a room six feet square, with berths on one side and a sofa on the other. Your companion has to go outside to give you a chance to dress. There is possibly a hundred feet or so of deck to walk on, but it is so unsteady that your reputation as a temperance man suffers the moment a promenade is attempted. The ship will roll and pitch and bump the passengers about, and necessitate gyrations that would do credit to an acrobat. When meal-time comes there is always an extra roll provided, —not of the French or Vienna bread, but the kind that brings dishes, soup, and the greater part of your dinner running down-hill into your lap, and then over the other side to your opposite neighbor. First one way, then the other, you and all about you are continually sliding down-hill; and the captain, with that bland smile which so greatly reassures you, says he never saw it smoother in his life. Half the passengers declare that there is a big, heavy box somewhere forward, rolled from one side to the other, to make the ship rock and keep passengers away from the table. But after awhile the "sea legs" are got on, and this rolling is not so noticeable, though it is a bad habit the vessel has, which she keeps up more or less all the sea over.

The chief thing done, however, on board ship is—nothing. The ten days' passage to Europe is the most complete exemplification it is possible to give of the meaning of that vulgar but expressive American word—loafing. The voyage is a prolonged and enforced idleness, varied by sea-sickness at the start and a growing anxiety for something to do as the goal approaches. The gong sounding for meals is the great event of the day, —it promises something to do. A passing vessel is a wonderful thing. All eyes watch her; all tongues guess her name, destination, and rig; dispute about her distance; and await with breathless interest the result of the signals. And when she is spoken and found to be the schooner Rappahannock, of Philadelphia, twenty days out, with hopes of being sold to the Russians for a privateer, or the Mary Jane, of Tuckahoe, laden with hoop-poles, all the passengers are happy. Then the Banks of Newfoundland are another subject of deep interest, most people supposing them to be dry land, and some willing, in the dire monotony of the voyage, to wager they are that or anything else, so that an interest is gotten up in something. The gulls and Mother Carey's chickens, porpoises and flying-fish, and occasionally a whale, also are subjects of earnest study. Some of the passengers help the captain sail the ship; others try to imitate the boatswain's whistle; others play games. We have some Philadelphians aboard who for fourteen years past have been steadily playing euchre, never changing partners, and have on this ship, according to the official record they keep, played their twenty-eight-thousandth game. Here is also a study for the ennuied passenger, that these four gentlemen, since 1864, in all the ups and downs of American life, have continued their games through weal and woe, with no break in their circle; no cheating at cards, and are now continuing them with a vim that even sea-sickness cannot shake. Then the dozen or so doctors we have on board as passengers discuss the 'pathies, and astonish the laymen by taking each other's prescriptions. Thus the voyage goes on, dreary in fog and storm, when all things are wet and cheerless; pleasant on the bright days, when all hands get up on deck, and the ladies recline in steamer chairs and sup their chicken broth, and the men watch the heaving of the log, and discuss the distance travelled, and the position of the ship, and the probable length of the voyage, or the proximity of icebergs. The passage is carefully scanned on the chart, which hangs in the companion-way, and occasionally an impatient voyager is told that we are within two or three miles of land, and upon asking where, is significantly pointed downward,—the nearest land being the bottom of the sea. And thus we go on, setting our watches a half-hour ahead every twenty-four hours, taking our four or five meals a day, with chicken broth on deck between meals,—and the children, of whom there are four in the cabin, run about to be petted by the passengers and sailors, and

2

beg oranges of the steward. But like Columbus, we are on the constant lookout for the approaching land, and will be glad indeed to hear the sailor's welcome cry announcing it. This is the experience of millions of transatlantic voyagers who have gone over the great ferry during all these years, and whose wonder is, that with all the vessels constantly passing between England and America, it is still possible for you to steam along for days together without seeing a single sail. With monotonous thump the screw goes on regularly, revolving day and night, making its thirty revolutions a minute, driving the great ship forward, and boring a gimlet-hole for three thousand miles through the Atlantic. The officer walks the bridge, peering over the sea, watching the compass and the lookout, and giving an occasional direction to the obedient seamen. The lookout stands at the bow, holding on to a brace, intently gazing out ahead, whilst the wind blows hard enough to sweep him off the forecastle. The steersmen hold the wheel, whilst the waves dash against the rudder and shake and rattle the chains. The ponderous machinery moves quickly, and away down in the hold the perspiring firemen and coal-passers keep pouring in the fuel, which comes up through the huge funnel in dense clouds of smoke, that lie in a long, black, narrow line of dark haze for miles over the sea in the wake of the vessel. But the harder the wind blows the brighter it makes the fires burn, and the easier is steam raised, so that it drives the steamer the quicker on her journey. Thus we go on, the machinery singing a lullaby at night, whilst the sea rocks us to sleep, and all hands trusting to the Divine Creator of the vast deep to take us safely across it.

## LETTER III.

### THE AMERICAN STEAMSHIP LINE.

ON BOARD AMERICAN LINE STEAMER OHIO, AT SEA, July 20.

We passed a ship the other day bound to America. She had every sail set. We saluted. She ran up the British Union Jack, for she was an English vessel. We ran up the

American flag. That flag is a scarce article in ocean commerce, but it is seen sometimes, and it was a proud thing to know that Philadelphia has raised it over as fine a fleet of steamers as cross the Atlantic, even if it is a rare sight to the sailor. This circumstance prompted the thought that possibly, if Americans were true to themselves, not only would our one American line increase in prosperity, but the lines themselves would multiply. The chief freight traffic across the Atlantic is carrying grain and provisions eastward to Europe. The vessels, both steam and sail, go with full cargoes, and the shipment is mainly controlled by Americans. Many a vessel comes out to America in ballast to get a return cargo that will pay the expenses of both voyages and give a profit besides. The greater part of this freight is through traffic shipped from the West on through bills of lading, and controlled as to its transatlantic carriers to a large extent by trunk railway influences. The railways can, if they wish, put much of this on board American vessels; and, in fact, they do so, and would do more were it not, as I have said before, that American vessels had become a scarce article on the ocean. West-bound freight is scarce, difficult to get, and in fact but partial cargoes are obtainable at any time, whilst many vessels come out to America without any cargo yielding freight. All the western-bound ships we have passed have been light, possibly only carrying ballast. The freighting that pays, it will thus be seen, goes from America, and can be to a great extent controlled as to its ocean carrier by Americans. On a steamship line the chief profit, excepting in special cases, is in the freight.

The passenger traffic across the ocean that pays the largest relative profit is in the steerage. Whilst it costs probably one dollar and a half per day to provide food for each cabin passenger, without calculating the extra cost of cooking and attendance, table-furnishing, cabin-space, etc., it will take not over one-fourth of that sum to feed a steerage passenger, where there are little or no extras that cost. Yet, whilst the cabin passengers—taking all classes, adults and children, and all rates of fare together—will average probably sixty-nine dollars income apiece to the vessel, the steerage will average twenty-three or twenty-four dollars apiece, which is one-third. Thus the relative profit is larger to begin with for the steerage, whilst it is increased the more by their closer stowage and the very slight cost of taking care of them. Locality to a great extent controls steerage travel both ways across the ocean, the passenger seeking the most convenient port, so as to save expense. But there is much of it controlled through agents operating for various lines, especially from inland points. Emigration of large communities is directed in this way, and there has been much competition in Europe to thus attract traffic for the various lines. For some time past the steerage travel to America, which a few years ago grew to large figures, had been declining, so that about an equal number of passengers were going each way; but latterly the movement towards America has considerably increased. The foreign element predominates in the steerage. In the cabin, however, the Americans are in the large majority. Englishmen, Frenchmen, and Germans travel for business; a few going for pleasure. The American, however, generally travels for pleasure, and as a race, comparatively speaking, the American probably furnishes proportionately more travellers than all other races put together. This is certainly the case on the Atlantic, and is probably the result of observation on all steamships sailing between the United States and Europe, whatever their flag. The statistics of the Cunard line show a large majority of Americans in the cabin, and the Inman, White Star, Anchor, and other lines will do likewise. I have heard competent judges estimate that this year, with the extra attraction of the Paris Exposition, three-fourths of the cabin passengers crossing the Atlantic will be Americans. Thus it will be seen that Americans in reality can, if they so desire, control the greater part of the transatlantic travel, both in freight and cabin passengers, and if they were animated by a proper spirit they could encourage not only one, but several American lines. A moderate estimate is made that over fifty thousand Americans are this year crossing the ocean, and paying the steamship lines four million dollars passage-money. What a magnificent subsidy this would be to American steamers, were there enough of them in existence to accommodate all the travel, and were the Americans paying it inclined to so spend it! Such a subsidy would be far better than any grudgingly given by Congress, and would enable American lines to raise their flags as numerously and as boldly as the Union Jack or the German tricolor. I think I have written enough to show that a good deal of the cause of the absence of American ships from the ocean lies with Americans themselves. If they put their own goods and trusted their own selves upon American vessels, there would be more of them afloat. They have it in their own power to create the demand that will again multiply American ships on the ocean, and enable ship-builders and steamer-owners to once more carry on business at a profit.

The American line itself enjoys a full share of the trade that is going All its steamers carry full cargoes eastward, and larger vessels and more of them could be filled, if they were available. As it is, outside steamers are chartered to accommodate the trade that the four American steamers cannot take. Of westward trade the American line gets a full share, and in fact carries more than average cargoes, compared with other lines when coming out to Philadelphia. It also has its full proportion of steerage travel, and the favorite ships, when sailing in the season, have full cabins. But there is still room for American encouragement, and particularly for Philadelphia encouragement, in the passenger lists of the line. Patriotism and local pride might, if exerted, give these steamers a fuller complement in the cabin, and thus encourage the building of others to increase the freight traffic, which they could easily get, if only in existence to receive it. There are on the Ohio some remarkable evidences of the work of patriotism, in making the passengers select the ship because it carries the American flag. The most of the passengers are Philadelphians, with a few Pennsylvanians; but with them the natural instinct directed the choice. We have, however, seven passengers who are not of this character, of whom two come from Canada, two from Baltimore, two from New York, and one from Springfield, Illinois. With these the principle of selection prevailed, and in some cases at the expense of their pockets. They wanted to cross the ocean on the American line. The two New Yorkers make no hesitation in avowing this intention, and one of them, a young gentleman from Fredonia, in probably the most remote part of New York State from Philadelphia, made his choice in spite of the persuasion of friends to take other lines, and his patriotic impulse makes him quite a lion on board. It is more of this impulse that is needed, and which, if exerted, would give the line an impetus that would make it not only an assured success, but might encourage its enlargement, and with this bring increased trade for Philadelphia.

It is a mistake, however, to suppose that Philadelphia unaided is able to support this line. In practice, whilst it furnishes a large share of the passengers, it provides very little of the freight. The metal importers of Philadelphia do very well in bringing out tin plates, etc., thus giving the ships west bound freight where it is most needed. But outside of this Philadelphia of itself does little. Chicago does better. The entire West does nobly. The greater part of the freight both ways is through traffic, which passes over the Pennsylvania Railroad. The ships are in fact an European extension of this great railroad, which stretches its arms so widely over the central portions of the United States. Both for produce going to Europe and dry goods and other articles bound to the West from Europe, the railroad and steamers together provide a line of communication unexcelled in its facilities. The terminal conveniences at Philadelphia, as is well known, excel those of any other transatlantic line. These advantages cheapen and increase traffic, and the Western shippers have found it out, so that they send the steamers actually more produce than they can carry to Europe, whilst the large houses in Chicago and elsewhere that deal in foreign goods find this the most expeditious and convenient mode of bringing them out. It may be considered that the American line, to the extent that it is able to carry goods, is the favorite freight route between the Western States and England. A similar remark may be made in reference to the Red Star line on the route between the West and the Continent.

There is a general supposition that the American line passages, on account of the greater length of the voyage, must necessarily be longer than those from New York. This, however, is not the case in any but exceptional instances. The American steamers can show as good average records as any crossing the ocean. Others may have made occasionally shorter passages; a few may be faster; but in the general statistics of transatlantic voyages the American steamers stand very high. Only a half-dozen out of a steamer fleet of over a hundred can do better, and the majority do a great deal worse. Some of these steamers have made very quick passages. The Ohio is now on her eighty-fifth transatlantic voyage. The eighty-four passages already made, according to Captain Morrison's record, show an average time between Queenstown and Cape Henlopen of ten days one hour and fifty-one minutes. This average is for all the voyages made, at all seasons and under all circumstances, winter and summer. Few steamers can show a better record. The relative distance between Sandy Hook and Ireland and Cape Henlopen and Ireland is against the latter voyage, but it is not so to any great extent. The shortest distance that can be made between Sandy Hook and Roche's Point (Queenstown entrance), by Cape Race, the direct route is 2772.3 nautical miles; whilst from Cape Henlopen to Roche's Point by the same route is 2848.5 miles, a difference in favor of Sandy Hook of 76.2 miles. By the usually-travelled route eastward, that crosses the 50th meridian of west longitude at the 42d parallel of north latitude, the distance between Sandy Hook and Roche's Point is 2875 miles; between Cape Henlopen and Roche's Point, 2944.5 miles, a difference in favor of Sandy Hook of 69.5 miles. The latter route from Cape Henlopen, it will be seen, is 76 miles longer than the former. These differences, while in favor of the Sandy Hook route, have not in the actual experience of the various voyages operated against the merits of the Philadelphia steamers. Their superior speed has made up for the somewhat greater distance. The passage through the Delaware River is the chief item in lengthening the voyage; and were the channel as thoroughly marked and dredged as it could be, this would be reduced to a minimum. The river and bay distance can be steamed over in six hours, but the difficulties of navigation and the large number of vessels always in the river frequently require reduced speed and great care. Abundant caution is, however, a rule of the line. With staunch steamers, well-officered and a thoroughly-competent ship's crew on each, the line has won its way into public favor, and has become a permanent American institution. It carries the American flag into Liverpool to appear there among the myriads of ensigns of all nations floating in the docks, and of its ships none is better or is more ably handled by its competent master, than is the Ohio by Captain Morrison.

## LETTER IV.

#### A SUNDAY AT SEA.

AMERICAN LINE STEAMER OHIO, AT SEA, July 21.

Sunday morning opened with the sea as smooth as a millpond, and the passengers were early on deck to enjoy the balmy air, and watch the passing vessels. All the sick had got well, and every one was on the lookout for the bold shores of Ireland, which we were approaching, but the land did not come in sight during the day. In the morning the captain made his regular daily inspection of the ship, and took me around with him. Accompanied by the chief steward, carrying the keys and a lantern to enlighten dark places, the captain made a minute inspection of all parts of the ship. This is the regular custom every morning, and the servants, standing in front of their respective departments, were on hand if reprimand for carelessness was necessary. But it was not needed. Everything was clean, bright, and attractive, showing evidence of the most scrupulous care and neatness. These careful daily examinations, and the fact that, in proportion to the number of passengers carried, the American steamers have a much larger relative number of servants, make these ships by far the cleanest that cross the Atlantic. Everything was in full operation at the time, and the cooks preparing for the noontide meal, but the neatness was as apparent as in the best-kept home in Philadelphia. Wholesale scrubbing and scouring and airing throughout the morning had secured the desired result, and did it every day the same. Down in the steerage-deck, forward in the forecastle, in the intermediate cabin, and in the myriads of little offices and apartments used for all sorts of purposes in these floating hotels, everything was as clean as in the main saloon. Nothing was overlooked in the inspection, and it gave an idea of the completeness of the ship's appointments in every respect such as could scarcely otherwise be obtained.

The inspection over, Divine service was held in the saloon. All of the steerage passengers who wished were brought in, and, with the cabin passengers, quite filled up the saloon. Ordinarily, in the absence of a clergyman, the captain conducts the service, but in this case he gave permission to a lady on board, bound to England on an evangelical mission, to do this. She conducted the service in accordance with the forms of the Methodist Church, making the prayers, singing the hymns, and preaching the sermon.

There were some things about this service which, to the hearers, made it probably one of the most remarkable that has ever occurred on a ship in the Atlantic Ocean. It was in two respects thoroughly typical of the great changes that have recently come over the American people. Mrs. Amanda Smith, who conducted it, is a colored woman, formerly a Maryland slave, and as I listened to her I could not help thinking of the change in American institutions that thus reversed the rule of a few years ago, and in the execution of the Civil Rights Bill not only permitted a negro woman to cross the ocean as a first-class passenger in the main saloon of an American steamer, but also allowed her to conduct religious service for the people on board. It is quite possible that such a thing has not yet occurred on any ship sailing under any other flag. But here, no clergyman being on board, she, in their absence, conducted the service, and thus made the Sunday at sea like a church-going Sunday on land. The ship's bells were tolled to summon the congregation, and for over an hour Mrs. Smith led the service, the passengers joining in the singing, and she preached a sermon full of sound sense, clothed in good language and illustrated with frequent appropriate similes, drawn from the scenes through which we had passed during the voyage. At the close the passengers, especially the ladies, crowded around and congratulated her. The deep faith and thorough religious zeal displayed; her versatile talents, developed evidently without much education; and her aptitude in drawing from what was occurring around her the lesson she wished to teach, were impressed on all. I do not believe there has heretofore been a case in which an emancipated slave-woman has conducted the religious service on a Sunday morning on any of our great transatlantic steamers.

## THE BRITISH SQUADRON.

In the afternoon the sky became overcast, frequent mists, with intervening sunshine, reminding us of the peculiarities of climate of the coasts we were approaching. Towards evening these mists disappeared, but clouds still obscured the greater part of the sky. About eight o'clock we were given a sight such as is rarely seen in crossing the Atlantic. We were about sixty miles from the Irish coast, and there we saw the North Channel Squadron of the British navy, which had come out for practice, lying-to for the night. There were seven of the large iron-clads of the navy in two parallel columns, separated about a quarter of a mile apart. The admiral's flag-ship led the starboard column, with three huge men-of-war following him at convenient distances, and the other three warships formed the port column. It was a grand sight, these ships, as it were, having come out to meet us and give the earliest welcome to the United Kingdom. The course of the Ohio was changed slightly to bring us nearer to the fleet, and as we passed under the sterns of the rearmost men-of-war our passengers gathered together and cheered our American flag as it was run up on the flag-staff at the steamer's stern. We could see crowds of British sailors peering over their bulwarks at us, and then as we dipped our ensign to the fleet, they politely dipped theirs in return. Then the admiral in his flag-ship, at the head of the column, about two miles off, ignited his powerful electric light, recently adopted in the British navy as a protection from torpedo-boats and other foes at night, and, fixing it upon us, this grand light came from afar over the waters, lighting up the intervening sea almost like noonday. By this time it was half-past eight, and the deepening twilight heightened the effect of this great light, which is the most powerful illuminator I have yet seen. For at least twenty minutes, as we steamed away, this light was kept bearing upon us, and it was finally put out when we were some ten miles distant. I have no doubt from its great brilliancy at that distance that it would be distinctly visible at least twenty miles at sea. For the purpose of illuminating the ocean within a circuit of a mile around the vessel there could scarcely be a more powerful method invented than a half-dozen of these lights, such as it is intended a man-of-war shall carry when in dangerous waters. The surrounding sea would be lighted up as with the sun, and the ship blazing with stars could discern and easily destroy an approaching enemy. By nine o'clock we had left this fleet far in the rear, the huge vessels lying-to for the night, but maintaining their position in double column. Many were the regrets expressed that the United States navy could show nothing like it. Thus closed our Sabbath at sea.

## LETTER V.

#### A PEEP AT OLD ERIN.

LIVERPOOL, July 23.

The arrival off the coast of Ireland by the transatlantic voyager is always eagerly anticipated. He wants to get out of the fog and storm and pitch and roll that make the ocean voyage usually so unpleasant, and to relieve the dull monotony of a trackless waste of waters by the sight of land. Hence no hour in the morning is too early to rise if the early rising will only bring a sight of Erin. We turned out at half-past two in the morning yesterday, and stretched out on the left hand, far over the waters, was the bold coast of the Emerald Isle. There is plenty of light in these high northern latitudes at that hour in summer-time, and there before us were the famous Bull, Cow, and Calf, with the light-house on the latter, towards which the steamer had been directing her prow all across the Atlantic. These are three isolated and curious rocks, rising abruptly in the water far out from the main-land, the tallest, about two hundred feet high, being the Bull, the broadest the Cow, and the little fellow modestly coming along behind being the Calf. The Calf, however, is the most important of the three, being the nearest to the course taken by the vast commerce which passes this way; hence it has the light-house, Calf-Rock Light being, with Fastnet, famous the world over as the beacons marking the approach to the English Channel.

It was a glorious morning, clear and beautiful, and the sun rose long before four o'clock over the Green Isle, as its bold headlands gradually passed in review before us; the precipitous rocks running abruptly down to the water, with breakers beating at their feet; the highly-cultivated fields, extending to the very edge at the top of the rocks; here and there a bay indented, opening up a smiling valley, with little clusters of white-thatched cottages scattered over the view. On nearly every headland was a light-house, its enclosing wall and outbuildings being painted white. Here, as indeed along all these coasts, the lighting system is complete, the beacons being placed in every position necessary for safe navigation.

For several hours, as we steamed on to Queenstown, we passed these bold headlands, with their ragged outlines, and the chief noticeable feature was the almost complete absence of trees. In about four instances, along the entire coast to Queenstown, there were slight patches of foliage, generally around mansion-houses; but Irish agriculture seemed everywhere else to have no room for trees. Fastnet Rock, which looks as if some giant had dropped it in the sea far off the coast for the especial purpose of building a light-house upon, was passed on the right-hand side, whilst the quartermasters were preparing to run up their signal-flags for Browhead Signal-Station, a little round-house stuck away up on a high rock on the main-land, whence is signalled back to America, and forward to Queenstown and Liverpool, the arrivals of all transatlantic steamers. The steamer talked with her flags, and the signal-station answered by flags run up on a staff above the round-house, and thus they made communication. This place, before the days of the Atlantic cable, was a great point for the collection of news from incoming Atlantic steamers, and during the war of the Rebellion all Europe waited for the outlines of news sent ashore there to be telegraphed. But now its more pretentious glory has departed, replaced, however, by the gratifying task of telling to awaiting friends all over the world the arrival of expected ships. Then we passed the "bold head of Kinsale," renowned in song and story, and rounding the more modest, yet broad, bold promontory, known as Roberts' Head, we saw far away in the base of the hills that spot dear to the Irishman's heart, the Cove of Cork. Guarding the entrance is Roche's Point, considered the end of the transatlantic voyage, and within is Queenstown, nestling by the hill-side, with the green fields and hedge-rows—for the country has no fences—enclosing it on all but the water side. Out of the harbor comes one of those low, black, curious-looking craft, belching forth black smoke from two funnels, so unlike what Americans are used to, which in these waters is called a steam-tender. The steamer did not enter the harbor, but remained outside, stopping the screw which had so steadily driven us day and night across the ocean; and the tender, which had been summoned by telegraph from Browhead, came alongside, and the passengers, mails, and luggage intended for Queenstown were quickly transferred. The passengers parted company with many regrets, and then the tender, which bore at the masthead a flag with the Keystone out of compliment to the steamer, started for Queenstown, whilst we steamed on for Liverpool. Hearty were the cheers as we parted, and the prominent figure in the view was a typical Irishman, dressed in the costume of a hundred years ago, knee-breeches, buckled shoes and all, who had come off to see the transfer, all unconscious of the admiration his quaint appearance elicited from the many American gazers, who had rarely seen such a dress before.

## LIVERPOOL.

The arrival at Liverpool, as at Queenstown, was also early in the morning, and it was before the town was out of bed that we bade good-by to the steamer and were set ashore to undergo the very slight customs examination required here, and seek our hotels. The Ohio we left anchored in the stream with twelve other transatlantic steamers, inward or outward bound, the thirteen huge crafts being stretched in a long line in the middle of the Mersey, in front of the city. The sight gave a good idea of the commerce of Liverpool, and the fact that they were anchored there was also an evidence of the rapid strides this commerce has recently made. The outgoing steamers had to come out of the docks, and the ingoing steamers could not enter them for the reason that this is the time of lowest neap-tides, when the flood does not rise high enough to float these large vessels through the dock entrances. Their cargoes, therefore, have to be lightered partially to and from them in the stream at great expense, until in a short period the time of higher flood-tides returns, when they can enter the docks. But even then there are only a portion of the docks having sufficient depth to float the large steamers now engaged in the transatlantic service. When the Liverpool docks were constructed, a ship of fourteen to sixteen feet draught was a large vessel, and no one dreamed of their some time drawing twenty-three feet. Hence the docks were constructed with the knowledge then possessed; but the commerce of Liverpool has, in this respect, outgrown many of these docks. A large, new dock is, however, in process of construction lower down the Mersey, capable of floating the largest ship of the present day, and will soon be opened. These docks are the great sight of the city, stretching along the entire river front, crammed with the ships of all nations, carrying every commercial flag; among the ensigns, however, the American flag being a somewhat scarce article. Huge warehouses line the quays. Steam railways have tracks all along the inside edge, but locomotives do not draw the cars, this being done by horses. The railway, however, is as convenient for freight shipments as that along our Delaware front, though I did not notice any sidings leading out on the piers alongside the ships. The most extraordinary specimen of a street-car for passengers I also saw running on this line, with broad wheels fitting the rails, but capable of running off the track whenever the driver wished to do so to get around the slowly travelling freight-cars. Only these passenger cars, called, in the language of the town, "trams," were allowed to run on this dock-border railway. There was another road alongside for ordinary wagons. Along these docks merchandise of all sorts in vast amounts is stored and being moved, the greater part of it apparently being American products, such as provisions, grain, cheese, cotton, and lumber. The excellent street pavements and the large breed of horses in Liverpool enable teams to haul astonishing loads. There are plenty of regular street passenger railways throughout the city, the tracks being laid by the city corporation, and being of a pattern that enables carriage-wheels to cross them and to turn out and in without the wrenching process that tears the heart and shatters the wheels whenever the attempt is made in Philadelphia to turn out of the tracks. The rail is laid so that the top is even with the pavement, and along the centre of the rail a narrow trench is cut, just wide enough to admit the flanges of the car-wheels, but not wide enough to let any carriage-wheel enter. Carriages, therefore, pass over at all angles without any apparent strain or even a jolt. Instead of the street railways controlling the city, as in Philadelphia, in England the cities control the street railways. The city corporation of Liverpool lays down all the lines according to a given pattern for the street-car companies, and charges them the expense. The cars are all two-storied, holding more on top than inside, and are without platforms. The question that has never yet been settled in Philadelphia, When is a street-car full? is settled in Liverpool by the legend painted plainly on every such vehicle here, and announcing that it is full when it has eighteen inside and twenty on top.

Liverpool contains many fine buildings, and a visit to the city and its suburbs will be well repaid. The usual fashion is to get out of Liverpool as soon as possible, the traveller regarding the necessity of remaining there upon landing from a steamer as an evil to be reduced to small compass. Besides being the best compact representation of trade which it is possible anywhere to find, Liverpool contains other objects of interest to more æsthetic tastes. It has a very fine new art gallery, the gift of a wealthy townsman; a most attractive public room in St. George's Hall, and any number of interesting old churches and other buildings. Like all English towns, its chimney-pots are its crowning glory. Every house has as many chimneys as is possible to put on it, and each chimney has from four to ten chimney-pots. Every new occupant of a house marks his tenancy by surmounting it with a new style of chimney-pot. Hence these strange pinnacles are of all sizes, styles, and colors. Whilst Liverpool docks and shipping cause wonder, Liverpool chimney-pots inspire amazement. Besides the large and noble horses seen in the streets, there are also many diminutive donkeys doing yeoman service as drawers of heavy burdens in unique carts. All the vehicles are in fact unlike ours; and among the strangest are the hearses and funeral coaches, huge black lumbering vehicles, entirely enclosed in black, and surmounted each with half a dozen large black plumes with spreading wings. A funeral procession when the wind blows looks like a confused army of dancing black children, these winged plumes when agitated by the wind executing the strangest gyrations. The outskirts of the city show unmistakably that an Englishman's house is his castle, for the roads run along between high stone walls and hedges, and whilst a peep here and there discloses many fine private houses, yet it is in every way evident that their owners desire not to be seen. The enclosures, however, are filled with grand old trees, and these cannot be hidden. Neither is it possible to conceal the constant evidence of thoroughness and completeness in building, road-making, etc., which constantly thrusts itself upon the eye. Liverpool has some very pretty, though not very large parks, with beautiful sheets of water interwining among their hills. There are also many quaint old inns in the outlying villages. It will interest my friends at Sixth and Chestnut Streets to know that one of these quaint old buildings in Gateacre is known as the Bear, and is kept by Joshua Ledger, whilst opposite is the Bull, and not very far off the Lamb, by Mr. Gudgeon. These seem, however, to get on very peaceably together. It will also be of interest to know that the Liverpool newspapers get out every day huge posters, which are set up on bill-boards about town, just like our theatrical posters, announcing their daily contents. Another quaint old inn is Childwall Abbey, once a religious house, but now an inn, as it has been, I am told, for three centuries, having opposite an old church and yard in which some of the graves date back to 1640, whilst on one tombstone I saw the names of seven persons inscribed, a family of five different generations, ranging from 1659 to 1772. Most of the stones are large flat slabs, laid over the graves, and the names of the dead are inscribed one after the other, like the entries in an account book, space being generally left on the stone for those who are to follow. This curious old inn and churchyard, five miles out from Liverpool, gets many visitors. Most of the private residences in the outskirts remind me of the style of architecture of St. George's House, and nearly all have fancy names, which are inscribed upon the gates in the walls enclosing the grounds around them. Thus we have The Hollies, The Towers, Ivy Cottage, Fullwood Park, Arequipa, and the like. This naming of private residences is almost universal in England, and adds to the charms of old homesteads, which have been for many years in the same family. The city, whilst showing great wealth, vast trade, and every attribute of industry, also presents, however, many sights indicative of poverty and vice; but I do not think these are so prominent as they were some years ago, though there is much room for improvement.

## LETTER VI.

### THE ANCIENT CITY OF CHESTER.

CHESTER, July 24.

It is quite possible that the readers of the *Ledger* in Chester, Pennsylvania, would like to know something about the ancient and venerable town of Chester, in England, after which their city is named. This town is about an hour's ride from Liverpool, and stands upon the river made famous in the song of "The Miller of the Dee." The Dee in this portion is by no means as wide as the Delaware, though farther towards the sea it becomes a very wide stream. It is a crooked, narrow creek at this part, running through a pretty valley, bordered by gardens and hop-vines. It formerly ran along the city wall on the west side, but its course has since been changed to a position farther west, and the old river-bed seemed, as we gazed upon it from the city wall, to be almost a perfect wilderness of garden-sauce and hop-vines. Few Americans of the thousands who land at Liverpool ever visit Chester, and yet it is one of the oldest of cities, containing within the half-mile square surrounded by its walls a collection of antiquities and curiosities such as can scarcely be seen elsewhere within as small a space. Some of its oddities are peculiar to the town. Its plan is a square bordered by walls, each of which contains a gate at its centre, facing the four points of the compass. These walls are very old, built, it is said, by the Romans, nearly a thousand years ago, and a considerable portion of the original Roman wall is still preserved. The tops of the walls, which are about five feet broad, are used as a promenade, so that the visitor can walk all around the town over the gates and past the frequent towers, covered outworks, and similar structures which were used for defence. Streets cross the town at right angles, connecting the four gates, and the sidewalks of these streets are in the second stories of the houses. At each street-crossing you mount up to the second story on stone steps, coming down again at the next street-crossing. This is the most original sort of sidewalk I have yet seen, but it is somewhat tiresome mounting up and down the steps, though the plan is a capital one as a protection from rain, and it also enables house-owners to utilize both the ground and upper floors for shops, the lower story also having a narrow sidewalk of its own, bordering the cartway.

The city is full of the quaintest-looking houses, with their gable-ends to the street, and the inhabitants are so proud of the flavor of antiquity which pervades everything that they build their new houses in a style which makes them look more venerable than the old. This adds to the oddity, and its deception leads to some amusing mistakes. Two or three houses that I saw which looked as if several centuries old, were built but seven years ago. The entire city is full of strange-looking buildings, including many venerable churches and one of the famous old castles of England. One quaint building of real antiquity is said to have twice shielded its residents from the plague, being the only house that escaped the infliction. This fact is recorded by an inscription carved on a board across the front, declaring it to have been the "Providence of God." Another strange-looking structure was called the "Pied Bull Inn." The finest modern building in the city is the new Town Hall, built nine years ago, to replace the old one, which had been burnt. It contains several fine apartments, and is ornamented with bas-reliefs illustrative of the city's ancient history, and many portraits of distinguished people. One of these is of William Offling, sheriff in 1517, and the inscription states that he had been twice married, and had twenty-six children; that his son William Offling had fifteen children; and that the father and five of his sons gave one thousand pounds to the poor of the city. The ancient castle of Chester is a curious old building, surrounding three sides of a court-yard, whilst remains of the old ditch which surrounded it are preserved in front of the court-yard. This castle is used as a prison and barracks, and a considerable portion of the Ninety-sixth Regiment are stationed here, part of them living in tents in the court-yard. The regimental band, of forty musicians, gave a concert during the evening in front of the castle. Dressed in their scarlet uniforms, they, with an admiring crowd, stood out in a rain for two hours, regardless of the wetting they were getting,—playing without shelter upon string as well as brass instruments, having their

CHESTER CATHEDRAL AND CITY WALL.

music upon stands before them, whilst their leader had an assistant in a red coat to turn over the pages for him, so that nothing interfered with his use of the baton. They were wonderfully proficient, and executed several difficult pieces with the greatest skill. Red coats were plentiful about the city all the time.

The most famous attraction of Chester, however, is the Cathedral, one of the most ancient and largest church edifices in England. It is being gradually restored to its original condition, the work being paid for by contributions from all parts of England, different persons and public bodies, religious and secular, providing for various parts. The greater part of the restoration is completed, but it is still going on in one of the transepts. It would be difficult to describe this wonderful old church, which has figures of wolves endeavoring to crawl over the eaves, and is filled with the richest of ancient carvings in oak and woods from the Holy Land, and ornamented by the finest mosaics. Days could be passed in examining it and the adjoining cloisters, which as yet are but partially restored, and, in fact, in some parts are almost in a state of ruin, from the action of the elements upon the stone. The choir of the Cathedral is filled with gems, and has been entirely restored. In this choir in the afternoon I attended a special service, held in accordance with the judicial custom of England, which requires the high sheriff to take the judge to church whenever he comes to the city to hold an Assize Court. Chief-Justice Coleridge to-day opened the assize at the castle, and yesterday, as a proper preparation, he went to church. The high sheriff, dressed in the uniform of a British colonel, scarlet coat, chapeau, sword, and spurs, took the judge in his state carriage from the hotel to the Cathedral, the coachman and two footmen standing behind wearing elaborate drab liveries. Preceding the carriage were about twenty men bearing javelins, and two heralds, who blew frequent blasts on their trumpets, closing with a sonorous peal, which resounded through the vaulted ceilings of the church, when the dignitaries, leaving their carriage, marched up the nave to the choir, preceded by the clergy and choristers in surplices. Vergers with their maces and officials with their staves walked before the sheriff and judge, whilst the latter had an attendant holding up his train. His appearance, in huge wig and scarlet gown trailing along after him, so disguised his sex, that my little girl, after gazing intently for a long time to solve the problem, finally in despair asked me to please tell her whether it was a gentleman or lady. With them came the sheriff's chaplain in a black gown, and whilst "God Save the Queen" was pealing from the organ they took their seats, and the service began. The entire service was intoned and chanted, the music being sung by a very strong male choir. The lessons and prayers, creed and sermon, were each assigned to a different clergyman, the sheriff's chaplain preaching. Vergers conducted each clergyman separately to reading-desk or pulpit, and then back again to their seats, and the lessons were read from a Bible whose magnificently-bound cover was inlaid with precious stones, whilst the markers were ornamented with pearls. This book was the gift of the Duke of Westminster and his family, the duke being one of the richest noblemen of England, and a sort of patroon in Chester, his magnificent home, Eaton Hall, being in the suburbs, and part of his vast estate in the city. It would be a very long story to tell of all the beauties and antiquities of this extraordinary town, which, having a wolf in its coat of arms, is, therefore, replete with wolves in its ornamentation. Visitors loving the ancient and the quaint, desirous of seeing how odd a city of English-speaking people can be, fond of old churches, castles, and Roman relics, will be well satisfied here. And American Chester, on the Delaware, may also be well satisfied with bearing the name of English Chester, on the Dee.

## LETTER VII.

#### CHESTER AND EATON HALL.

HOLYHEAD, July 25.

There is in Chester a venerable structure known as the Church of St. John Baptist, which is said to be as old as the Cathedral. Much of it is in ruins, with ivy and moss overrunning the broken arches and half-destroyed stone-work. It is preserved with scrupulous care, railed in to protect it from vandalism, and is regarded as one of the greatest curiosities of this very curious town. It adjoins Grosvenor Park, a very fine bit of beautifully-ornamented grounds, running down to the river Dee, and containing a statue of the late Marquis of Westminster, and two large cannons captured from the Russians at Sebastopol. In this park I observed our well-known weed, the mullein, growing in the flower gardens, and evidently cultivated very carefully. I asked a native what it was, and was told it was a "hexotic, and very rare, indeed, sir." Among other curiosities of Chester were four battle-flags, set up in the nave of the Cathedral, two of which had been at Waterloo and two at Bunker Hill; but the latter were British flags. The old inns of Chester are some of them very curious, and, like many of the other houses, are ancient buildings, set gable-end to the street, and sometimes protruding upon it. Whether they violate street lines and boundaries or not, they are carefully preserved in their old-time condition. I saw among these inns the "Bear's Paw," the "Liver," and the "Old Nag's Head." Some of their signs were very odd. They announced that they kept newspapers, also "tea, coffee, and hot water;" and in one case "ham and eggs, good beds, and beer." The Grosvenor family, who are the chief people here, and of whom the Duke of Westminster is the head, appear to be most liberal benefactors of the city. The home of the duke, at Eaton Hall, outside the town, is one of the famous great houses of England, surrounded by magnificent grounds, and itself a palace of large proportions. Its interior decorations are magnificent, among them being a small tessellated pavement, which cost eight thousand dollars. It contains many costly paintings. Its architecture is Gothic, and repairing and altering are continually going on, the duke being one of those unsatisfied men with full purses who are always tearing down and building up. It is probable before he dies he will get the house so built as to suit him; but then, as we were told, his son, when he comes into possession of the title and estate, intends to tear it all down and build it over again, as it does not please him at all. "But it is all right, you know," said our informant; "makes trade, you know"

## THE IRISH MAIL.

The great mails between England and the United States, although carried upon steamers sailing to and from Liverpool, do not pass through that city. They are taken from and put on board the steamers at Queenstown, and they are carried to and from London on one of the fastest trains that run in this country of fast railway travelling. This train is known as the Irish mail, and it passes through Dublin, Holyhead, and Chester, crossing the Irish Channel by express-boats, so that the time occupied in making the journey is several hours shorter than the steamer time between London and Queenstown, thus expediting the mails. The road over which this mail goes is one of the most costly in Great Britain. It runs from Chester west along the river Dee to the sea, and thence along the bases of the Welsh mountains westward through Wales, Anglesea, and Holy Isle to Holyhead, the most westerly projecting point of Wales, jutting out into the sea and surmounted by a revolving light, which is one of the great landmarks of this coast. It passes through a rugged and picturesque country, but is so frequently interspersed with tunnels to get through the mountains that it really seems as if one-fourth of the entire distance ran through the bowels of the earth. The entire line is a succession of rock-cuttings, galleries, retaining-walls, tunnels, and costly bridges, which must have cost millions of money to construct. On this railway is Stephenson's tubular bridge, erected across the Conway River in 1848, and also the stupendous Britannia tubular bridge which crosses the Menai Strait, and is famous the world over. This bridge was erected by Stephenson, is one thousand five hundred and thirteen feet long, cost five million dollars, and stands one hundred and four feet above the water, being elevated to allow vessels to pass under. It was nearly five years building, and gets its name from the Britannia Rock, which stands in mid-channel, and supports the central pier. It consists of a pair of square wrought-iron tubes, through which the trains run as through a tunnel. Huge lions, carved out of the solid rock, stand on both sides of each entrance, elevated high above the track. This bridge, and, indeed, the entire line of railway, is a monument to the genius of Robert Stephenson, whose engineering skill is held in fond memory throughout the entire country, and is marked by frequent statues and other memorials. The railway runs through rich pasture-lands in portions, in which graze many sheep and large herds of coal-black cows; in fact, cows of any other color seem to be scarce in this part of Wales. It runs past collieries, slate-mines, and any number of castles perched on the hills, relics of feudal times, and of the days when the Welsh had to keep a sharp lookout for marauders from the sea. Nearly every station is a watering-place, and bathers could be seen going into the surf from the cosy little bathing-machines, which are wheeled out into the water. The railway train shoots past the ponderous ruins of Conway Castle, and almost under the bastioned and crumbling walls of that ancient burgh. In St. Mary's church-yard of that city are many ancient tombs of the good people of a day far gone, and among them is the tomb of a Welshman, of a family who, evidently, served their country well,—Nicholas Hookes, of whom it is recorded that his father had forty-seven children, while Nicholas himself had twenty-seven children. The American tourist, however, in this land, should not venture far away from the railway carriage door, unless he does not fear getting lost. If he once got out of sight of the railway he would have difficulty in inquiring his way back again. In order to make a record of the route followed by the railway between Chester and Holyhead, through Wales, I will mention that it passes by stations known as Gwyrck Castle, Prestalyn, Rhyl, Colwyn, Tal-y-Caln, Bettws-y-coed, Pennmaenmawr, Llanfairfechan, Pontrhytholtt, Cwmyglo, Llanwnda, Tycroes, and a few other important places of the same sort. If the tourist cuts this out for reference he will stand some chance of not going astray on the Irish mail line through Wales. But if he should get lost in this neighborhood it is only necessary to inquire for Tanyrallt, Caen Gwyllym, or Caerheddynog, and all will be right.

## HOLYHEAD.

Holyhead gets its chief importance from the fact that it is the point of transfer from train to boat on the route to Dublin. It evidently has a large trade, for no less than nine steamers of the through lines were in harbor when I sailed. It is an ancient city, and has various quaint buildings, whilst the proprietors of its inns spend their time chiefly in endeavoring to get the passengers to stop for refreshments,—a task which seems to be but poorly rewarded. Holyhead has a good harbor, protected by a fine breakwater, and is used as a port of refuge for vessels in the Irish Channel. The railway is building a new station, which, when completed, will be a finer station than any we have in Philadelphia, and apparently as large as our largest. Like all the railway construction here, it is being built in most imposing style, of cut-stone and brick, and in connection there is being constructed a basin, so that the steamers can enter at all stages of the tide. Five dollars per week seemed to be the prevailing wages for labor on this work, the men working from 6 A.M. to 5.30 P.M., with a half-hour for breakfast and an hour for dinner. This seemed to be the standard rate for most male labor, so far as I could learn, whilst female domestic servants get from one dollar and twenty-five cents to one dollar and fifty cents per week. At Holyhead I was much impressed with the fact that the schools kept all summer. We saw a school dismiss at 5 P.M., and asking for a look at the boys' books, found they were learning to write, presenting very fair copy-books. They were all chubby-faced Welsh boys, in perfect health, and claiming a thorough knowledge of English. They understood our language when spoken to, but when they answered I found their English was not the kind that I had learned. The attempt to talk finally became so ludicrous that the boys could stand it no longer, but pointing to our straw hats, which seemed to amuse them very much, they gave us three cheers as we retreated discomfited before this new Welsh invasion. We discovered enough, however, to be able to note that in that school at least there was no summer holiday. How the teachers must long to emigrate to free America, where education works somewhat differently!

Holyhead is among the high hills, which run down abruptly to the water, presenting an iron-bound coast, but a most picturesque one. As the steamer receded from the shores of Wales we saw the white light-houses ranging along the coast. The excellent lighting of all the British shores was again most forcibly impressed upon us.

## LETTER VIII.

### BROWN STOUT AND THE PHŒNIX.

DUBLIN, July 27.

Dublin, as most Irishmen and a few Americans know, stands on the Liffey River, a beautiful stream, but full of shoals, and navigable only a few miles from its mouth. The entrance from the Irish Channel is beautiful, the renowned Hill of Howth guarding it on one hand, and Kingstown on the other. Very large amounts have been spent in keeping the channel open so as to maintain navigation up to the city, but only with indifferent success, for as soon as dredging ceases the channel fills. The entrance is, therefore, a perfect marvel of light-houses, buoys, dykes, etc., showing that only the utmost perseverance will accomplish the result desired. The buoys are huge beacons, some with balls, others with lights, and three or four dredging-machines were at work as we passed. This work maintains a large and valuable commerce. The quays are lined with vessels, and the trade of the city, judging from the shipping in port, is of great importance. In fact, the largest ships are able to enter the port through the means employed to maintain the channel, and, as the second city in the British Islands, Dublin deserves an open road to the sea.

You no sooner land at Dublin than you find unmistakable evidences of being in an Irish city. At the quay, when the baggage is brought to the place of delivery—a hundred or more trunks piled on a huge car—a score of Irishmen rush at the pile with a cheer, and carry it off with a struggle suggesting Donnybrook Fair. You select your man, show him your trunk, and without check or any other certificate he grabs it, upsetting whatever may be between. Mounting on a jaunting-car, with your legs dangling over the sides, you travel to the hotel; and then, when you put your hand in your pocket to pay the fare, it is naïvely suggested by the cabby, " Your worship, for the love of your children, plaze remember the driver." There's luck in odd numbers, said Rory O'More;

therefore, when the hotel guests sat down to dinner, the head-waiter carefully counted them, and finding the number even, he sent out for a representative of the house to come in and sit down, so as not to spoil the adage; and not to forget old friends, this Irish hotel, remembering the ancient alliance, served dinner with a French bill of fare.

Most tourists visit Dublin to see the buildings, and, like the rest, I thought this the necessary thing to do. But whilst outside of Dublin, the Cathedral, the Castle, Christ Church, the Bank, the Four Courts, Custom-House, and Trinity College were greatly praised,—yet inside the city, in the estimation of most of the denizens with whom I came in contact, these were cast in the shade by the greater glories of Brown Stout and the Phœnix. The buildings I have named are all of them fine structures, well worth going a long distance to see. The Castle, with its broad court-yards and its beautiful little chapel; the huge Four Courts; the spreading greens and spacious buildings containing the one thousand students of Trinity College; the grand semi-circular front of the Bank of Ireland, with its imposing colonnade; the beautiful ornamentation of Christ Church, the Cathedral of the English Church; the hundreds of magnificent private buildings; the columns, statues, monuments, squares, and quays,—all make Dublin one of the most attractive cities of the Old World. The atmosphere gives them all the sombre appearance customary in every town in the United Kingdom, and this flavor of antiquity adds to their attractions. It is probable that the Bank of Ireland is historically the most famous of all these buildings. Before the Union Act was passed, at the beginning of this century, which united Great Britain and Ireland under one parliamentary government, the Irish Parliament met in this building, with its two Houses of Peers and Commons. The last sitting of this Parliament was held October 2, 1800, when the Irish Union bill was put through by methods which the Irish people will never forget, and which dwarf anything that is told of American legislative doings. It cost, to get a majority sufficient to pass the bill, according to the standard guide to the city, fifteen million dollars compensation to members, twenty-nine new peerages, twenty promotions in the peerage, and six million three hundred and sixty thousand dollars compensation to boroughs; or, as the guide-book says, "rather to those who considered themselves, from their influence, owners of the same." It evidently paid in those days for a politician to "run his division" in Ireland. The Bank of Ireland now has its chief office in the spacious hall formerly occupied by the Irish House of Commons. St. Patrick's Cathedral is probably the largest church in Ireland, and is a beautiful structure, which was not long ago reconstructed at the expense of Sir Benjamin Lee Guinness, who paid about one million dollars for the work, an act of munificence which has enhanced the Dublin veneration for brown stout,—A. Guinness, Son & Co. being the great brewers here, and being known in the remotest parts of the world, wherever their single or double stout may have penetrated.

A visit to the brewery will very well inspire equal veneration in the stranger. It is a brewery covering forty acres, compactly occupied by brew-houses, malt-floors, stables, packing- and cleansing-rooms, and, vast as the establishment is, it is evidently not large enough for its growing trade, as there is building another huge brewing-house of large dimensions with the necessary adjuncts. Everything necessary to the trade is constructed on this ground, even the water being pumped from its own well, over one hundred feet deep, and the latest appliances are in use for every part of the work. Machinery does almost everything, and yet fourteen hundred men are employed in the establishment. A railway siding enters the works; a special narrow-gauge railway with five locomotives and one hundred cars connects different parts of the brewery and transports the casks to the quay on the Liffey River, in front, whence they are shipped on nine steamers to the lower portion of the river, where they are transferred to the shipping; and one hundred and thirty horses are necessary to draw the wagons serving the town, and provide other transportation not covered by steam. The extensive stables are among the great curiosities of the place. Each horse has a wide stall with separate hay and feed boxes and drinking basin, supplied by a separate faucet. On the wall above the horse's name is inscribed on a plate.

The brewing capacity of the works is about two hundred and fifty thousand gallons daily, and for storage, prior to shipment, one hundred and fifty vats, each holding nearly one hundred thousand gallons, are used, and yet there is not enough room. Everything is done on the most enormous scale. There are acres covered with machines washing, steaming, and drying barrels, of which over four hundred and fifty thousand are in use, and long lines of pipes filling barrels. Everything is utilized. The waste that flows over the bung when the cask is filled is run into drains and pumped into vats. The yeast skimmed off is put under a press, drained of every drop of beer, and then, when in a condition resembling oil cake, is sold to distillers, who manage to extract spirits from it. So vast an establishment is well calculated to increase any one's veneration for brown stout.

The Phœnix, which is also the admired of all Dublin, stands on a high column in the centre of Phœnix Park, surrounded by rural loveliness of every description. The beautiful green sward, the grand old trees, the brier and furze, the deer and cattle in the grand old park, with its long vistas of view disclosing the Wicklow Mountains, and its lovely slopes down to the Liffey, here a narrow but pretty stream, are well calculated to win admiration. This, some seven or eight miles in circumference, and covering over seventeen hundred acres, is said to be the largest park at any city in Britain. It reminds me in many respects of Fairmount Park, though it has nothing like the river views, for it is generally level, and its gardeners seem to endeavor to preserve nature in the shape of green grass, fine trees and shrubbery, rather than pile up artificial views and mounds and dig out artificial valleys at enormous cost. The Phœnix, indeed, well deserves to be the Irishman's delight, and his home is one of the loveliest on the face of the earth. In Dublin we were reminded of Philadelphia by finding the Baldwin Locomotive Works Catalogue and the Pennsylvania Railroad excursion route book in the hotels; both being well studied by the visitors.

### THE DUBLIN SUBURBS.

The suburbs of Dublin, in every direction, are beautiful. There is every variety of hill and vale; of landscape and water; of highly-ornamented and cultivated grounds, with pretty hedges, and solid stone fences dividing the fields. Occasionally there is seen a wooden fence, but they are rare. Some of the houses are ornate, and there is every evidence of wealth and refinement in the villas of the gentry surrounding the city. The country is also full of low-thatched cottages, generally one-story stone buildings, with steep roofs. The thatch is very thick, and fastened down with wires. Ruins are occasionally seen, which are turned into dwellings. In one case—a small church—families lived in the nave and transepts, and hung out their wash-clothes and kept their donkeys in the roofless choir. All the roads are good, but the wagons, as in all parts of the British Islands, reverse the American rule, and keep to the *left* instead of the *right*. This is the ancient British custom, allowing the vehicle approaching to pass on the side on which the driver sits, and is more convenient than the American rule. But I am told it was reversed in the United States after the Revolution, our people desiring to do nothing in the same way as the mother-country did, and, therefore, determining to "keep to the right," whilst the Englishmen did the other thing. I do not vouch for this, but give the tradition as told to me. There are plenty of little donkeys on these roads dragging loads that would be sufficient for most horses. In many cases women guide them, and look very odd trudging along with their shillelahs and having confidential talks with the "baste," the object of which is to get him to go faster. Throughout all this region, as in England, the idea of privacy and exclusiveness prevails, as shown by the height of boundary walls and the wholesale manner in which broken glass is stuck endwise in mortar on the top to keep people from clambering over. The fashion in the United States of tramping at will over any man's land is here repressed with severity. Dublin, like most English cities, is a sufferer from the smoky atmosphere, which makes everything dingy, and the appearance of its many statues is marred by their very dirty faces. Dublin street naming and numbering might also be improved by adopting the Philadelphia system. A street will have a new name every few squares, and each section of the street has its own set of numbers, which begin at one end, run along consecutively on one side to the other end, and then back again along the other side to the place of beginning, the last number on the street thus being exactly opposite the first.

In the Hill of Howth, however, Dublin has its greatest admired suburb. This is a hill six hundred feet high, jutting out into the sea and guarding the entrance to the river. It commands a glorious view and slopes down abruptly to the water, the breakers beating against its base. Whilst the Liffey washes one foot of this hill, a deep bay, converted at large cost into a harbor of refuge, is at the other. This bay was filled with fishing-vessels with dark-brown sails. The base of this grand hill has an occasional beach, which is availed of as a bathing-place, and its slopes are very beautiful, covered with heather and furze, with variegated wild-flowers, scarlet, yellow, and blue, adding to the charm. It is just such a place as would attract vast crowds if near an American city; but, excepting on Sunday, but few seemed to visit it from Dublin. Near by is a strange rocky island, called Ireland's Eye, while the Devil's Bed was a curious rock near the shore. Howth, we were told at the inn, was the last place his Satanic Majesty stopped at in Ireland, and he slept the last night in this bed. He did not leave for good, however, our informant added, as he now comes back occasionally to look after all persons "who take lodgings in the town, but are too mane to ate anything at the howtel." We lunched there to avoid any difficulty.

## LETTER IX.

### CROSSING BOYNE WATER.

BELFAST, July 29.

Irish politics transferred to America usually culminate on July 12, when the anniversary comes of the famous Orange crossing of Boyne water. I never could understand why this conflict of two centuries ago should be transferred to American soil, and I understand it less now that I have also crossed Boyne water, and found it a very peaceful stream of small dimensions, dyked in to preserve the channel, and in this way narrowed to but little more than the width of the canal through Smith's Island. Although it was only about two weeks after the anniversary of the crossing, I saw nothing of any indication of party conflict about it, and at Drogheda, on the river, I asked a native what he knew about the famous battle, and he replied that he had lived in those parts these five-and-thirty years, and no "foight" had taken place there to his knowledge. Yet the result of the Battle of the Boyne was that Drogheda surrendered to the Orange party, and James II. was overthrown, though the Droghedans of the present day may care little about it. There is certainly ground for the belief that Irishmen going to America are foolish in carrying over that water the strifes which may distract the old country they have abandoned. I crossed Boyne water in the opposite direction from the Orangemen. I came from Dublin, whilst James II., after his defeat, ran away to Dublin on his way to France, and, blaming the defeat which his own weakness and incapacity caused upon the Irish troops who stood manfully by him, he said they had run away very fast. To this an Irishwoman, Lady Tyrconnel, quickly retorted, that His Majesty had certainly won the race, as he had got to Dublin first. The Boyne at Drogheda is a beautiful stream. The railway bridge is raised high above it, affording a charming view up and down the river, where the slopes of the old banks have been highly cultivated, and most of the riverbed outside the dykes has been reclaimed and converted into rich fields. The Boyne was as peaceful and its verdant banks as smiling as they could possibly be. Although the train was chiefly laden with red-coat soldiers there were no other signs of war.

These red-coated soldiers and some in darker uniforms have been a leading feature in the scene ever since I landed in Her Majesty's dominions. Large numbers of them have been met everywhere, with their short-tailed scarlet coats, almost dazzling the eyes, and their little apologies of visorless caps stuck on one side of the head, which the wind would blow away were they not fastened at the chin. The darker uniforms are not so glaring. These soldiers are chiefly the reserves, got under arms and put in camp during the conflict with Russia, but now being disbanded and sent home. They appear by hundreds everywhere, but in a few days will probably all be sent home; then only the regulars in the garrison towns will be seen. Crowds assemble at the railway stations to welcome the returning troops, and give the scene somewhat the appearance of that at the close of the Rebellion, when our regiments were returning home to go out of service. These British troops carry their clothing in white canvas bags, usually tucked under the arm. They have only very small knapsacks.

From Dublin, past Dunkalk, Balbriggan, Newry, Portadown, and Balmoral to Belfast is a beautiful ride. At first the line skirts along the Irish Sea, and gives splendid views over the water. Then it strikes inland into a rich agricultural country, interspersed with bogs, and gives an idea of this part of the Irish life. Sometimes when the railway ran along a hillside a beautiful view would be disclosed for miles across a country, showing the richness of the land and the thoroughness of the agriculture. The view from Basbrook across the valley of Newry was particularly fine, reminding one of the Chester Valley, excepting that hedges and stone walls replaced the fences of that beautiful region, and low thatched cottages represented the thrifty farm-houses. Hundreds of women as well as men were working in the fields, for it was harvest-time. Before we left Philadelphia we had seen the hay and wheat-harvest there, but now, more than three weeks afterwards, came upon the Irish gathering their crops. And such crops! especially the hay. The yield is enormous, larger than it has been for many years, and much larger per acre than around Philadelphia. The oats, barley, and potatoes are still growing, and promise also a good yield. The smallness of the fields particularly surprised me, for it was a rarity to find one of over four acres. The carefulness with which every inch of available ground was cultivated was also plainly shown. They even mowed the railway embankments, and gathered crops from every portion of the land not actually occupied by the tracks. The women worked as hard as the men, stopping a moment to look at the train and then going on again. The peat-bogs were being dug for turf, which was cut out into pieces resembling large bricks and piled up to dry. Much of this sort of work was going on, as a large portion of this country seemed boggy. Nearly every cultivated field was provided with underground drainage, showing what an expensive business farming in this moist country is. As the railway—which, by the way, was in some portions so constructed as to give more exercise to the mile than any American railroad I have ever been on—reached Belfast, a change came over the scene. The large linen-factories, for which this section is famous, began to appear, and the ground was covered with myriads of pieces of linen laid out to bleach. It was laid upon delicate green sward, each field having a pond in the centre, where the water to be sprinkled upon the linen was obtained. Millions of yards were thus spread out, in long pieces, all around us, presenting an odd sight. And then we soon came to Belfast, the headquarters of the trade, nestling under the high limestone hills, which not only make the scene so picturesque, but also give the city protection from the severity of northern and western gales.

#### LINEN AND THE ABSENTEE.

The crowning summit of the range of hills protecting Belfast is a noble peak known as Cave Hill, from the slopes of which there is a glorious view over Belfast Lough, the city and the sea, whilst from the summit, on a clear day, Scotland is visible. On this hill-side is the castle of the Marquis of Donegal, about a mile from the highway, and in a park said to be four miles in circumference. The marquis owns the land on which the city is built, whilst linen has built it up. Yet, with an income from his leases estimated from one million to one million five hundred thousand dollars, the host of this princely estate has never made it his residence, and only built the castle five years ago, to which he makes probably one or two visits a year. "The Estate," as it is popularly called in the town, spreads everywhere, being managed by agents. Imagine a city, one-fourth the size of Philadelphia, paying rent to one man, giving him a princely income, and he spending his time and money elsewhere. Such a thing would be in conflict with every American idea, yet it seems to be the rule with Irish landlords, and is the absenteeism of which the Irish so justly complain. Belfast, however, barring the rents, is as well off without as with its absent patroon. It is the only Irish city that grows, and in many characteristics reminds one of an American city, although there is a continual reminder of "the Estate," by seeing on signboards announcements of "this building ground to be let forever;" "this concern to be let in perpetuity;" "apply to the Estate Agent." Belfast has all the bustle, vigor, and push of an American town, and its streets and buildings and the smart movements of its people are a continual suggestion of the American way of doing things. Excepting that it would be wider and generally better paved, a section of a business street in Belfast is much similar to a section of a business street in Philadelphia. It is entirely unlike the other Irish cities in being just the opposite of them in the aspects of the people. Dublin appeared sleepy and languid, whilst Belfast rushed about with overflowing life. Yet Belfast keeps Sunday most rigorously; the street-cars do not run, and everything is closed tight, the streets, excepting at church-time, being almost deserted. Whilst Belfast is up at daylight on week-days, it is very lazy on Sundays, and the morning church services do not begin until half-past eleven. The city is full of churches,—the Presbyterians being exceptionally strong,—and many are very fine buildings. The Scotch-Irish race impresses its marked characteristics upon everything about the city. St. Patrick's Catholic Cathedral is also a beautiful building, and the front is adorned with a statue of Ireland's patron saint. The Queen's College, the Ulster Bank, the Presbyterian and Methodist Colleges, the Custom House, and several other structures, are also ornate buildings, though none of them are on the stupendous scale of similar buildings in the large cities of England. The Albert Memorial, on High Street, is a very fine clock tower. The Royal Botanic and Horticultural Society's gardens are a fine enclosure, containing most beautiful flower-beds, exceeding anything of the kind yet attempted in Philadelphia. St. George's Episcopal Church, a square structure similar to the olden style Philadelphia church, and much resembling it in the interior, required four clergymen to conduct the morning service, though it was done without the superfluous ceremony of Chester Cathedral. Rev. Dr. McIlwain, the vicar, rather astonished me by *not* preaching from a written sermon, but making an extemporaneous address from the pulpit, illustrated by quotations from a small pocket Bible, to which he frequently referred. The address, which was a fine specimen of educated Irish eloquence, was a strong political argument, urging that if the honor of the kingdom was at stake it was the duty of the people to fight; praising the Ministry for having maintained the nation's rights and yet secured peace; and declaring it to be the height of folly at this late day for Irishmen to keep up the Orange feud and on Orange day go out for a "commemoration," which meant getting drunk and into a broil. This doctrine he thrust home with strong illustrations from his small Bible, and he certainly made a good and sensible argument, declaring that in Ireland now all reputable people of whatever politics or religion abstained from Orange commemorations.

The dwellings of Belfast all look comfortable, and nearly every house has its window garden, giving a very cheerful appearance. The suburbs contain many fine villas, and jaunting-cars jog merrily along the well-paved roads, while the populace, of all degrees, ride in them, these being the chief method of conveyance. Many of the sidewalks are made of cobble-stones,—not the uncomfortable kind that we have at home, but small ones, about two inches in diameter, carefully laid, and presenting a surface almost as good to tread upon as brick. The street numbering is also upon the satisfactory plan of odd numbers on one side and even ones on the other. Whilst Belfast has a large trade in cattle and agricultural products, and has to keep open its road to the sea by continual dredging, and is also a large cotton-manufacturing place, yet the chief glory of Belfast is the linen trade. For this it is renowned in all parts of the world, and by this its wealth has been made. Enormous mills surround it for miles, and its Exchange is known as "Linen Hall." Around this structure, which stands in a park and has a fine court-yard, cluster rows of warehouses, in which are stored the manufactured fabric, which, when bleaching, covers the fields for many miles around the city. One of the great mills, that of the Messrs. Mulholland, is an enormous pile of buildings, the firm employing in one way or another twenty-five thousand persons, of whom over three thousand work in the Belfast mill. Here the whole process of ordinary flax manufacture can be seen, from the rough hackling to the final weaving of the linen cloth, which is sent out to the greens in the country to dry. On entering the engine-room of this great factory, I heard the familiar sound of the Corliss cut-off on the huge steam-engine which was driving the machinery. The engine was a new one, having been run but six months, and had been built expressly to have the Corliss attachments, which the Centennial Exhibition had brought to the attention of the house, and which the engineer warmly praised. Said he, though this new engine has seventy per cent. more power than our old one, this attachment enables us to drive it with less fuel; we save thirteen bushels of coal a day. Only the cheaper linens are made by steam-driven machinery in the mills, of which there are a great number in and around Belfast. The finer linens and damasks are all made by hand, and, unless specially ordered, the finer qualities rarely reach America. The most famous Belfast factory for the character of its work is M. Andrews' royal manufactory of linens and damasks, at Ardoyne, in the suburbs of Belfast. Here, on hand-looms, are woven the finest fabrics for the royal families of Europe, goods being made to a fineness of one hundred and sixty threads to the inch. This factory, which is cheerfully shown, is one of the curiosities of this part of the world, the mysteries of weaving the beautiful patterns seen in table linen being of great interest. When I was there, three special patterns were going through the looms, decorated with special crests and coats of arms,—one for the Duke of Edinburgh; another for the Fishmongers' Company of London, one of the famous corporations of the metropolis; and the third, an American order, which was a great rarity, was a pretty and appropriate design for Battery M, of the First Regiment of United States Artillery. This linen traffic appears in all parts of Belfast as its prominent industry, and as a bustling business city, full of life, and, as it were, of American ideas and systems of doing things, it has no rival in Ireland. Belfast is well worth a visit from any American who desires to see a good representation of industry and thrift, and to get in what he sees a reminder of what he is used to at home.

## LETTER X.

### THE GIANT'S CAUSEWAY.

PORT RUSH, IRELAND, July 30.

To go to the great Irish national curiosity, the Giant's Causeway, you take the Northern Counties of Ireland Railway, between Belfast and Londonderry (or, as it is universally called here, 'Derry), to Port Rush, on the extreme northern coast. This railway passes through a rich agricultural region, cultivated down to the very edge almost of the Atlantic Ocean,

GIANTS' CAUSEWAY.

and on the way stops at the well-known towns of Ballymena, Culleybackey, Templepatrick, Ballykelly, Moneymore, Linavady, Magilligan, Ballymagarrettknock, Cookstown, Carrickfergus Junction, Ballymoney, and several other places of like repute. These are all pleasant villages, and some quite large towns, with great linen-factories raising up their tall chimneys. They have first-rate railway stations, and exhibit a general appearance of thrift, beggars being few, and the industry of the Scotch-Irish race strongly developed. On all sides there are green fields, divided by hedgerows or walls, cultivated to the highest degree, peat bogs being industriously dug for the turf, which is stacked in piles to dry; neat thatched cottages with their stacks of peat fuel; flax ponds, around which the manufactured fabric is laid out to bleach; and among all these is seen the gathering of the hay and flax harvests, both men and women working in the fields, making hay with their hands, without rake or fork; or pulling up the flax and leaving it in long rows behind them, getting for their labor, as I was told, from thirty-five to fifty cents per day, according to whether the landlord provided their food. In one flax-field of about fifteen acres I counted forty of these working men and women gradually crossing it in a long row, pulling flax, which is dragged by hand out of the ground, roots and all. Around nearly every cottage are little flower-beds, the prominent growing plant being the fuchsia, which grows to large size in the open air and flowers beautifully. Nearly every window also has its garden. Throughout all this north end of Ireland, so far as I could judge, there was but little outward evidence of poverty, and the humblest thatched cottages I saw seemed cleanly and well cared for. This region has good landlords, I was told, who looked after the popular interests, and were well thought of. Across, on the west side of Lough Foyle, however,—the lough that leads up to 'Derry,—there was a different story. There were the estates of the late Lord Leitrim, and the people had no good word to say of him.

Whilst the railway approach to the Causeway is thus pleasant, the continuation of the journey from Port Rush eastward along the coast is decidedly primitive. Here is one of the wonders of the world, of equal fame with Niagara, yet no railway goes within eight miles of it, though, so far as engineering is concerned, its construction would be easy. These eight Irish miles have to be travelled in a jaunting-car, and the journey fully maintains the elastic reputation of the Irish mile, for it grows to about fifteen before the Causeway is reached, and requires nearly an hour and a half of fast trotting to accomplish, over a road which is a very good one. When St. Patrick measured the Irish mile he had with him a mad dog, whom he held with a woollen string. At the end of the mile the dog gave a leap, stretching the string, and this accounts for the elastic character of the Irish mile. It has only been within a brief period that there has been a well-kept hotel at the Causeway; and in fact this great wonder is shown in the most un-American style possible. It was the height of the season, and one of the finest days of the summer, yet not over a dozen visitors were at the place. If this great curiosity were as near Philadelphia as it is to Belfast, we would be running cheap excursion trains to it over broad and narrow gauge railroads, emptying out thousands of passengers to cut their initials in very bad letters upon the basalt rocks. It would be overrun with booths selling questionable drinks, and basket merchants vending peanuts. Yet not a booth was to be seen anywhere near the Causeway, and I do not believe there is one peanut in all Ireland. That great American institution is yet to be introduced into Her Majesty's dominions.

To the credit of the Earl of Antrim, the lord of the manor, it should be said that, without getting a penny of revenue from this noted possession of his, he has thrown it entirely open to the public, free of any fee or reward, and is in every way protecting it from vandalism. The Causeway is carefully preserved from relic-hunters, and I did not see any one's name carved or written upon any portion of it; or any one's advertisement of soap or bitters or pop-corn adorning the rocks. The freedom of access is in marked contrast to the system at Niagara, where it is impossible to get a near view of the Falls without paying a tax to the proprietor of some garden or bridge, who purposely obstructs the view to gather the toll. Beggars and print and specimen venders are, however, the annoyance at the Causeway, and to an extent unknown in America. They dog the footsteps of visitors, and interfere seriously with the enjoyment of the visit. When the Emperor of Brazil was here, in 1876, a force of constabulary had to accompany him to keep off the horde who would quickly have despoiled him of all his loose change. A vigorous application of Anglo-Saxon is the best protection, for the kind of English an angry American talks is an unwonted tongue to these harpies, and it strikes them with awe.

Fin McCool was the Irish giant who made this region famous. He constructed this Causeway as a road to Scotland, landing at Staffa, for the purpose of inviting over a Caledonian giant for a fight. The Scot came, and, as the story is told in Ireland, got whipped. Perhaps if the story was told in Scotland the result might be different. Be that as it may, however, Fin McCool, with true Hibernian magnanimity, became the friend of the Scot, induced him to marry and settle in Ireland, " which everybody knows is the best country in the world;" and then the Causeway being no longer wanted by the giants, it was sunk under the sea, only leaving a portion visible here, a little at Rathlin Island, ten miles off the coast, and the portals of the entrance at Fingal's Cave, in Staffa. Thus originated the Causeway, according to tradition. Geologists have some idea that it had a different formation, but as no two of them can agree on a theory about it, possibly we will be as well off if we adhere to the tradition. All the way from Port Rush to the Causeway are seen relics of the great Irish giant. The entire coast is a wonderful formation: a high, bold, rocky coast, of limestone and basalt, towering sometimes as high as four hundred feet above the water. These rocks are hewn and wrought by the constant action of the waves into caves, archways with natural bridges, enormous cauldrons, curious profiles, honeycombs, and every sort of fantastic shape. Here we have Fin's Punch-Bowl, wherein the sea, when a northern gale blows, boils around furiously; his face, a rock one hundred feet high, which is a colossal forehead, nose, mouth, and chin of almost perfect form, and a much larger formation than the profile on the White Mountains in New England; his grandmother, a perfect representative of an old woman stooping over and bent with age, this rock, weighing seven tons, being declared to be a petrifaction of his grandmother, thus punished for having three husbands; his loom, whereon he formerly knit his garters and stockings, and his wash-tub at the mouth of a cave, always filled with soapsuds, wherein he washes his shirt in the mornings. On the Causeway itself we have the giant's crown; his pulpit, from which his sermons when he preaches can be heard all the way to Scotland; his church, with its steeple; his organ, which every seventh year on Christmas morning plays while all the rocks dance, the tunes being "St. Patrick's Day in the Morning" and "Boyne Water," both being adopted so as to secure strict impartiality; his chimneys, which rise up like so many chimney-pots above the Causeway, and the Scotch cap of his foe, which was dropped in the water when the Scot was vanquished. These things are no mere fanciful representations, but are almost as perfect resemblances of the things named as if the sculptor had gone there and carved them. The organ has all its pipes. The Scotch cap has the knot tied behind. The church has nave, transept, and peaked roof. The crown is massive, but true to its name. The chimneys possess everything but the smoke. There is also a rock called the Lion's Paw, an extraordinary formation, jutting out into the sea, and looking just as if some colossal lion had gone there and laid down his foot upon a huge pedestal. On this coast there is also a remarkable ruin, which is a curiosity of human work, as strange as the natural ones referred to. This is Dunluce Castle, also belonging to the Earl of Antrim. It stands upon an isolated rock rising precipitously over one hundred feet above the sea, standing close to the rocks on shore, but cut off from them. On this rock, and entirely covering it, are the roofless ruins of the old castle, hoary with age, with vines overrunning them, and dating back no one knows how far. The dark-brown ruins are very picturesque, and are accessible only by a narrow bridge, raised high above the water, and not three feet wide. It is the subject of endless tradition and romance, and is underlaid by a cave only accessible from the sea at low water. This entire coast is honeycombed and washed by the sea into extraordinarily fantastic shapes. Against it beat the waves of the broad Atlantic, no land being interposed between this coast and the hyperborean regions.

Of the Giant's Causeway itself it is difficult to give an intelligible description. It is certainly unlike anything I have heretofore seen, and also unlike the idea I had formed of it from reading descriptions. If descriptions could not give me the proper idea, I must hesitate to communicate it by any words of mine. Two grand amphitheatres facing the north are hewn in the rocks on the coast, their background rising to a height of four hundred and twenty feet above the water. On the upper faces of those amphitheatres are columnar rocks, not unlike the palisades of the Hudson, but more perfectly formed. On the easternmost verge a high, bold headland extends into the sea. Between the two another headland not so bold, but broken down at the end, also extends into the sea. On the side of this is the organ, and from the top rise the chimneys. In front is the Lover's Rock, a leap from which, four hundred feet, into the sea, is a sure cure for love. These two amphitheatres are the setting enclosing the Causeway. It stretches out from the western amphitheatre for one thousand feet into the sea. It is low down,—so low that during gales the water entirely covers it,—and it gradually slopes down until lost to view under the water. Suppose that some one had driven about four thousand piles into the water, as closely together as they could be placed, with their tops very nearly levelled off, though somewhat irregular, and an idea can be got of the Causeway. Suppose, further, that all these piles were stone columns, accurately cut and polished into prisms varying from three to nine sides, no two of them shaped exactly alike, yet all of them so accurately fitted together that water can scarcely penetrate the seams, and there will be an idea of the formation. Then take every column and break it into pieces from one to two feet long, but leave them all standing, and cut off the tops so that some will be a foot higher than others, and there will be an idea of the surface. These columns, whilst so accurately fitted, can yet be taken apart without trouble, and, in fact, the Causeway was in danger, some time ago, of being carried away bodily, until the lord of the manor stopped it. No stonemason could do better work than this wonderful formation shows, and it looks as if set up block by block in the amphitheatre, and then gradually sunk into the sea. The visitor can tramp all over the Causeway, excepting where the water covers it, and in doing this will walk over the heads of some four thousand columns. In the midst of it, he can take a drink from a spring which has some wonderful quality which I have forgotten, the water of which is said to weigh one ounce less per pint than any other water in Ireland. He can also sit in the "wishing chair" and have his desires fulfilled in a twelvemonth. Cows and sheep were grazing on the borders of the Causeway where the grass grows among the rocks, and I learnt the important fact that white sheep eat more in Ireland than black ones, because there are more of them.

Two extraordinary caves are shown adjoining the Causeway, one of which penetrates over three hundred feet and the other over six hundred feet; both being very high, one having an ornate Gothic arch at the entrance, and into both the boat into which you get to visit them is rowed for some distance, a pistol being fired off and noises made to develop the echoes, whilst the coloring on the rocks under water is magnificent. It is no easy task for the four stout oarsmen who pull the boat to breast the waves of the Atlantic, and force her around the rough rocks to get at the entrances of these caves. At the same time it is impossible to get a view of the surroundings of the Causeway, which are very grand, without going in the boat, whilst a guide is also necessary. This great natural curiosity ought to be made more accessible, but it is still possible by an early start to see it all and get back to Belfast in a day; and at a cost, including all fees and swindles,—for there are some practised upon the visitor,—of not over five dollars for each person, if there is a party. The railway fare is two dollars and twenty-five cents, the jaunting-car fare sixty-two cents, the boat two dollars, and the guide one dollar and twenty-five cents, all reasonable, and the fees for boat and guide being the same for one person or a half-dozen. But the jaunting-car driver wants sixpence and each boatman sixpence extra for himself, besides forcing you to buy specimens at fifty cents a box, and raising a commotion if you don't buy a box from each boatman. These are swindles, and ought to be suppressed, especially as good specimens can be got on shore for half the money, but the aggregate swindle does not amount to any great sum, and is, probably, much less than it would be if a genuine Yankee were imported to "run" the Causeway. As it is impossible to see such an extraordinary formation anywhere else for less, or indeed for any money, we may possibly be willing, in the interests of sight-seeing, to permit these descendants of Fin McCool to swindle us to the modest extent which seems to content them.

## LETTER XI.

### THE TWO CLYDES.

GLASGOW, August 1.

It is a very common thing in Philadelphia to speak of the Delaware River as the Clyde of America, but, excepting that iron ships are built on both and both run down to the sea, there is no resemblance between them. Glasgow would be a proud city and would have saved millions of money had she such a noble highway as the Delaware leading to her quays. She would make very much more of her facilities in such a case than Philadelphia does. But, instead of a river of the width of the Delaware, I found the Clyde a stream much smaller than the Schuylkill, and corresponding about to the Rancocas Creek. It would be perfectly feasible to make the Rancocas as famous and as deep as the Clyde (it is now as wide) if it had Glasgow located upon it, with Scotch energy to do the work. There is no better evidence of the ability of human hands to make a seaport where nature did not intend one to exist than is to be seen at Glasgow. In former times, Greenock was the port of Glasgow. Greenock stands at the point where the Clyde River debouches into the Firth of Clyde, and above it in those days the river was an insignificant stream, with barely nine feet depth in the twenty-two miles of water up to Glasgow. But the canny Scots determined to have a port, and their achievements in deepening, embanking, and preserving the river, and making their city one of the great ports of the world, have brought them renown.

I came across the Irish Sea in a Cunard steamer from Belfast, Ireland, one of a fleet of no less than seven large steamers, that leave Belfast every evening for British and Scotch ports, laden with cattle and food supplies, for which Ireland is drawn upon so largely to feed her neighbors, and carrying hundreds of passengers. The commerce between these islands is very great, and requires a large amount of tonnage. On our steamer were no less than a hundred beef cattle. On another were large droves of sheep. Ireland is the grazing farm for Britain. The journey is performed during the night, and the Firth of Clyde is entered about three o'clock next morning, it being already almost sunrise. The Firth has high bold shores, beautiful in the extreme, but partially obscured by fog, which overhung the water all the way to Glasgow. The Firth narrows into the river as Greenock is approached, and this partially decayed port, overshadowed by her greater neighbor's second growth, is, nevertheless, seen to have a large commerce, her docks being full of shipping. At this point begins the evidence of the hard work that has made the Clyde what it is. Constant dredging is necessary to maintain the channel, and I saw no less than six huge steam-dredges, of a pattern very different and much more effective than those we are accustomed to, at work in the river between Greenock and Glasgow, and learnt that more were employed, besides others building. Where rocks have been encountered in opening the channel they have been blasted out, and this has been extensively done, adding to the cost of the work. The nine feet depth of water has been deepened sufficiently to float the largest ships, although these vessels are too long to turn round in the channel excepting at certain points, and then at high water. The crooked parts of the river have been straightened, and this work is still going on. For a few miles above Greenock the channel is marked by a series of buoys, towers, and other beacons, sometimes in rows only about two hundred feet apart. Above this the river is embanked for miles, with masonry walls, faced with broken stone to resist the action of the wash from passing vessels. There are range lights and towers, numerous tidal gauges, and, in fact, the channel is fenced in with buoys and banked in with walls so effectually that it is impossible to go astray. The river, from a short distance above Greenock to Glasgow, is not more than three hundred and fifty feet wide, and in some places narrows to two hundred and fifty feet. At Glasgow itself it widens to almost the dimensions of the Schuylkill to permit of vessels lying at the quays, for there is no room for piers, and the steamers have to be strung along lengthwise. This famous river is in effect a wide canal, and navigation is conducted somewhat upon the principles governing a railroad. Signboards are posted at various places ordering " Dead Slow," and officers are stationed at intervals to see that pilots obey the order. There is no such thing as steaming at full speed along the Clyde. It is like a crowded street, a stream of vessels passing up and down, their steam-whistles blowing frequent signals and their crews standing often with fenders to prevent collisions. Navigation has to be slow and very cautious. Such a marked and governed river I never saw before. It is in reality a canal constructed for ship navigation, and used apparently to the utmost extent of which it is capable. There is not in any other part of the world such extensive buoying and marking, and at night the signals line each shore like rows of lamps along a street.

But to come back to the " Clyde of America" in its point of resemblance to the Clyde of Scotland,—in ship-building,— I was told that trade was very poor, and that every one was complaining. The ship-yards are strung along both banks for probably twelve miles below Glasgow. Some of them have huge travelling-derricks erected over the vessels building, so as to facilitate heavy hoisting. It appeared to me that not much more than one-third of the ship-building capacity of the yards along the river was being made use of, judging from the unoccupied launching-ways, yet this one-third, if on the Clyde of America, would make the hearts of our iron ship-builders leap for joy. I counted forty-eight iron steamers, most of them of the largest size, in course of construction, whilst a half-dozen more were lying at quays receiving engines. When we launch an iron ship on the Delaware it can shoot out into the river without fear, but this cannot be done on the Clyde. There is no ship set up at right angles to the river. They are all built at an angle almost parallel with the shore, so that when launched they will float up or down stream, and thus get room to clear the ways. Most of these vessels looked longer than the river is wide. It was not an unusual thing to count ten different launching-ways in one yard, but the largest number of vessels constructing in any one yard was five. At the same time I counted over one hundred steamers in the river, besides many sailing-vessels. The great commerce of this stream is compressed into smaller compass than that of Liverpool, but, although eclipsed by that port, it is large enough to yield Her Majesty's government twenty million dollars annual customs duties. It has given Glasgow great growth, that city now

c*

having a half-million population. But I do not think that a broad and noble river like the Delaware ought to be dwarfed by being named after this narrow, cramped, and artificially constructed creek, which is navigable barely twenty-five miles, and would close up were not dredge-boats constantly at work. The Mississippi, on the same principle, might as well be called the Clyde of the West.

### GLASGOW.

The great Cathedral, seven hundred years old, is the chief curiosity of Glasgow, and behind it rises the Necropolis, an abrupt hill elevated to the top of the Cathedral roof, which is the chief Glasgow cemetery. This hill forms a beautiful background to the brown walls of the Cathedral, the steep hill-sides being terraced with tombs, covered with monuments to the dead, and surmounted on the peak with an elaborate memorial to John Knox. The Cathedral has been thoroughly restored, and one of its most pleasant features is the memorial windows presented by people far and wide to complete the restoration. Within it on the walls are ornate tablets to soldiers who have fallen in England's wars, and deep down in the crypt, which is the most spacious in the kingdom, is the shrine of St. Mungo, Glasgow's patron saint, from whose effigy zealous Glasgow reformers long ago cut off the head, leaving the headless trunk to be wondered at by surprised visitors. Several curious things appeared in this interesting city. On the public offices, my American ideas of the laborious character of official work were somewhat shocked by finding signboards announcing that the offices are kept open from 9 A.M. to 5 P.M. When vacant lots are to be disposed of the announcement reads, "To sell or to feu." All the chief streets are provided with horse railways or " trams," as they are called, laid with the peculiar rail I have heretofore described, which prevents jarring or any interference with other traffic; and all the tramcars are two-storied structures, whilst a considerable portion of them have roofs over the upper story. These huge structures look very curious on the streets. Glasgow is thus far the champion city for chimney-pots, in a kingdom which has devoted probably as much ingenuity to those extraordinary productions as it has to anything else. Glasgow has more chimney-pots per house, more queer ones, and more strange con-

GLASGOW.

trivances to prevent wind blowing them down, than any other town I have yet seen. From twelve to seventeen pots on one chimney are frequent, and in one case I counted twenty of them on a single chimney of an ordinary-sized house. What possible use there could be for so many I could not conceive. It was not infrequent to see pipes run from one chimney to another, as if a man were entirely disgusted with his own achievements in this line, and wanted to try his neighbor's. What a glorious business the terra-cotta and smoke-pipe manufacturers' must be in Her Majesty's dominions! Glasgow has two beautiful parks, both on high ground and commanding views of the city. Kelvingrove Park is a small one, but beautifully situated on the Kelvin River, which runs along a deep valley through it. In this park is the City Industrial Museum, and adjoining it the University of Glasgow, in a commanding position overlooking the city, the latter being one of the finest buildings in Scotland. Rows of large dwellings also face the park, and are built on terraces behind it in a most eligible situation. The Museum contains a fine exhibition, chiefly of industrial arts, with a large portion devoted to steam-engine and ship-building. Models are shown of Watt's earliest steamers. In this museum I found, in a prominent position, the fine exhibition of the agricultural products of Kansas, which was at the Centennial. The Queen's Park, on the other side of the city, whilst not so ornate as Kelvingrove, occupies a fine position, and from it can be seen the battle-ground of Langside, where Mary, Queen of Scots, was defeated, and the tree marking the spot where she stood to witness the battle's disastrous result. Glasgow honors her great men. St. George's Square, in the centre of the city, on which the chief hotels front, contains a monument to Sir Walter Scott, whilst around it are statues of Sir John Moore, Robert Peel, James Watt, Lord Clyde, and other famous natives of the city. It is a good Scotch representative town, showing prodigious energy, vast and ramified trade, but is unfortunately overhung by the fog and begrimed by the smoke that obscure so many British cities, but at the same time give all their buildings the venerable appearance that increases their reputation.

## LETTER XII.

### THIRTY-SIX HOURS IN THE HIGHLANDS.

EDINBURGH, August 3.

To get a glimpse of the Scottish Highlands there are various routes from Glasgow, all leading down the Clyde by steamer, and after leaving that river taking various lines by water or land. The excursion business is conducted here as extensively as with us at home, and requires many steamers, most of them being extremely comfortable boats, but built very narrow, as all Clyde steamers are, the necessities of the navigation of that contracted, tortuous river forbidding the use of wider craft. In passing down the Clyde a good idea is given of the difficulties of its navigation and the risks encountered. The moving steamers and dredge-boats keep the mud constantly stirred up, so that there is a very disagreeable smell from the water. Part way down-stream we found the huge Anchor Line steamer Ethiopia run ashore, and lying partly careened over in the mud. She had come down stern foremost several miles from Glasgow to get a wide enough place to turn around preparatory to sailing for New York, and was waiting for high water, though in a position which evidently must be a severe test of her staunchness. Further on a fine excursion steamer was seen seriously injured by collision with another steamer, and our boat had to take her passengers off. They were in quite a fright, and were glad enough to get transferred. All hands came off, including the Scotch lassie who dealt in cakes and candy, and who passed her stock over the rail with celerity. Groundings and collisions seem of constant occurrence in this narrow, crowded river. On the way down Dumbarton Castle is passed, one of the famous Scottish strongholds, and opposite there were gangs of men fixing the bank, repairing damage from some vessel running ashore and displacing the stones protecting the bank. This sort of work has to be done all the time, and the promptness of repair keeps everything in order. I doubt whether this river in some places can be over two hundred feet wide. Dumbarton Castle stands on a rock six hundred feet high, with precipitous sides. A flagstaff rising among the trees on top is all that can be seen of the castle from the river. Farther down, on a high, isolated rock, almost split in two, and looking as if it had been thrown down on the sand bordering the river, is Cardross Castle, the ruins of which are plainly visible. This was the last home of Robert Bruce, who died there in 1329.

Greenock, as we passed it, was gayly dressed in colors—the shipping, the buildings, and the quays. All the flags they had in the town and on the shipping were brought out in honor of a great event. Greenock has been stirred up in her rivalry with Glasgow, and, in order to hold fast to her commerce, has determined to construct a new dock at a cost of two million dollars. This dock is to have twenty-six feet depth of water, is to be two thousand feet long, and to be provided with jetties giving no less than a mile and one-third in length of quays. The first sod of the new work was to be turned, and the town was full of excitement preparing for the event, the provost being provided with a silver-mounted spade and wheelbarrow with which to perform the ceremony. The new work is to be called the James Watt Dock.

The excursion business is conducted very extensively among the beautiful islands adjoining the mouth of the Firth of Clyde and the region known as the Kyles of Bute. Steamers laden with passengers can be seen flitting about in all directions. The one I was on carried at least one thousand passengers, who were getting on and off at the many pretty places at which it stopped. The Scotch predominated,—some in kilts and some in breeks, and wearing strange hats and clothes such as are rarely seen in America. There were plenty of children and plenty of luggage. In fact, although the boat was large, it was at times uncomfortably crowded. It showed, however, that the Scotch are as great travellers as some of the rest of mankind, and that they love the exceedingly beautiful scenery of their own land well enough to go and look at it. The steamer wound in and out among the lovely islands, which gave to the Duke of Rothesay the title of Lord of the Isles, and about which Scott has written, and stopped at many pretty places. Here are portions of the domains of the Marquis of Bute and the Duke of Argyle, and one of the homes of the Marquis of Lorne, the heir to the latter title, who is to be the new Canadian Governor-General, and whom the Court Circular describes as "Her Majesty's son-in-law." Here centre the scenes of volumes of romance and all sorts of traditions; whilst centuries ago, Norwegians and Danes, and Picts and Scots, and Celts and English fought many a battle amid these beautiful scenes.

Passing through the Kyles of Bute, the steamer sailed up the beautiful Loch Fyne, skirting the peninsula of Cantyre, and to avoid the long journey around this peninsula, debarked the passengers, who adopted the primitive navigation of the canal to get across it. Here we were introduced, as indeed at all the landings on this journey, to the toll-levying methods adopted by pier-owners. All passengers are mulcted various sums who pass over piers to or from vessels, as a sort of wharfage. Paying the tax, we embarked on a steam-barge on the Crinan Canal, which, availing of a depression in the peninsula, crosses it at a narrow part, passing through fifteen locks, the highest stage being seventy-two feet above the lowest level. The canalling and locking were rather exciting, especially as Scottish pipers, dressed in Highland costume, availed themselves of the stoppages to play their pibrochs for half-pence, whilst bare-legged damsels danced the Highland fling. The canal passed through a pretty country, but did not seem to have much trade, though, like all British public works, it is very substantially constructed. The canal-barge brought us alongside another steamer, as fine and almost as large as the one on which we embarked at Glasgow, and we were soon steaming through the Sound of Jura into Loch Craigneish on our way to the heart of the Western Highlands. As we proceeded the scenery became constantly more romantic, the steamer threading among islands and hills that grew bolder and higher as the day advanced. On the left we passed Benmore, the mountain of Mull, over three thousand one hundred feet high, and we entered the domain of the Earl of Breadalbane, one of the largest Scotch landed proprietors. Here we touched at Oban, the chief town of the Western Highlands, and a fashionable watering-place, which sits on a low, narrow strip of land, backed by high hills, the hotels running up the hillsides in terraces, as it were, whilst the harbor in front is filled with pleasure-boats, including two or three steam-yachts. Continuing the journey the ruins of Dunolly Castle are passed, the old-time stronghold of the Lords of Lorne, standing on a high rock, with everything gone to pieces excepting the donjon-keep, around which ivy creeps, giving it excessive beauty. A short distance farther, and guarding the entrance to Loch Etive, though standing on a low point, is the famous ruin of Dunstaffnage Castle. Here the ancient Scottish kings were crowned on the Dunstaffnage stone, or the stone of Scone, which is now the seat of the coronation chair in Westminster Abbey, and on which every English sovereign has been crowned since James I. Steaming on through higher, rougher, and steeper hills, and among regions but sparsely cultivated and still more sparsely inhabited, with long vistas of hazy view opening up between them; passing among pretty islands and through narrow channels, and into a region that reminded me very much of the Juniata, though the water expanse was broader, our boat at sunset turned a sharp angle around a hill six hundred feet high, partially covered with fir, and we were in Loch Leven. Here, at the little town of Ballachulish, of which the chief buildings seem to be a hotel and a post-office, guarding the entrance to the famous pass of Glencoe, and on the banks of the Loch Leven that poets have sung about and romancists written of, the journey was broken for the night. But it was eleven o'clock before the night began, the twilight lingering late in summer-time in these high northern latitudes.

### THE PASS OF GLENCOE.

Next morning, adopting another old-time method of travel, —for there are no railroads in this celebrated though sparsely-inhabited region,—we took the stage-coach through the Pass of Glencoe. This pass is said to excel every other glen in Scotland in dreary magnificence, and in history it is associated with the massacre of the Clan MacDonald by the English in 1692, the chief of the clan being the famous MacDonald of Glencoe, and the massacre taking place in the glen where the clan had received their treacherous foes with free hospitality. Relics of the massacre are pointed out at several places in the entrance to the glen, but they are fast going to ruin. A monument marks the residence of the chief, whose story is interwoven into most of the traditions of the glen. This famous pass is not visited by many Americans, though the route certainly gives the best idea of the Highlands that can be got in a hasty tour. The sail above Oban and the entrance to Loch Leven give the water scenery, whilst the Pass has all the dreary, inhospitable, cold, cheerless, and gigantic magnificence that can be put into a mountain and valley landscape. A little brook called the Coe, rising at an elevation of about nine hundred feet above the sea, flows westerly among the huge peaks of this portion of the Highlands, and at a distance of about ten miles from its source falls into Loch Leven. It makes a deep glen of the wildest character, the peculiar character of which is the almost entire absence of trees. The peaks rise from two thousand to three thousand five hundred feet, without a tree upon them, and look like gigantic sugar-loaves, with their precipitous, rocky sides run into ravines by the action of the water. The very few trees that are in the glen are scattered at the bottom of the valley. The Coe is an insignificant stream, a torrent in the rainy season, but now almost dried up, but the valley in which it flows has considerable breadth, and on both sides the bold peaks rise up, the whole scene presenting an appearance of utter cheerlessness and inhospitality.

Nothing that is of value seems to thrive there. Before entering the glen, on the shores of Loch Leven, there are extensive slate quarries, but the glen once entered there seems not a living thing. The sparse vegetation is not fit for pasturage. There are no horses, no sheep or cattle, such as fill the valleys elsewhere; not a sign of life, excepting at the little stable near the head of the glen, where the coach-horses are changed. Such a thorough abolition, as it were, of living things from the face of the earth I never saw before. The situation of the glen is not unlike the Lewistown Narrows, on the Juniata, if we can imagine the Juniata dwindled to a dried-up brook, its valley widened to a half-mile, and the enclosing mountains entirely denuded of trees and surmounted by rows of isolated peaks, whilst every building and every living thing is removed from the scene. It is the peculiarity of these Highland hills that, instead of running in ridges, they are composed of separate peaks, each independent of the other, and elevating their pointed, rocky, treeless tops in all directions, with intersecting glens and valleys between.

Having passed out of this dreary scene, with the three forbidding "Sisters of Glencoe" elevating their haughty heads

on the right, the "Lord Chancellor" on the left, and the
"Shepherd of the Glen" in front, all high, isolated peaks,
the route crosses the heads of Glen Etive and Glen Orchy,
and passes over a ridge fourteen hundred feet above the sea,
from which the highest mountain in Britain, Ben Nevis, can
be seen at about twenty miles distance; the route then seeks
the valley formed by a tributary of the Tay, and gradually
descends along the top of a deep cañon towards the railway station at Tyndrum, thirty-six miles from Ballachulish. Glencoe, I am informed, is partly the property of Miss
Downie, a wealthy Scottish lady, and partly of the well-known
family of Stuart. Having passed out of the glen, the route
is through the extensive domain of the Earl of Breadalbane.
This portion of the journey is much like a wagon-road up and
down hill across the eastern slopes of the Alleghenies. There
is a certain hill at Altoona, where a southern view can be had
across the railroad of ridge after ridge and spur after spur of
the mountains, until the horizon cuts it off. The view from
the summit near the King's House, across Glen Orchy, is not
unlike this, though it is entirely denuded of trees. The Earl
of Breadalbane rents all of this territory to the Earl of Dudley, a wealthy English nobleman, for shooting purposes. Lord
Dudley has the privilege of bringing his friends here to shoot
deer during about seven weeks in autumn. For this he pays
a rent of twenty-five thousand dollars a year, besides maintaining sixteen houses in different parts of the domain for his sixteen gamekeepers who protect the domain from trespass. These
keepers get, besides their houses, four thousand seven hundred
and fifty dollars salary. Lord Dudley also maintains a "shoot-
ing-box" here, in a beautiful position near Tyndrum, the
"box" being, in fact, a large hotel, capable of accommodating
thirty to forty guests. There in splendor he entertains his
friends during the deerstalking season, the Prince of Wales
being usually among them, and to aid the sport has had planted
extensive forests of pine, fir, and other trees, in which the deer
harbor along the valleys adjacent to Tyndrum. He certainly
pays dearly for a few weeks' sport, but then his income is one
of the largest in the kingdom.

The stage-coaches used on this route are great lumbering
vehicles, built about twice as heavy as an American would
build a coach to go over such hills. The road is a good one,

and does not need such heavy vehicles, which almost exhaust the horses, though there are four changes in the thirty-six miles. At Tyndrum the railway is taken to either Glasgow or Edinburgh. I took the latter. It passes through many historical and romantic scenes, whose tales in song or story, as indeed the history of the entire route described, have been told by Sir Walter Scott. It passes Coilantogle Ford, where Roderick Dhu, having chivalrously conducted Fitz James thus far in safety, according to promise, challenged him to mortal combat; then goes through the land made famous by the exploits of Rob Roy; then leaving the Highlands for the Lowlands, passes the famous Castle of Donne and Abbey Craig, with its monument to William Wallace; next goes over the bridge of Allan and into Stirling, and alongside the ruins of Stirling Castle, the most famous castle of Scotland; then over the battlefield of Bannockburn, the Bannock River being a peaceful brook running between gently-sloping green banks, with but enough water to cover its pebbly bed; through Falkirk and by the ruins of Linlithgow Palace, into the ravine through Edinburgh, landing its passengers almost beneath the walls of Edinburgh Castle and Holyrood. The route ended amid the green and highly-cultivated fields of the rich and level country near Edinburgh, and the puny, hairy cattle of the Highlands were quickly exchanged for the fat ones of the Lowlands; whilst arriving in the modern Athens, and landing at the Waverley Bridge, I found that I had to unlearn the lessons taught me in school, for all the kilted and breeked Scots and people who ought to know were pronouncing the name of Edinburgh as if it was written Edinborough.

## LETTER XIII.

### PROUD DUN-EDIN.

EDINBURGH, August 5.

Few views with more charms burst upon the traveller's eye than the sight he beholds upon coming into Edinburgh from the west, and being set down by the North British Railway

EDINBURGH CASTLE FROM WAVERLEY STATION.

at the Waverley Bridge Station. The railway, after running through two tunnels under portions of the city, passes along the bottom of a deep ravine, and sloping up from both sides are gardens surmounted by magnificent buildings, whilst towering above all, on the right-hand side, is Edinburgh Castle. Then emerging from the station, crossing the Waverley Bridge, and going around the magnificent Waverley Memorial into Prince's Street, the sight, as one passes along in front of the great hotels, is grand indeed. No wonder Dun-Edin and her people are proud. Even the Champs Elysées, of Paris, cannot compare to the front view from any one of the hotels on Prince's Street across the ravine to the hills beyond, splendid edifices meeting the eye on every side, the Castle on its massive rock in front, with red-coated sentinels guarding the ramparts, the bottom of the ravine a series of lovely gardens, and all made into a landscape in the heart of a great city that I believe is without a rival on either continent. The modern Athens enjoys from nature a position of the highest beauty, which art has adorned in the most thorough manner. No visit to Europe is complete without a visit to Edinburgh.

Imagine, if you can, a great city with two ranges of peaks scattered through it,—miniature mountains, as it were, rising from a rolling plain. Streams of water, with occasional lakes and morasses, originally ran through the bottoms of the intervening valleys; but the one in the central valley has had its course stopped, all the water being diverted so as to supply the city, whilst the former bed has been converted into the line of railway I have spoken of, and the Prince's Street gardens. Towering five hundred feet from the former bank of this stream, and in the heart of the city, rises the rugged and precipitous rock on which stands the famous Edinburgh Castle, still a garrisoned post, but the hill being also availed of now for the more peaceful object of furnishing a water reservoir for the city. Farther down are the rugged Salisbury Craigs, which terminate in the abrupt peak, eight hundred and twenty-three feet high, looking like a recumbent lion, which is known as Arthur's Seat. On the country side of this range, and at some distance, are the Pentland Hills, nineteen hundred feet high, whence these water-courses take their source. Across the city, and on the other side of the ravine, are other hills, three hundred to four hundred feet high, the most prominent being Colton Hill, and these slope down to the little stream known as the Water of Leith, whilst on the other side the land rises upwards again. On these hills and in these valleys Edinburgh is built, with the Castle in the centre, the "Old Town" on one side of it, and the "New Town" on the other. The configuration of the ground gives scores of situations for magnificent edifices, and they are thoroughly availed of. The city is a succession of statues, memorials, commemorative edifices, churches, castles, and historical buildings, and no townsman has done anything to merit fame who is not commemorated in some way. Edinburgh is handing down to posterity in "storied urn and animated bust" the memories of all her great people.

Three famous names, however, eclipse all others in the decoration of Edinburgh,—Sir Walter Scott, Mary, Queen of Scots, and John Knox,—and their memorials are seen everywhere. Scott revived the chivalry of a former day, and the city of his birth and chief residence is doing everything to keep his memory green. On the corner-stone of the magnificent Waverley Memorial, which is an emblematic structure, built two hundred feet high, covered with statues of Scott's chief characters, and enclosing also one of the great writer, Lord Jeffrey inscribed words declaring that Scott's admirable writings had given more delight and suggested better feeling to a larger class of readers, in every rank of society, than those of any other author, with the exception of Shakspeare alone. The designer of this magnificent memorial was drowned before its completion. In and around the city you are pointed to hundreds of memorials of the writer and his characters, which the town has marked so as to preserve their fame. His dwelling-house is shown; George Herriot's hospital and schools; the site of the Tolbooth, where Effie Deans was confined, as told in the "Heart of Mid-Lothian," this spot being marked by the figure of a heart formed by the stones in the street pavement where it stood; Effie's trysting-places at St. Andrew's Well and the cairn; Jennie Deans' cottage; the "closes" and "wynds," and inns and buildings told of in Scott's songs and stories; every man, woman, and child in the city being familiar with them all, and ready to tell of them, and showing a veneration for the great writer such as is scarcely found for any one. As we have passed through Scotland this has been the prominent trait of the people, and the admiration of the Scots for the author of Waverley stands out as conspicuously as the veneration of Americans for Washington.

Of Mary, Queen of Scots, many precious relics are also kept. Buildings that were her favorite resorts in and near the city are guarded with scrupulous care, but the chief relics cluster around the Castle and Holyrood. The Castle, to which there is but one entrance, over the drawbridge across the old moat, which is now used by the garrison, Her Majesty's Fiftieth Regiment of Foot, in the peaceful occupation of pitching quoits, is maintained as far as possible in its original condition. The chief objects here are Mary's room, with the adjoining apartment, about ten feet square, where her son, James I., was born, and from the window of which he was lowered when eight days old, in a basket, down the precipitous sides of the rock at night to trusty friends below, who carried him off to a place of supposed greater safety. Both rooms are dark and dismal, looking more like prisons than a palace. The little room, which is historically so famous, is a photograph-shop at present. Then there is the regalia-room, which was reopened chiefly through the exertions of Sir Walter Scott. Here are exhibited the crown of Robert Bruce, the sword of state, and jewels of the throne of Scotland, set with gems, and very valuable. These articles, when Scotland was united with England in the early part of the eighteenth century, the Scots were afraid would be carried off to London. Their custodians enclosed them in their chest, and closed up the doors and stairways leading to the apartment. Here they rested for over one hundred years, until Scott, in delving through the musty records of the city, searching for materials for his novels, discovered papers indicating their whereabouts. Every one had forgotten them; but Scott had a royal warrant issued for a search, and by dint of breaking locks and entering into hidden places the crown regalia-room was ultimately opened to public view in 1818. These priceless gems, which, it is said, Scotland would raise a rebellion if their removal was attempted, are now exhibited, together with the huge old chest that contained them, on the spot of their hiding. They are enclosed in an iron cage, jealously guarded, and Scott's description and history of them is at hand ready for visitors. This apartment is adjacent to Queen Mary's room in the Castle, but is so situated as to be easily overlooked.

On the highest pinnacle of the Castle, opposite the grated pan wherein the alarm-fires were kindled in former days to rouse the clans upon a Southern invader appearing, and pointing at the New Town, almost over a little adjoining graveyard which attracts fully as much attention, is the famous old gun "Mons Meg," supposed to have been made at Mons, in Belgium, in 1486, and to have been at the siege of Norham Castle, a few years later. This gun is thirteen and a half feet long, seven feet in circumference at the largest part, and of twenty inches diameter of bore. It is made of longitudinal iron bars, wrapped around by other bars to hold them together, and fired stone balls, several specimens of which are at hand. It was kept in Scotland until after the union of the kingdoms, when it was sent to London, and was one of the great curiosities of the Tower. It was restored to Scotland in 1826. The gun is very rough and is mounted on a modern carriage. It has no trunnions, and originally sat in a wooden box on wheels. The little graveyard which this effete monster guards is used by the troops in burying the pet dogs of the garrison. It is a triangular space, covering about fifty square feet, wherein are set up the modest tombstones recording the virtues of Tiny, Flora, Toby, and Topsy. They have more exalted graves than the kings and queens of Scotland, whose dust lies in the ruins of Holyrood Abbey, but so commingled and desecrated in the religious wars of the country that their tombs are not recognizable. St. Margaret's Chapel, a small, low apartment, about twenty-five by ten feet, with arched roof, is the oldest part of the Castle, and has been restored. It is a bare, dungeon-like apartment, with no attractions but its antiquity. It is said to be eight hundred years old.

Holyrood Palace, like the Castle, is also chiefly famous for its relics of Queen Mary. Here she lived with her husband, Lord Darnley, and here the latter got up the conspiracy to murder the Italian Secretary, Rizzio. Mary's apartments are shown, with her furniture and bed. They are antiquated relics, time-worn and moth-eaten, but gazed at still with wondering eyes. Here is the narrow, winding, stone stairway, circling around like the stairways in factory towers, up which the con-

HOLYROOD AND BURNS'S MONUMENT.

spirators crept into Mary's room; the closet where they hid themselves; and the little circular apartment in the corner tower of the palace where they fell upon Rizzio and killed him, and his blood-stains (it is alleged) are there on the floor. The palace surrounds a square court-yard, and adjoining on the left-hand side are the ruins of Holyrood Abbey. The stone roof has fallen in, breaking down part of the walls and some of the massive columns along the nave; but the formation of the roofless building is completely shown, and its floor is partially paved with flat gravestones and partially a grass-plot. The palace contains a gallery of execrable portraits of Scottish princes, going back two thousand years, which all look alike; and most of them were evidently painted by the same person by wholesale contract. Queen Mary's is the chief, and seems to have been recently brightened up. Old tapestries hang on the walls of the smaller rooms, dingy with age, but withstanding time's ravages with success in other respects.

To get a view of the Old Town, a walk along the High Street and into the famous Canongate is the best way. There are tall, weird, old houses on either hand, and among them the narrow home of John Knox, a strange-looking building, adjoining a church. Nearly every house in these two streets is historically famous, and out of these streets run curious alleys known as closes, and bearing quaint names, such as " Big Jock's close," " Bakehouse close," "Strathie's close," etc. " White House close" leads to a famous inn. All these old houses, some of which are sad-looking rookeries, were in former days the homes of the nobility. The dukes and earls of the olden time were evidently satisfied with very rude accommodations. Among the relics of John Knox is shown St. Giles' Cathedral, where he preached, an ancient edifice since restored. Behind it was the graveyard where he is buried. I say *was*, for that graveyard is now a street in front of the Parliament House, and among two or three plates let into the pavement marking famous graves over which carriages run, is a modest one marking Knox's grave. It bears simply the initials " I. K." and the year 1572. On coming out of the Canongate are seen the lines of stones across the street marked with the letter " S," across which Edinburgh debtors rush to secure safety from creditors, and keep out of jail till they can make a settlement.

It would be impossible to write of or remember, in a hasty visit, all the attractions of this wonderful city. It has a magnificent drive around Arthur's Seat, known as the Queen's Drive, from which there are a series of lovely views across the Firth of Forth to Fifeshire, and over the land towards the Pentland Hills, disclosing a beautiful country. Up near the top of this hill is a pretty little lake, whereof it is told that a befogged guide, on one occasion, informed some strangers that the Ark, after the deluge, rested on Arthur's Seat, and this lake was a "piece of the flood." But the Scot who told me this story volunteered the further information, in justice to his race, that this guide was an Irishman. Fettis College is a modern building, across the Water of Leith, constructed in admirable style, from which there is a fine view; as, indeed, there is from a dozen points of vantage in and around Edinburgh. Also bordering the Water of Leith is Dean Cemetery, where the famous people of the present day are buried. Here Lord Jeffrey rests, and the peculiarity of the graveyard is that there are no mounds over the graves, the cemetery being a dead-level, with plain flat grass-plots covering the graves. Some of the tombs are very fine. Occasionally, in wandering around the city, there are reminders of America, the most prominent being a sign, "New York Ox-Beef Company," showing that American meat sometimes gets here. Weeks could be spent in examining this great place, and there is no wonder that the Edinburgh people are proud of their city, or that the Scots carry its fame all over the world. Dun-Edin has many things to be proud of.

#### A SABBATH AT ROSSLIN CHAPEL.

Edinburgh keeps Sunday strictly. The street-cars do not run. Scarcely a vehicle is in the streets. The red-coated soldiers of the Castle garrison are marched without drum or music to church. The bells ring, and almost the entire population seems to attend the churches, judging by the crowds going to them and the deserted appearance of the streets after the service begins. But the thing for the visitor to do appears to be not to go to church in Edinburgh, but to attend the service held in that remarkable little edifice, about eight miles out of town, known as Rosslin Chapel. So thither we went, crossing the North and South Bridges and out past the college which now stands upon the ground where the house formerly stood in which Lord Darnley was blown up, through the pleasant suburb of Newington, south near Lasswade to the chapel. Lasswade stands on the Esk, and they show you there a photograph of the girl carrying a man on her back across the Esk, he telling her, "Jenny, lass, wade," from which circumstance the village standing at the spot gets its name.

Rosslin Chapel is by no means an ancient church, having been built in the fifteenth century, beginning in 1446. It was intended for a large church, but only the choir and a portion of the transept walls seem to have been completed. Near by is one of the seats of the family of the Earl of Caithness, Rosslin Castle, from which the chapel derives its name. This chapel is considered the most beautiful specimen of church architecture in Scotland. It is small, being only about seventy by fifty feet inside, but its Gothic architecture is of varied and singular character. Inside and outside it is most elaborately ornamented by curious carvings in the stone. The high Gothic arched roof is supported by fourteen massive pillars, from which cloistered arches are sprung right and left. There are no less than thirteen different kinds of arches within the church, each being ornamented with gorgeous designs carved in the stone, and of a different character for each. Such profuse and elaborate ornamentation, covering and carved into almost every stone forming the pillars, walls, or roof, I never saw before. This church was desecrated during the religious wars of 1688, by a mob from Edinburgh, the statues thrown down and much injury done, the outside especially showing the effects of ill-treatment. But it is carefully preserved now in its half-destroyed condition, standing on a lawn enclosed by an ivy-covered wall. Its chief curiosity is the "'prentice pillar," around which garlands are twined, carved in the stone. It is related that the builder went to Rome to get a design for a pillar that would exceed all others in beauty. When he returned he found that an apprentice had erected this one, which outshone his design, and in anger he struck down the apprentice with a hammer and killed him. The column is beautiful, but the story is apocryphal. In former times the chapel belonged to the Barons of Rosslin, and several of them are interred beneath it, clad in full armor, and this, with the romance connected with it of the chapel appearing in flames whenever one of these Barons died, Scott tells in the ballad of "Rosabelle."

The service of the Episcopal Church was conducted within it, beginning at noon, by a single clergyman to a congregation of about two hundred, all that the old-fashioned seats and the stone benches around the walls would accommodate. They were chiefly strangers, and their wandering eyes showed that the curious chapel, more than the prayer-book, was occupying their minds. Returning from Rosslin, by a different route through the suburb of Morningside, there was passed the villa of Rockville, a strangely-built house of large proportions, ornate and attractive, constructed of various-colored stones, which had come into port at Leith and elsewhere, as ballast in vessels from all parts of the world. There was also passed the old and partly honeycombed stone, the Lore stone, whereon was set up the Scottish standard at the battle of Flodden in 1513. This stone is placed on a column by the roadside, with an inscription, quoting its history from "Marmion." All the suburbs of Edinburgh are fine, and from all, for miles away, there tower up as the central point of view towards the city the Castle rock and Arthur's Seat.

## LETTER XIV.

### CROSSING THE BORDER.

YORK, August 6.

The railway from Edinburgh southward over the border to England, the Great Northern line, passes along the east coast, running by the banks of the Firth of Forth and the edge of the North Sea. The route lies through a country of great beauty and deep historical interest, made famous by the border wars and by Scott's writings. For miles north and south of Berwick-upon-Tweed the cars run almost upon the edge of the ocean, elevated on the cliffs high above the water, giving a glorious view far over the sea, whilst the boundary between

Scotland and England is passed upon a bridge, built by Stephenson, one hundred and twenty-five feet high, two thousand feet long, and costing six hundred thousand dollars. Here a brisk wind blew. An incautious Englishman on the train, looking out the window, had his hat whisked off his head, and the accommodating Scotch engineer of a locomotive following the train stopped his engine and picked it up, a proof of border courtesy. On the way through Scotland the route passes the battle-field of Preston Pans, where the Pretender, in 1745, defeated the English; Carberry Hill, where Queen Mary surrendered to the Scottish nobles, and was afterwards imprisoned in Loch Leven Castle; Gifford Gate, the birthplace of John Knox; the old castle of Hobgoblin Hall, mentioned in "Marmion," which is now Yester House, the seat of the Marquis of Tweeddale; Tantallan Castle, now in ruins, the former stronghold of the Douglas family, where Marmion bearded the "Douglas in his hall;" Dunbar Castle ruins, eight hundred years old, the scene of many memorable conflicts, Edward II.'s refuge after his defeat at Bannockburn, and Queen Mary's refuge before her surrender at Carberry Hill; Broxsburne House, Cromwell's headquarters at the battle of Dunbar, and now a seat of the Duke of Roxburgh; near Fast Castle, the Wolf's Crag of the "Bride of Lammermoor"; the ruins of Lamberton Kirk, where Margaret, daughter of Henry VII., and James IV. were married, which was the origin of the union of the kingdoms of England and Scotland; and finally Berwick itself, taken and retaken and destroyed over and over again during the border wars. South of Berwick the route passes near Alnwick Castle, a magnificent establishment, now the seat of the Duke of Northumberland, and dating anterior to the Norman conquest. Here are the ruins of the ancient abbeys of Alnwick and Hulme, and of Warnworth Castle; and then the line goes through Newcastle-upon-Tyne, which is famous the world over as a bad place to send coal to, and which gets its name from the New Castle, an ancient-looking ruin at least seven hundred years old. This town enjoys the usual fortune of cities in the Old World, in having its fame as a shipping port for coal spread far and wide, but it does not send away as much coal as the Reading Railroad sends from Port Richmond, and the Tyne, which carries this commerce, is only about half as wide as the Schuylkill where it passes by Newcastle, though below it empties into the sea as a wider estuary, and here accommodates the shipping. Newcastle itself is a strange-looking town, with red tiled roofs, narrow, dingy, crooked streets, and numerous chimneys belching forth smoke from the many iron-works. These mills and furnaces are also numerous in the surrounding country, whilst the neighborhood is a perfect net-work of railways carrying coal from various lines to the shipping piers. The centre of the city, away from the river, contains, however, several fine streets, squares, and buildings, secured by clearing away and modernizing the ancient structures in that section.

Crossing the river Wear, a stream about the size of Wissahickon Creek, there rise up on precipitous rocks bordering the river, high elevated above the red tiled roofs of the town, the towers of Durham Castle and Cathedral, of both of which, apparently adjoining each other, a fine view is had from the railway, which runs on a high level above the tops of the houses. The Cathedral is seven hundred years old, and the castle was built by William the Conqueror, and both seemed, at the distance from which I saw them, to be in good condition. All the country hereabouts is thoroughly cultivated, and the little streams running through deep valleys, past sloping green fields and occasional bits of woods where the land is too steep for cultivation, add to the picturesque scene; an occasional tall chimney pouring out smoke, reminding, however, of the iron underlying this entire region. Huge heaps of slag and refuse surround the furnaces as with us, the English not knowing how to utilize it any better than we do. At Darlington the iron-mills are in abundance, and the railway station bristles with announcements of " Ozokerit Candles," whatever they may be, whilst an occasional donkey is seen toiling along the roads, carrying a pannier on each side and a baby in each pannier. Here there came to greet us a Pullman palace car on the railway, and an announcement of the American line of steamers hung up in the station. We had got into Yorkshire and, at North Allerton, found an Agricultural Fair in full progress, with plenty of red-painted farming-machines and fat cattle, but no " horse trots" as at home. The ladies, although it was August, were going about the streets clad in furs, having probably brought them out for an airing at the fair. The farther south the train progressed the riper became

DURHAM CATHEDRAL FROM THE WEAR.

the grain-fields, and the nearer seemed the harvest, and the trees also became more numerous, being generally planted along the hedges, though there were frequent pieces of woodland. Then we passed the North York Wolds and the Hambleton Hills, and came gradually down upon the almost level plain on which York stands, the drab-colored towers of the Minster rising from afar, as the first indication of the approach to the city, into which we ran alongside its famous river, the Ouse, a stream about one hundred and fifty feet wide. We were now in York, and knew we had successfully crossed the border into England by the butter being salted when placed upon the hotel table. Scotland serves up its butter without salt, and I am told this is one of the best ways of detecting when you have crossed the Scottish border.

### THE ANCIENT CITY OF YORK.

Of all the old things in England York claims to be the oldest. She has Roman antiquities by the acre; her people talk of the Romans as familiarly as of the events of yesterday, and they trace their genealogy back "to the great grandson of Æneas, who was contemporary with King David." York was the Roman capital of Britain, and here Constantine the Great was born. This ancient town boasts of structures a thousand years old, and has Roman antiquities of all kinds lying around, whilst the people have so little relish for modern things that they almost stopped making history after the "Wars of the Roses." The white rose of York is introduced into pretty much everything in the city, albeit the people put up the head of Richard, Duke of York, as a warning to traitors, upon the chief entrance to the city, Micklegate bar. The two and three-quarter miles of old and carefully preserved walls, towers, gates, battlements, and bastions, almost surrounding this ancient city, enclose a sort of condensed Boston, although the streets outrival anything that Boston can show in the matters of crookedness and irregularity. They are not only crooked but of varying width, and run into and out of each other at all sorts of angles and by all sorts of curves. Every house is ancient and Roman-like in appearance. Even the few new ones put up are made so as to imitate the curious and cumbrous construction of the olden time. It is a very easy city to get lost in, but then the towers of the Minster stand out as a landmark, which can be sought for a fresh start. The streets are nearly all named "gates," such as Petergate, Castlegate, Newgate, Friargate, Fossgate, Cripplegate, Goodramgate, Fishergate, Monkgate, Skeldergate, and the like; whilst the gates are all called "bars." The old Castle of York is of little account now, all that is left being a flattened, broad, round tower, called Clifford's Tower, dating from the Norman conquest. The remainder of the present Castle is a comparatively modern structure within high walls, and used as a jail. The city has any number of churches. They appear in all directions. There are several of them under the very walls of the Minster. A chief use to which they seem just now to be put is as public bill-boards. All the church doors contain announcements to the public to step up and pay their taxes, and also long lists of voters, for York is about having an election, and this is the way the polling lists are put up. Might not Philadelphia get a hint from this antique city and put up her election lists on the churches as well as on the taverns? York's chief present pride seems to centre in an old stage-bill and her Minster. Jealously guarded as a precious relic is this old stage-bill, about six inches by four, printed in ancient type, in 1706, and announcing the beginning of the regular stage-line, between York and London, on which the stages were to start three times a week, commencing April 12, in that year. This line, the little bill tells us, "performs the whole journey in four days (if God permits), and sets forth at five in the morning."

York Minster, the Cathedral of St. Peter, is worthy the pride of the city. It is the largest Gothic church in England, and contains the largest church-bell in the kingdom, "Old Peter" weighing ten and three-quarter tons, and struck regularly every day at noon. The Minster is of huge size, five hundred and twenty-four feet long, two hundred and twenty-two feet wide, ninety-nine feet high in the nave, and about two hundred feet in the towers. The nave would hold our Masonic Temple without its tower, though one can stand under the central lantern of York Minster and look up one hundred and ninety-six feet to the roof, it being two hundred and twelve feet high. These are large proportions, and there is no wonder this massive pile was two centuries in building. Its great charm is its windows, most of them containing the original stained glass, some of it dating back as far as the year 1300. These windows are of enormous size, the East Window being the largest stained-glass window in the world,—seventy-seven by thirty-two feet,—and of exquisite design, made in 1408, by John Thornton, of Coventry, who designed, stained, and glazed it, doing the whole work on wages of four shillings a week, and ten pounds gratuity when finished. Then there is the famous Five Sisters Window at the end of one transept, designed by five nuns, each planning a tall, narrow sash ; and the beautiful Rose Window at the end of the other transept. This old glass is among the most famous in Europe. The Minster, like most other church edifices, has been desecrated in the religious and civil wars, some statues being thrown down and others beheaded. Curiously enough, however, the desecrators left the statue of St. George, which stands high up in the nave, untouched. He defies the dragon, which pokes out its head on the opposite side, and they concluded to let them fight it out. The Chapter House, an octagonal building, sixty-three feet in diameter, surmounted by a pyramidal roof, is one of the gems of the Minster. Seven of its sides are composed of large stained-glass windows, and the ceiling is a magnificent work. It is no wonder that an Archbishop, Bishop, and about thirty other clergymen of various grades are required to conduct such a grand church as this. Its tombs are among its curiosities. All its walls are full of memorial tablets, a few modern ones to fallen soldiers of recent English wars, but most of them ancient. There are strange tombs set in the walls bearing effigies of the dead. Sir William Gee stands there with his two wives, one on each side, and his six children, all eight statues having their hands folded. Others sit up like Punch and Judy, the women being dressed in hoops and farthingales and ruffs, in the highest fashions of their age. There are scores of graves of archbishops, so plenty as to be almost unnoticed. Here is buried Wentworth, second Earl of Strafford ; also the famous Hotspur, whose body rests in the wall underneath the great East Window. In one tomb the effigy of an archbishop lies on the ground covered by a stone canopy, and the corpse, instead of being underneath the ground, is up overhead in the canopy. This tomb is six hundred and twenty years old. Here is buried Burke's friend Saville, his epitaph having been written by that great statesman. Underneath the Minster is the crypt, the walls of which were those of a church standing there before the present one was built. Some of the effigies on the tombs represent skeletons, others wasted corpses, the faces being life-like, but depicting the agony of death. Some of these reproduce the diseases that caused death. One archbishop died of a white swelling, and his effigy reproduces it, one knee being made much larger than the other. The outside of the Minster has all sorts of grotesque protuberances, which, according to the ancient style of church-building, represent the evil spirits that religion casts out.

This strange old city of York ranks next in dignity to London, and is the only other English city which has a Lord Mayor. It has not grown much for a good while, but stands still at about fifty-one thousand population. Its walls and gates are great curiosities. Nearly all the walls have outside them the old ditches, dry now, but carefully preserved and plainly visible. The gates are surmounted by towers and battlements, and are very strong, giving an excellent idea of the system of defensive works in the middle ages. The utmost care is taken to preserve these precious relics, and there are a few remains of an old arched wall, overgrown with ivy, which is all that is left of Cardinal Wolsey's palace. The Multangular Tower, with its ten sides, is also carefully preserved, a Roman relic, and near it stand a row of ancient Roman stone coffins, which were exhumed in different parts of the town. A little way out of town is the village of Holgate, which was the residence of Lindley Murray, the grammarian.

It does not do for an American, however, to venture alone far from home in this ancient city, for he quickly discovers that the kind of English he has learnt is not the kind that is spoken in this part of England. The antiquity of everything seems to have affected the language, for it is not the modern dialect as taught in Philadelphia, and for all I know may be some antique version of our mother-tongue. In fact, I have discovered, since landing in this kingdom, more about the English language and its versatility of pronunciation than ever I dreamed of before. In Liverpool I was at once recognized by my pronunciation as an American, whilst in Wales, as soon as I talked, I was accused of being an Irishman. In Ireland they thought me a Scotchman, and in Scotland an

Englishman. Now, however, in York they do not seem to recognize me at all—or I them, for that matter. A Frenchman's English has a better show than an American's in this antique city. If any of my countrymen wander this way let them not boldly venture to pronounce the name of the city as we do at home, " Y-o-r-k." If they do, the Yorkshireman will understand it to be and write it down as " Newark." But let them pronounce it " Y-a-w-k," and all will be well.

## LETTER XV.

### AN ENGLISH WATERING-PLACE.

SCARBOROUGH, August 7.

Scarborough, says the guide-book, is " the queen of watering-places" in England, and, therefore, I hied thither. It is certainly a place that its owners may well be proud of, and it has no counterpart on the American coast. About a half-dozen miles above the famous Flamborough Head, on the Yorkshire coast of England, there juts out for a mile into the North Sea a lozenge-shaped promontory, having on each side semi-circular bays,—looking like miniature bays of Naples,— each about a mile and a quarter across. Steep cliffs, from two hundred to three hundred feet high, run precipitously down to the beach all around these bays, and on these cliffs is the town of Scarborough. At the extreme point of the promontory, and fully three hundred feet above the sea, which washes it on three sides, is the Castle; whilst myriads of fishing-vessels cluster around the breakwater piers constructed there to make a harbor of refuge. As may be imagined, a seaside town, giving four or five miles of bluff, elevated two or three hundred feet above a smooth sand-beach, would be considered a grand watering-place; but when to this is added the Spa, two famous mineral springs, coming out of the hill almost at the water's edge, its rank becomes first-class. It is Long Branch, Saratoga, and Cape May combined. It has the bluff, the springs, and the beach.

The town is old, and the older streets crooked and confused;
D*

but in the newer portions millions of money have been expended in adornment and buildings. Everything is built of brick or stone or iron, in the most substantial manner. The roads are solid, the bridges ornamental and strong, the hotels of large size. Whilst the bluffs on the northern bay are left almost as nature formed them, so precipitous that their sides are nearly perpendicular, the cliffs on the southern bay have been converted into a beautifully-terraced garden and promenade. Here, amid flowers and summer-houses and terraced walks, is the fashionable promenade, the foot-paths twining up and down the face of the cliffs, or broadening into the garden on the shore, where music is provided and there are attractive illuminations at night. Over two million dollars have been expended in beautifying the front of the cliffs which adjoins the Spa, and there is now being erected there a grand music hall, and refreshment- and conversation-room, at a cost of four hundred thousand dollars. All these buildings and other structures are made of solid brick and stone, built to stay, whilst the pier, which runs out over the water, is of iron, and, for about five cents fee, one can go out to the pier-end and listen to the music there provided, and, at the same time, watch the water. The views from the cliff-tops, however, are the great attractions of the place.

Yet, with all its beauty and attractiveness, and the crowds thronging it, for this is the height of the season, Scarborough has no surf equal to or approaching that of Cape May. It has the broad beach, but the North Sea only rolls upon it the tamest kind of waves. The Gloucester ferry-boats do as well for the little boys who watch for "rolleys" along that sand-girt shore. The North Sea can, I am told, knock things about in a storm, but it cannot provide surf-bathing at Scarborough to suit an American. They would probably give a million or two to get here a piece of the surf that washes our New Jersey coast. Hence the bathing does not come up to the other attractions of the place. Rows of little boxes on wheels—the bathing-houses —are drawn by horses into the water, and their occupants get out and bathe, whilst the box waits for them, and when they re-enter it is drawn back on the beach. This is the English system of surf-bathing. You change your clothing in the little box. The Scarborough surf ruffles playfully about its wheels. The New Jersey surf would knock it all to pieces.

The Scarborough beach forms a fine drive, and the hackmen are glad enough to haul people all around the place at twelve cents apiece. Hundreds of patient little donkeys stand on the beach for juvenile riders, and give little boys and girls a half-hour's ride for six cents. Scarborough prices are not high, which may account for its popularity. I was only charged twelve cents to enter the Spa, the gardens and terraces, and enjoy all the attractions for which so much money has been expended, and the refreshments sold in its gorgeous saloons were at reasonable prices. Possibly if American watering-places were to imitate some of these moderate charges they would get more custom. As it is, Scarborough finds a railway station almost as large as that of the Pennsylvania Railroad in West Philadelphia necessary to accommodate its travel, yet the town has but twenty-five thousand population. The season, which begins in June, is at its height in August and September, and is over by December. For six months everything is shut up, and, like our sea-coast cities, it is partially deserted. Of course time is necessary to build up such a grand place, and by the time two hundred years have passed over our watering-places, as they have over Scarborough Spa, we may find it a worthy rival.

## LETTER XVI.

### TWO ENGLISH HOMES.

ROWSLEY, August 8.

Nestling among the limestone hills of Derbyshire, at the point where the Wye flows into the Derwent, is the pretty little village of Rowsley, whereof two Dukes divide the ownership, part of the land in the neighborhood being the estate of the Duke of Rutland, and part the estate of the Duke of Devonshire. This village stands almost midway between two of the famous homes of England, one a home of the olden time, and the other more modern. To get to Rowsley, either from Manchester to the North or Derby to the South, the visitor has to pass over one of the most costly-constructed railways in the kingdom. The country is rugged,—high hills and deep valleys,—and this portion of the Midland Railway is almost entirely a tunnel or a deep rock cutting. It winds its way through and under the great limestone rocks, until it passes probably forty tunnels, many of them a mile in length. Such boring and cutting as are here exhibited are rarely seen even in this land of costly railways. Among these rocks marble and limestone are quarried, and the lime-kilns are frequent. The country is full of antiquarian remains, and at Buxton and elsewhere there are Roman relics and famous medicinal springs; but none of these things have the attraction that draws to Rowsley, and has made its little old-fashioned "Peacock Inn" one of the famous hostelries of Europe. A quaint building is this old-time inn, with its low ceilings and thick walls, its narrow stairways, and Queen Elizabeth window-panes. How old the house is no one seems to know; but it mounts upon the roof the famous peacock, which is the crest of the ducal house of Rutland, to which estate it belongs, and, long after it was built, some one carved on the stone over the door, in rude characters, the name "John Ste-venson," divided into two lines where the hyphen is placed, and the date, half on each side of the name, "16-52." It has been an inn for over two centuries, and before that time it was the manor-house to Haddon Hall, which has not been occupied as a residence for over a hundred years. The gardens of the inn run down to the edge of the Derwent and are a little paradise. To this ancient place I went, and slept in a high-post bedstead up under the peaked roof, so as to get a proper start next morning for a visit to the two famous English homes near by, which are entirely the opposite of each other in every respect.

#### THE ANCIENT BARONIAL HALL.

American readers have probably noticed that in every British Conservative Ministry during recent years there has appeared the name of Lord John Manners as Postmaster-General. Manners is the family name of the Duke of Rutland, and Lord John is the Duke's younger brother and heir. Proceeding up the Wye from Rowsley, the Rutland estate covers almost all the land, and its chief centre is the renowned old house, or rather series of houses, known as "Haddon Hall." This ancient baronial home, with its court-yards, towers, embattled

COURT-YARD, HADDON HALL.

walls, and gardens, is located on a hill-side sloping down to the Wye, whilst the railway has pierced a tunnel through the hill, almost under the ancient buildings. It is maintained not as a residence, but to give as perfect an idea as is possible of a baronial hall of the middle ages. It did not always belong to the family of Manners, though their most famous possession now, but came to them through a romantic marriage. Scott has woven its history into several of his absorbing tales. Parts of it go back to the Norman conquest, and from "Peveril of the Peak" it passed to the family of the Vernons, a daughter of which house eloped with Sir John Manners, clandestinely married him, and in 1561, inheriting the estate from her father, brought it into the family now owning it. This lady casts a halo around the old hall which cannot be dissociated from it. We are told that she fled away with her lover whilst a ball was progressing. The long, narrow ball-room, with its low ceiling and rich oak carvings on the walls, is shown, and with it Lady Dorothy's stair, and door, and postern. She fled down the stair and out the door into the garden at night, then across the flowers and grass to the outer wall, and through the postern, where her lover was waiting, and they disappeared in the wood covering the hill-side.

Haddon Hall is an ancient place, and kept so purposely. Its stone courts, floors, and stairways have been worn by busy feet. Everything is aged, ponderous, old-fashioned, and as we regard it from to-day's stand-point,—uncomfortable. The tables, chairs, windows, furniture, and utensils are of the rudest description. The buildings are ill arranged, the ceilings low, and there is a damp, unwholesome odor pervading the whole place. Yet it is a faithful preservation of a baronial hall, of Cromwell's age and before, kept as well as time will permit, and this is its great attraction. The buildings surround two court-yards, paved with large stones, and cover a space probably three hundred feet front by two hundred feet deep. The entrance is by an arched gate into the first court-yard, outside of which is the low thatched cottage used as a porter's lodge. To get to this gate the visitor toils up a rather steep hill, and passes on the way two remarkable yew-trees,—one cut to resemble the peacock of Manners, the other, the boar's head of Vernon. There are scores of apartments inside,—banqueting-rooms, a chapel, chambers, a prison, and rooms for all sorts of domestic uses. The great hall is the Martindale Hall of "Peveril of the Peak." Once in a great while the old hall is lighted up for a ball, and to such a use it had been put by the Derbyshire volunteers to celebrate their disbandment from service, the night before I visited it. Hence it was redolent with the stale fumes of beer and tobacco, which probably were about the same as those left after a roust two or three centuries ago when Haddon was in full glory, but this rather took the romance out of Haddon of the present day.

When this baronial hall was in its heyday a retinue of one hundred and forty servants was necessary to maintain it, but its glory departed when the Dukes of Rutland determined to change their home to the Castle of Belvoir, in Leicestershire. Yet the family faithfully maintain it as a relic of an age gone by. In the Journal of the British Archæological Society it is recorded that portions of the buildings were constructed at various periods from 1070 to 1624, the most of them prior to 1470. Here, then, we have carefully preserved a home which reproduces life in England prior to the discovery of America, showing much of the furniture, utensils, armor, etc., of that time. It was worthy a pilgrimage to see, and presented the sharpest contrast, in its quaintness and age, to the gorgeous modern glories of the palace on the other side of Rowsley.

THE MODERN DUCAL PALACE.

American readers, who care anything for British politics, will have frequently noticed the name of the Marquis of Hartington, one of the Liberal leaders in the House of Commons. The Marquis, if he lives long enough, will become the Duke of Devonshire, and succeed to one of the greatest estates in the kingdom. William Spencer Cavendish, his father, the Duke, is the owner of the finest palace in England,—Chatsworth,—one of the great show-houses of the realm, maintained as such at heavy expense to exhibit the glories of wealth and the pomp of titles. To be a rich duke is said to be the great aspiration of Englishmen; for a half-dozen wealthy dukes, with a number of other noblemen, really govern the kingdom, and influence the Queen, whose worldly possessions they could probably buy without materially reducing their bankers' balances. Yet Chatsworth, with all its fame and grandeur, is said to be positively hated by the Duke, who prefers Barrow, in Yorkshire, a more comfortable home of less pretensions, whilst the Marquis, his heir, very rarely visits it. But it is, nevertheless, maintained in costly splendor, if not to please its owner, at least to gratify the thousands of visitors who daily pour through the park and house and gardens.

Chatsworth has been written of by Scott as the " Palace of the Peak," for it stands not very far distant from that remarkable limestone formation known as the Peak of Derbyshire. The chief part of the palace is about one hundred and eighty years old, but an extensive wing was added fifty years ago. It stands in a park covering over two thousand acres, the walls surrounding which extend over a circuit of eleven miles. The Derwent flows in front, with a lawn gently sloping up to the buildings, behind which sharply rises a wooded hill, crowned with a tower embosomed in trees, over which a flag floats whenever the Duke is at home. In the midst of busy, crowded England, two thousand acres of lawn and woods can thus, by the peculiar custom of the country, be emparked for the benefit of a herd of deer, which were wandering over it in detached parties. There are about a thousand of them in the park, and there were also some cows and sheep feeding, which belonged to the Duke's tenantry outside the park, but the land is never planted with a crop, and so it has been kept for centuries. It may all be very well to do this to add to the glory of a show-house, but Englishmen frequently ponder as to the use of it,—two thousand acres of idle land in a country that has to send to America for food. Yet it is only one instance of many of similar emparking.

The palace is of a brownish-yellow, a square flat-topped house, with a modern and more ornate wing. It is of vast size, fronting at least six hundred feet, and in parts is of probably equal depth. Like all such structures, it consists of masses of buildings around court-yards. It contains some of the most magnificent apartments in the kingdom,—rich in every decoration. As you go from one room to another and look at the paintings, sculpture, mosaics, carvings, gildings, rich furniture, magnificent vistas of view, and see all that money and art can produce in the decoration of the house, you wonder if there can be any limit to the purse of the man who, with his ancestors, has piled up all this splendor. Yet the place is too magnificent. In some respects it is gaudy,—

too much ornamentation in too small a space,—and the grandeur becomes dreary, so that you wander through the state apartments and do not marvel that the Duke is not enamored of this white elephant his ancestors have left him to maintain. The people troop through it, and gaze at all the grandeur, but few are envious. They do not want so much glory at such a price. It was the grandeur of Chatsworth that Edward Everett used to contrast with the "modest mansion on the banks of the Potomac," when that great orator in the later portion of his life devoted his talents to. the reclamation of Mount Vernon.

The gardens are, to my mind, the gem of Chatsworth. Such apartments and such furnishing one may see elsewhere, but not such gardens. There are one hundred and twenty-two acres of these gardens around the palace, so arranged as to make a beautiful view out of every window. Everything that can add to rural beauty is here provided. There are fountains, cascades, waterfalls, lakes, running streams, rocks, woods, sylvan dells, and every possible thing that can enhance the attractions of flowers and trees and shrubbery. Sir Joseph Paxton, who was the Duke's head-gardener, and received a salary equal to that of the President of the United States, designed these gardens, built the great hot-house and conservatories, and acquired such fame that he was afterwards selected to design the London Crystal Palace. He married the daughter of the Duke's housekeeper, which fortunate lady gave her one hundred thousand dollars dowry, and left her five hundred thousand dollars, all accumulated from the shillings and sixpences "tipped" her and her retinue of assistants by the thousands of visitors to the palace. The revenues are said to amount sometimes to two hundred and fifty dollars a day from this source, but they are no longer a perquisite, otherwise the housekeeper might some day be able to buy out the Duke. Now, the money taken in the house, I am told, is partly used to support the servants and keep it clean; whilst the money taken in the gardens goes into a fund for the maintenance of a large hospital. Such a little bit of history as this will show what there is in the business of "tipping," a curse of European, and fast becoming a curse of American, life.

It would weary the reader to tell all there is in these gardens. The celebrated cascade flows from a stone temple,

CHATSWORTH, FROM THE RIVER DERWENT.

which it completely covers, down among dolphins, sea-lions, nymphs, etc., over a series of waterfalls, until it disappears among rocks and seeks an outlet underground into the Derwent. They have no weeping willows here, but have devised one,—a tree which, at the touch of a secret spring, weeps from every leaf and branch. Enormous stones, weighing tons, are nicely balanced, so as to swing as gates, or rock at the touch. Others overhang far above, as if a puff of wind would throw them down. The Emperor Fountain, so named in honor of the Czar's visit to Chatsworth, throws a column of water two hundred and fifty feet high. Here is an oak five years old, which the Prince of Wales planted, and another planted by the Queen, when a Princess, in 1832. Scores of other trees are shown, planted by the great people of Europe; but the finest tree of all in this aggregation of fine trees, is a noble Spanish chestnut, of sixteen feet girth. The great botanical glory of Chatsworth, however, is the famous Victoria Regia, the seed of which was brought from Guiana, and first bloomed here in 1849. It grows in a tank thirty-four feet in diameter, the water being maintained at the proper temperature and kept constantly in motion as a running stream.

This great ducal palace and the baronial hall at Haddon show the present and past glory of England; but it is only the enormous fortunes piled up by the system of entailing vast estates that can maintain such houses. I doubt whether either of the Dukes whose glory centres in these famous halls has a tithe of the happiness and content of the old lady in a neat white cap who presides over the modest house that lies between them,—the " Peacock Inn."

## LETTER XVII.

LEAMINGTON.

LEAMINGTON, August 10.

The Royal Leamington Spa, in Warwickshire, is the great English saline spring, whither invalids come in large numbers to drink or bathe in its waters, and to participate in the dissipations of a fashionable watering-place. The population dutifully visit the "Royal Pump Rooms" every day, and then practice archery or battledore in the lovely Jephson gardens, while the military band attached to the garrison discourses fine music, or else ride through the streets on tall bicycles as a proper preparation for dinner. These modern abominations on the highway are common in this very idle town, as well as elsewhere in the kingdom, and lank English youths turn sharply round corners and glide swiftly over the smooth roadway, to the dismay of the invalids who are hauled about in Bath chairs. Leamington is thus attractive now to the invalid and the idle, whilst later in the season it is the headquarters of the "Warwickshire hunt," one of the most famous in the kingdom, there being one hundred and forty hounds in this combination who are let loose after the unfortunate fox, whilst troops of red-coated squires jump hedges and ditches, and course across country after them. For the foreign visitor, however, Leamington has other and better attractions. It is a convenient point to fix as a base of operations for a visit to three of England's greatest curiosities,—Warwick, Kenilworth, and Stratford, which are but a short distance out of the town.

## WARWICK.

Warwick Castle, since I last saw it, has suffered from a severe fire, but the destroyed portions, which fortunately were the modern structures, have been restored, and the inestimable treasures they contained, which were not seriously injured by the fire, really present a much better appearance in their new quarters, and the whole Castle has put on a far more attractive guise. In Warwick, therefore, I was agreeably surprised, and can safely say that its range of new apartments fronting on the Avon exceed Chatsworth in glory, notwithstanding the grandeur of that palace. These apartments contain priceless gems, in armor, furniture, and ornamentation, far exceeding Chatsworth's furnishing in value. I do not believe there is such another series of apartments in Europe, and the disposition of these gems sets them off to so much greater advantage that one is charmed with the view. The Castle is one of the best exhibitions of the feudal castle there is in England, and it occupies from every point of view a lovely position. Its grand towers, its embattled walls, its spacious court-yard, its sloping gardens running down to the Avon River, giving the windows so beautiful a view, all command admiration. There is not at Warwick the dreary grandeur of Chatsworth, but it is comfortable, homelike, and attractive, whilst its gems depend upon themselves for glory and not upon their setting.

Guy of Warwick, the great giant, nine feet high, and his staff, and club, and sword, and armor, and exploits, I was told of, as before; but the story of the prowess of this mythical personage is given in the porter's lodge, at the outer gate, and not in the Castle,—and, therefore, I, like the Earl of Warwick of the present day, may be permitted to doubt it. There is nothing doubtful, however, about the existence of the redoubtable Guy's huge porridge-pot, which holds over one hundred gallons, and is used as a punch-bowl whenever there are rejoicings in the Castle. This huge bronze cauldron, weighing eight hundred pounds, stands in the porter's lodge, and sounds as clear as a bell when struck, just as it did ten years ago, though it is kept cleaner now than then. In fact, the great fire did a deal of good in furbishing up everything about Warwick Castle. The Castle had got into the condition of a certain building at Third and Chestnut Streets, which, in former days, was only cleaned when it caught fire and the engines deluged it with water. I hope, however, that the gray towers of Warwick may never be in danger again. It is too precious a relic, and contains too much of the olden time that cannot be replaced. Its destruction would bring sadness to the " Malt Shovel Inn," and the Warwick tailor, who announces on his sign that he is " breeches-maker to the Warwickshire gentry;" and to the old pensioners in that quaint building, Leicester Hospital; and to all the people who cluster about the ancient gateways and old gabled houses of the town and have so long looked up in reverence to the home of Guy and Nevil, the King-maker. No title in England has in its day had more renown than that of the Earl of Warwick, though the present incumbents, the Grevilles, had little to do with its fame.

### KENILWORTH.

In Warwick Castle was once the home of Dudley, Earl of Warwick, known as the " good earl," who was the brother of the famous Leicester, Queen Elizabeth's favorite, about whom there has been probably more romance written than about any other Englishman. All that is left of Leicester now, besides the ruins of Kenilworth, is his tomb in St. Mary's Church, near Warwick Castle. There lies his effigy with hands pointed to heaven and folded together, and beside him lies his third wife in similar position. He is in armor, she in the latest fashion. An elegant tomb supports and covers these figures, whilst the corpses lie beneath the pavement. All that remains of the proud Leicester, and of a half-dozen other noblemen of his time, is now exhibited there to the curiosity-seeker by a young woman for a shilling "tip." Kenilworth, which is the subject of so much romance and the object of so many pilgrimages, is a pile of well-preserved yet decayed ruins overrun with ivy, an occasional grand window, a gateway and towers, and a general mass of dilapidation surrounding the green sward of the court-yard, being what remains of the most splendid palace of Queen Elizabeth's day. There has been some restoration going on recently, and an attempt at clearing away rubbish, but the hand of time is evidently lying heavily on this famous ruin.

### STRATFORD-ON-AVON.

The Avon that flows by Warwick is the Avon that Shakspeare has made famous, and no American could pass within reach of Stratford without making a call there, even though the Stratford inns, as I find to my cost, give poorer refreshments for a higher price than any others in England, unless it be those at Kenilworth. But cost what it might, the visit had to be made. I will not attempt any description of what has been told ten thousand times over about Shakspeare's birthplace and tomb. The old house where he was born is still exhibited for a sixpence admission fee, as likewise is the church where he is buried, this system being far better than the "tipping" expected at "free" exhibitions elsewhere. The most remarkable feature of the old house is the success with which the public have managed to write their names all over it, and cover every particle of space on walls and ceilings with their initials, even including the scribbling all over a bust of the immortal bard exhibited there. This writing has in later years been stopped, however, though the names of the millions who did it prior to 1860 are carefully preserved, to the exclusion probably of many later visitors better deserving of such fame. I had thought this scribbling propensity an American vice, but an inspection shows it to be world-wide in Shakspeare's case. The writing is by people of all nations, though the Americans generally did the boldest characters, as if putting their initials there "to stay." There is nothing to see in the house that has any proved connection with Shakspeare, excepting a portrait said to have been painted when he was about thirty-five, and vouched for as authentic. This portrait is kept in a fire-proof safe. The sign of the butcher who did business in the building before it was purchased by the Trust now holding it is also exhibited, and announces that "The immortal Shakspeare was born in this house."

Of the house where Shakspeare died nothing is left. It was pulled down, and a green arbor in a yard, with the initials of his name set into the fence in front, is all that now marks the spot. The church where Shakspeare is buried is by far the most interesting relic. It is the Church of the Holy Trinity, and five flat stones in a row across the chancel, which is about twenty-five feet in width, cover the graves of Shakspeare's family, Anne Hathaway, his wife, lying next the left-hand wall; then he alongside her, and then their relatives. His monument is on the wall almost over Anne Hathaway's tomb, whilst almost over it, and, in fact, the nearest window to the tomb, is the American memorial window, now in process of construction. The window, which is highly prized by the townspeople, is constructed by American subscriptions of pennies and half-pence dropped in a box beneath it, and will cost about twelve hundred and fifty dollars. It represents the seven ages of man,—five panes being already completed and set up in the window. These are (1) the Infant, represented by Moses; (2) the Scholar, by Samuel before Eli; (3) the Lover, by Jacob and Rachel; (4) the Warrior, by Joshua; (5) the Judge, by Deborah; (6) the Old Man, by Abraham; and (7) the Very Old Man, by Jacob blessing Ephraim and Manasseh. The Judge and the Very Old Man are yet to be placed in the window. The most imposing building in Stratford is the "Shakspeare Memorial," which is fast approaching completion. The main portion is almost finished, but the tower is yet to be built. It is a large and will be a highly ornamental structure, emblematic, and thoroughly worthy of the memory which will do it honor.

## LETTER XVIII.

### A SUNDAY IN LONDON.

LONDON, August 12.

Like Philadelphia, London pays all possible respect to the Sabbath. It is the characteristic of the English in contradistinction to the French people, that Sunday is kept sacred to holy duties. In Paris the shops are open on Sunday, and the opera and theatres give their grandest performances, the chief elections are held, and the great horse-races take place at Chantilly and in the Bois de Boulogne. Paris devotes Sunday to just those things which England and America would think least appropriate to the day; but London keeps Sunday as closely as Philadelphia, almost all the population going to church or taking innocent recreation in the afternoon in the parks or suburbs. Consequently the London Sunday, with the stores closed, the streets almost deserted, except by church-goers, and all the church-bells ringing, has a close resemblance to an American Sabbath. At this time so many American clergymen are in England, particularly of the Episcopal Church, whose great Conference has just closed, that many of the pulpits are being filled with my countrymen, and at the two great churches of London, St. Paul's Cathedral and Westminster Abbey, American bishops preached the sermons yesterday. In England a bishop is always a "lord bishop," so that on making the inquiry at St. Paul's I was informed that the " Lord Bishop of Nebraska" was preaching the sermon, and was given a printed notice, announcing that the " Lord Bishop of Pittsburg" would preach the sermon there next Sunday morning. I hope the laity of Western Pennsylvania will properly appreciate the honor done their prelate.

I went to church twice yesterday, in the morning at St. Paul's and in the afternoon at Westminster Abbey. It is no common privilege to attend service in these two wonderful buildings, and it will, I hope, condone for occasional failures in church-going at home, such as afflict the journalist. St. Paul's, with its vast interior space, filled with the sunlight from its grand windows, contained probably ten thousand people under its great dome and in the adjacent portions of the nave and transepts. The service was solemn and impressive, though it was impossible to distinguish the words in the chaunting, intoning, or singing, on account of the great distances within the building and the echo. Yet this echo wonderfully increased the impressive solemnity of the music, and made the service one of the greatest I have ever heard. In England everything is intoned, and it is, therefore, impossible, with these echoes, to follow what is said; but the service, nevertheless, addresses itself most deeply to the imagination, and the organ music swells and reverberates through the grand old Cathedral in a way almost unknown to us at home. The sermon, however, could be distinctly heard, possibly because preached from a pulpit located under the dome, and near the centre of the church; but also owing its distinctness to the clear enunciation of the preacher.

There is, however, a sharp contrast between this London and a Philadelphia congregation in the irreverence shown. With us it is the height of indecorum to move about in church during the service. But here, in St. Paul's, the congregation was most restless and uneasy. People were constantly coming in or going out, moving about from one part of the congregation to another, changing seats and walking around the portion of the Cathedral unoccupied by chairs. At every lull there could be heard the pattering of scores of feet, and yet the clergyman went on, as if accustomed to what would with us have brought down a stern rebuke from the pulpit. It looked as if a large portion of the congregation had only dropped in while sight-seeing, and sat down a few moments to rest, getting up again and moving off when it suited them, without regard to what was going on. I could well understand why placards were hung up about the Cathedral, imploring visitors to keep quiet during divine service. Whilst the service was thus grandly solemn, the uneasy, restless spirit shown by the congregation detracted greatly from its sacredness, especially as, whether the service was prayer or praise, hymn, creed, or absolution, the restlessness was the same. But there must be something pardoned to the weakness of mortality. Here is a church filled with grand tombs and memorials,—one of the great sights of England. How can one keep from gazing at the tomb of the Duke of Wellington, or up into the great dome, or through the vast vista over the chancel, and in the awe-struck spirit thus inspired forget for the moment what is going on! The irreverent restlessness ought, however, to be stopped if St. Paul's is to be maintained as a pattern house of worship.

At Westminster Abbey they have learned better how to deal with this difficulty. This church exceeds any other in the world in its famous tombs and memorials, and its attractions for visitors. Days will not suffice for its close inspection; and, knowing how the mind wanders, the Sunday service is confined to the transept, the nave being railed off and kept closed whilst the service is going on. This crowds the congregation into a comparatively small space, and, this being filled, the people cannot move about if they would. Hence, although there is every inclination to wander, it is a physical impossibility, excepting for the eyes. The Abbey, like St. Paul's, on account of its size, produces the same effect on the service. It is as grandly impressive, the music swelling and echoing through the lofty vaulted roof, though the intonation and singing are practically undistinguishable. But the reverence and solemn stillness of the vast congregation were as marked as the irreverence at St. Paul's. The eyes would wander,—for with the memorials of Britain's greatest heroes, statesmen, poets, and authors around you, how could the eyes keep still? But the feet were quiet, and the ears lent attention to the service. It was certainly to me one of the greatest religious services I ever attended,—the place adding impressiveness to the ceremonial.

Westminster Abbey is filled with the tombs and memorials of the princes, heroes, and great men of Britain in every walk of life. There is method in their arrangement. In 1400 the poet Chaucer was buried in the south transept, and that portion of the Abbey has been since devoted to literary men, and is known as the Poets' Corner. The north transept is devoted to statesmen and warriors, the first distinguished burial here being that of the Earl of Chatham, the elder Pitt,

WESTMINSTER ABBEY.

who died in 1778. The organ stands in the north side of the nave, and here the eminent musicians repose. In the side chapels are buried the great nobles, and in the chancel and its adjoining chapels the kings and princes, the most noteworthy and elaborate tombs being those of St. Edward the Confessor, Henry VII., and Mary, Queen of Scots. Isaac Newton, in 1727, was the first scientist buried in the nave, and that portion is devoted to distinguished scientific men, humanitarians, and other similar classes. There are several things in the Abbey which more particularly attract the attention of Americans. One of these is the tomb of Major John André, whose remains were brought here from Tappan, New York, where they had been buried for many years after the Revolution. Another is the magnificent monument to the Earl of Chatham, the first great statesman buried in the Abbey, and the friend of the American colonies during the Revolution. This tomb, which stands on the right hand as the visitor enters the north transept, is one of the finest in the Abbey, and upon it is the inscription: "Erected by the King and Parliament as a testimony to the virtues and ability of William Pitt, Earl of Chatham, during whose administration, in the reigns of George II. and George III., Divine Providence exalted Great Britain to a height of prosperity and glory unknown to any former age." This tomb was erected in May, 1778.

The memorial window erected by Mr. George W. Childs is also eagerly sought for by Americans visiting the Abbey. There are not as many stained-glass windows in the church as there are windows of ordinary glass. Out of the twenty-two stained-glass windows, I could find altogether only three memorial windows which were so marked, two alongside of each other, on the north side of the nave, erected to Locke and Stephenson, and the other to which I have referred on the south side. Excepting these three, the entire stretch of the nave on both sides contains only ordinary glass windows. Mr. Childs's gift is in two parts,—or, as it were, two complete windows, one in memory of Herbert and the other of Cowper. It is the extreme western window on the south side of the nave, and is in the baptistery, somewhat secluded on account of the high tombs standing in front, and the stone arched railing separating the baptistery from the nave, but pouring a rich flood of mellow light over them. The window is a high one, and is a fine piece of work, greatly admired. The Dean and Chapter desire to encourage the enriching of the Abbey with stained glass.

One of the greatest curiosities in the Abbey is the coronation chair. It is in the chapel of St. Edward the Confessor, which contains the tomb of that sainted king, around which to within a twelvemonth it was the custom of crowds of pious devotees to kneel, until it was stopped by the absolute necessity of preventing such adorations, which were frequently made the cover for carrying off pieces of the tomb once inlaid with precious stones, most of which have been purloined. In this chapel, which is a sort of eastern extension of the chancel, two ancient, high-backed chairs stand on the western side. In their present positions these chairs are immediately behind the grand altar of the Abbey. They have hard wooden seats, are most unpretentious in appearance, and are probably as uncomfortable chairs as any one ever sat in. The one on the left as you face them is the famous coronation chair, in which every sovereign of England has been crowned since Edward I. The one on the right was made in imitation of this at the time of William and Mary, when it was necessary to have two chairs, both king and queen being crowned and vested with equal authority. As these chairs stand to-day they are, as it were, guarded by several monarchs in death, for the kings of England lie entombed all around them. At the next coronation they will be brought out covered with gold tissue, and one or both of them will be placed before the altar in the centre of the chancel, prepared for crowning the Prince of Wales, should he live so long. The coronation chair has fastened under its wooden seat the celebrated Stone of Scone, on which all the monarchs of England, and previously of Scotland, sat for crowning.

This dark-looking, old, rough and worn-edged stone is about two feet square and six or eight inches thick. It is said to have been a piece of Jacob's pillar, and all sorts of legendary tales are told of it. Such is the reverence of royalty for it that I suppose the next monarch of England could not be crowned if this stone, on which all have sat for six hundred years, were missing; but it looks as if it had been purloined from some old wall, and was yet covered with almost black dirt. Edward I. brought this famous stone from Scotland, where many generations had done it reverence, and in 1297 the old chair was made to contain it. And such a looking old chair! The wood has grown black with time, and in every part of it the energetic Briton has carved his name. This carving and cutting of rude initials has covered it all over,—seat, sides, back, arms, legs, and rounds. Some of the names are in full, and when the Prince sits there at his coronation, he will press upon the signs manual (made by a knife) of any number of his own and his ancestors' subjects. The most prominent name upon it is " F. Abbott," whoever he may be. I could also detect the names of " Sheppard" and " Bourk," whilst " J. Smith" stands out in bold characters, but he neglected to inform an anxious world whether he was the immortal " John." Some of these names have old dates attached to them ; one was as early as 1718.

There is certainly a short step from the sublime to the ridiculous. Here is this ancient chair which has encompassed the royalty of Britain for six hundred years, and has been the chief agent in the grandest pageants of the monarchy; yet, instead of its being marked with the royal names of those who sat there, their subjects have most ridiculously covered it with their names carved by inexpert hands, mostly in shocking bad characters. This sort of thing went on to such an extent that recently guards had to be placed over these chairs, and now lynx-eyed vergers closely watch them. " Whose names are these?" I asked of one of the guardians. " Henybody's ; heverybody's," he replied ; " but they haint doing it henny more," and then he told me that if that particular portion of the Abbey were not closely guarded, the public would probably not stop with cutting their names, " but carry hoff the chairs haltogether." Westminster Abbey is the Collegiate Church of St. Peter, and among the latest tombs placed there is that of Lady Augusta Stanley, wife of Dean Stanley, whose long service to the Abbey has brought him much renown.

## LETTER XIX.

#### THE UNDERGROUND RAILWAY.

LONDON, August 14.

To an American, the method of rapid transit adopted in London is one of the great sights of the city, and, although portions of the Underground Railway have been in operation for several years, the system is still being extended and constantly becomes more complete and useful. It is simply an impossibility for cabs, omnibuses, or any of the ordinary means of locomotion, to successfully overcome the great distances between the centre and circumference of London. They take too much time, and were reliance to be solely placed upon them the streets would be so crowded that it would be impossible for any one to move with any celerity. For twenty years at least London has been endeavoring to improve her means of transit between the business section or "The City," as it is called, and the suburbs. New streets have been cut, viaducts built, improved pavements laid, and all sorts of outlets provided, but there has been nothing which gave so much general satisfaction as the construction of the Underground Railway. There are over ten thousand cabs and two thousand omnibuses in London, besides private coaches used for popular conveyance, and were it not for this railway they would not begin to accommodate the public. Probably two million people daily require conveyances of some sort in London, which, in addition to its own millions, has always a vast floating population. The cabs and omnibuses find abundant occupation, and as they grow in numbers, together with the vast aggregation of vans, wagons, and trucks, the problem was how to provide room for them to move about. As London was ten years ago, the avenues between the City and West End were almost unable to accommodate the vast mass of moving vehicles, whilst the problem is yet unsolved how to increase the capacity of London Bridge to carry its moving stream over the Thames. To increase the road-surface leading westward out of the City the fine new Holborn Viaduct was built, which

LONDON BRIDGE.

gives a broad road to Oxford Street and its line of streets leading westward, whilst Fleet Street and the Strand, also leading westward near the Thames, were relieved by constructing an entirely new street from the Mansion House, in the City, to the Parliament Houses, in Westminster. This new street was cut through the heart of London from the Mansion House to the Thames at Blackfriars Bridge, this portion being known as Queen Victoria Street; and then it was run westward, a noble street along the river, known as the Victoria Embankment. A grand carriage-way running between rows of trees, with broad sidewalks and an ornamental stone balustrade on the river-side, forms the surface, whilst beneath runs the Underground Railway. These new constructions cost millions of money, but they gave London two new streets, each almost as wide as our Broad Street, leading from the heart of the city to the West End, and thus provided needed relief. It is now possible to avoid the "jams" that formerly occurred, whilst the steam facilities for transportation have probably put a limit to the increase in the numbers of cabs and omnibuses. London, in the portion served by the Underground Railway, does not incline to street railways, and, in fact, the distances are too great for horse-cars to satisfactorily overcome them. There is still, however, the unsolved problem of London Bridge. It is the easternmost bridge over the Thames, yet it crosses only in the heart of the city. The commerce of London will not permit the river to be bridged below it, so London Bridge, therefore, has to carry all the centre and east end traffic across the Thames, and do the work that half a dozen bridges above it do for the West End. It is on week-days a grand moving mass of vehicles and humanity,—one stream north, the other south. The police are busy keeping everybody and everything moving. Four lines of vehicles pass over the bridge, two each way. The outer lines go at a walk; the inner at a trot. Thus the heavy and light traffic is assorted before going on the bridge, and the capacity is increased by adopting this plan. But whether to widen the bridge or build another, London is undecided. The only solution of the problem seems to be to roof over this portion of the Thames.

The original idea of the Underground Railway seems to have been to connect the various stations of the railways leading out of town. This and the furnishing of means of rapid transit within the City were combined, and resulted in the construction of the Metropolitan Railway across the northern part of the city, connecting one steam railway station with another. By this means seven stations, the termini of the great railroads leading west, north, and east through the kingdom, were connected. The line was opened by sections, and was so successful that it was extended both ways. Its eastern end was turned southeast through the heart of the City to Aldgate, on the eastern side of the business portion, whilst the western end was divided into various lines, extending beyond Paddington, through the extreme West End. These lines worked so successfully that another corporation, the Metropolitan District Railway, began construction at a later period, and going west from the Mansion House, and along the Thames Embankment, ran its line past Westminster Abbey and Victoria Station, until it joined the other in Kensington, and then extended farther westward to the suburbs of Hammersmith, Kew, and Richmond, on the Upper Thames. This District Railway, besides giving a direct line out of the city, also connected all the stations, on the north side of the Thames, of the railways leading south, southeast, and southwest, whilst the junction of the two practically connected the whole out-of-town railway system. The Underground Railway thus makes an irregular ellipse, open at its eastern end, and as all the lines and branches are run in unison, the system is practically that of one company. To complete it the portion between the Mansion House and Aldgate, in the heart of the City, is yet to be constructed, and when this is done the ellipse will be complete. The route for this has been surveyed, the line giving a broad sweep farther east, so as to take in an additional portion of that section, and last week the Metropolitan Board of Works authorized the construction, and work is at once to begin. When this is done the underground circuit of London will be complete. These lines, it should be understood, are all north of the Thames. The city south of the river is as yet unprovided with this convenience.

The Underground Railway is in all portions a double-track railway. Trains, keeping to the left, run all around the city from the Mansion House to Aldgate, and *vice versa*. Thus the passenger can go anywhere he wishes by following the circuit around. Other trains run from both the termini mentioned, out the various extensions at the West End beyond Paddington and Kensington. For the out-of-town railways, this system provides each with some fifteen or twenty sub-stations, at which their passengers can buy tickets and begin the journey; and likewise on coming into London the passengers can at will land at any of the underground stations. Here at once is a vast relief to the cabs and omnibuses, as these stations are located at intervals of a half-mile, and sometimes less, along the underground routes. All the stations are large and roomy, with fine entrances from the streets above, and plenty of light below, as they are generally open to the daylight. The tickets are punched on entering the station, and are taken up on leaving it, thus avoiding any necessity for ticket examination on the trains. The trains run every three minutes; long trains, capable of carrying three hundred to four hundred passengers; and at the busier parts of the day they run as quickly as they can be despatched. In its practical operation the waits are no longer than for a Philadelphia horse-car. Each train, as it comes towards the station, has on the front of the engine, in bold letters, the name of the terminus towards which it is going,—the Mansion House, or Aldgate, or the various branch lines, such as Hammersmith or Richmond, so that the passenger has no difficulty in determining whether it is the right train. This is also aided by different arrangement of lights on the front of the engine for each train. The cars are divided into the three classes usual on English railways, and the fares are very cheap. The great convenience of the lines is shown by my own experience. Since I have been in London I have seldom used any other vehicle in going about. Whatever direction or whatever great building I desired to reach, the most convenient route was sure to be the Underground Railway. I am staying in the West End, four miles away from the centre, —say at Blackfriars,—yet I can make the journey in fifteen minutes, at a cost of eight, ten, or twelve cents, according to the class I take. I presume that one-half the moving population in London goes on the Underground Railway, and it is such a perfect solution of the "rapid transit" problem for the city, that, excepting in the case of London Bridge, that problem is no longer discussed.

This railway has been the costliest in the world, and a considerable part of the cost has been defrayed by subsidies from the public funds. Thus, for the completion of the circuit which I have referred to above as having just been authorized, the Board of Public Works voted a large subsidy, and gave orders to pay over two hundred thousand dollars immediately, as the first instalment. Large loans also provide the means, and there is a heavy share capital besides. Sir John Hawkshaw seems to be the principal engineer in planning and constructing the works. They are underground railways only in the sense of being constructed at a level lower than that of the city, but are not a continuous tunnel. On the contrary, they are sometimes through open cuttings and sometimes on the level of the ground. They are a succession of tunnels, sometimes very deep, going far down when it is necessary to go under some great sewer, or under another railway. Thus, beyond Paddington, where the Great Western Railway comes into London, the underground railway runs alongside and on a level with the other at Westbourne Park, and then gradually sinks, goes under, and comes up on the other side at Paddington again to a level with the Great Western Railway. The underground lines turn sharp curves and have considerable gradients. Their routes are pursued without regard to street lines on the surface above, often passing diagonally under blocks of houses. One of the lines passes almost under the room in which I sleep, and I can hear the suppressed rumbling of the trains, but it is not unpleasant, and by no means as loud as the passing of a cab in the street. The construction of these underground lines, besides its enormous cost, has taxed engineering ingenuity to the utmost. Huge buildings have been undermined, and their foundations removed, and have had to be held up by enormous arched walls and girders. I have looked with wonder at some of these constructions, where the cellar has been devoted to the railway, and immense iron beams have been let in to hold up the houses. At Blackfriars, where there is a large underground station, the arches sprung over it, and the beams and pillars constructed, have not only to hold up the line of the London, Chatham and Dover Railway, which crosses there, but also two streets leading from Blackfriars Bridge, across the Thames, and a huge six-story storehouse. Every sort of beam, girder, retaining wall, arch, pillar, column, buttress, and support that can be devised is used in thus holding up the structures tunnelled under,

and, wherever possible, openings are made to the daylight
There has also been much ingenuity shown in carrying sewers,
water- and gas-pipes across and along these lines, siphons being
frequently adopted. The system is the slow growth of years,
and as it progressed solved its own difficulties. The travelling
on these lines is pleasanter than is usually the case in going
through tunnels, for the engines consume all their own smoke,
and there are no dirt and cinders to fly into the car windows.
The cars are so well lighted that all the passengers read their
newspapers the same as on surface railways. Thus has London
successfully solved its problem of rapid transit, at enormous
cost it is true, but to the public satisfaction.

## LETTER XX.

### SOME LONDON SKETCHES.

LONDON, August 16.

Most of the great sights of the metropolis are well known
by reputation in America, but there are others that are not so
well known, and it may be interesting to devote a few lines to
some of these. Most visitors go into that ancient building
around which clusters the honors of the city, and within which
the civic dignitaries eat their feasts,—the Guildhall,—and view
the two Brobdignagian statues of Gog and Magog. These
uncouth beings are supposed to preside over the destinies of
London, and they stand up in the gallery where the band
plays at the feasts. Most visitors also stand in the street
known as the Poultry, and in front of them look upon the
Bank of England and the Royal Exchange, with Threadneedle
Street between, and Lombard Street on the right hand, and
think that this is the region which controls the monetary
affairs of the world. Then turning round to look at the Mansion House (the Lord Mayor's residence), behind them they
see the centre of the city government. Crossing over and
passing through the Exchange, they find its rear to be that
mysterious institution known as "Lloyds," where the marine
insurances are underwritten, and risks of millions are taken

E*

every day. They also gaze at the buildings of the Goldsmiths' Company, and the Merchant Taylors' Company, and the Fishmongers' Company, the headquarters of guilds that are rolling in wealth, and that seem to have little else in view but feasting. Then they wander through the little crooked streets of the old City, each with a famous name and history, and get lost in the maze. They go down to London Bridge to watch the mass of moving humanity crossing it, and on the way stop at the Fire Monument erected on Fish Street Hill, to mark where the great fire in London, over two hundred years ago, stopped, and endeavor to read the inscription upon it,—but being in Latin, this is difficult for the untutored American mind, and, therefore, refuge is had in reading the only inscription on this grand monument in plain English, which in bold letters announces that the practice so long pursued of beating and cleaning mats and carpets against the monument must be stopped. They take a boat-ride on the Thames, under the bridges and past the shipping, and up and down the very crooked, dirty, swift-flowing river, which bears so great a commerce; they look at the grand semi-circular sweep of the Victoria Embankment, with the Temple and Inns of Court behind its eastern portion, and the broad front of Somerset House rising above its western portion; and then at Westminster upon the noblest scene of the river,—St. Thomas' Hospital, with its groups of buildings upon the one bank, and the Houses of Parliament, with their noble front and great towers, upon the other,—the finest building of London. The visitor goes to Hyde Park to see the equipages; to the Zoological Garden to see the animals and promenade on Sunday afternoons; to South Kensington for the great Museum, and probably to Billingsgate on Saturday morning to see the fish handled and learn rhetoric; or to Smithfield, where the railway brings through a tunnelled line all the dead meat that feeds London, and it is hauled up to the great new market above to be sold. The visitor, if an American, is also very likely to go to that peculiar British institution, the Heralds' College, for I am told it gets its chief support from the liberal fees paid by Americans who seek crests and coats-of-arms to take home to astonish their neighbors. But most of these things, and many more, are the well-known sights of London, and too much written about to need repetition.

## CLEOPATRA'S NEEDLE.

Of some other things, however, matter that is new may be written. Cleopatra's Needle and its eventful journey to London are familiar themes, but it may not be so well known that all the cost of bringing this huge obelisk to England and setting it up in the metropolis is defrayed by two public-spirited citizens, John Dixon and Professor Erasmus Wilson. This stone weighs one hundred and eighty tons, is over sixty-eight feet long, and tapers from about seven feet square at the base to between four and five feet near the apex, which is then sharpened to a blunt point. It is a coarse granite, with gray and red grains intermixed, and is covered all over with large hieroglyphics, some of them five or six feet long and quite rudely carved. All the edges of the stone seem more or less injured by abrasion, whilst the base is partially rounded. It is intended to be set upon the outer balustrade of the Thames Embankment, midway between the Charing Cross and Waterloo Bridges. A low pedestal has been prepared for it, and it has been lifted by hydraulic power out of the vessel that transported it, and thence moved back over the embankment until it now lies horizontally on its supports, over the position it is to occupy. The Needle is yet to be lifted up and swung into position, so that it will stand upright. To do this a wooden scaffold and derrick of great strength are being erected, whilst a semicircular shoe of iron is being fitted on the base of the Needle. It will be gradually lifted upright by hydraulic power, great care being taken lest it should break. The process will be slow and laborious, but there are no fears of its failure, as excessive care is taken to guard against accidents. England has been endeavoring to get this obelisk removed since the beginning of the present century. When, in 1801, the English conquered the French in Egypt they were given the Needle, but endeavored in vain to remove it. A week's hard work only moved it six inches. But it was successfully carried off by the improved appliances of the present day, and will soon be one of the great sights in London, standing in an excellent position for its exhibition.*

---

* Cleopatra's Needle was successfully swung into position a few weeks after this letter was written.

## THE BANK OF ENGLAND.

Few visitors go inside the Bank, or pass beyond its interior portals. Yet the Bank contains a mine of wondrous information, and its vast stores of money make impecunious fingers tingle. Here are machines weighing with the nicety of a hair; machines that automatically separate the good coins from those of short weight; printing-machines of exquisite finish, for making the notes; electro-plates, from which the notes are printed, and curious mechanisms for constructing the cloths by which the very effective water-mark is put in the Bank note-paper, which is the main reliance for preventing counterfeiting and forgery. You are shown great stores of gold and notes, and for once are made rich by being permitted to hold in your hand, at one time, five million dollars, though the vanity of earthly riches is at the same time taught by the celerity with which all these millions slip through your fingers —and back into the vault. You are shown great rooms full of money, with gold a perfect drug,—piled up in ingots, hauled around on trucks, carted about in kegs, and shovelled from one place to another, like so much coal. My eyes were allowed to look upon an accumulation of ninety million dollars of gold coin and bullion, but I could not carry any of it off. I was offered a sack if I could lift it, but it seemed fastened to the floor. Picking up a little twenty-pound ingot, I was told to beware lest it fell, and an attendant who was limping about in a slipper said that one of them, of value equal to his next year's salary, had, the day before, almost mashed his toe. There were cart-loads of silver in bricks, most of it, like the gold, coming from America; but there was not in all this great store a single Bland dollar,—a famous coin at home, but which does not flourish in London as yet.

The Bank does all its own note printing, and also all the assorting of light-weight coins. It is the great corrector of the British coinage, returning to the mint for the melting-pot all the light-weight, defective, and defaced coins that come into it. By this means it keeps the coinage up to the standard, as only the good ones are allowed to go into circulation again. The loss on the silver coinage the government bears, but the depositors have to bear the loss on the gold coinage. Every coin that comes in on deposit or otherwise is weighed, and the light ones are immediately cut almost in two, by an ingenious little machine that works with great celerity. For every short-weight sovereign the depositor is charged a uniform discount of eight cents, which covers the average loss from this cause. For gold bullion and foreign gold coins, the Bank pays by weight, at the rate of seventy-seven shillings and nine pence per ounce for gold.

The Bank transacts all the Government business in connection with the Public debt, and, so far as this department is concerned, it acts similarly to the Treasury at Washington in paying interest and making transfers. The debt is all registered stock, however, and separate accounts are kept with every holder. There are about two hundred and fifty thousand of these debt accounts, some being in very large amounts. I was shown a signature of Glyn & Co., where they had just received interest on nearly two million one hundred thousand dollars of one class of the debt. The business of the Bank is divided into three great departments,—the Government Debt, the Issue (bank-notes), and the Private Deposits. Each of these is separately conducted, and the deposits aggregate about one hundred and thirty million dollars. I told some of the Bank officials that this sum possibly was not all the deposits, as several of my countrymen, in Camden and elsewhere, were inquiring about one hundred and fifty or one hundred and sixty millions on deposit in the Bank for the Jennings estate, but they did not seem to be aware of any such deposit, but they were very sure that the total actual deposits footed up what I have named.

There are, among the great curiosities of the Bank, its method of tracing the history of every note it has issued, done with great labor by means of ingenious indexes. The smallest note is for five pounds and the largest for one thousand pounds. In their collection of redeemed notes, all of which are kept, is a redeemed note that had gone through the Chicago fire. This note had been burnt to a crisp, yet it had been carefully opened out and the charred remains spread upon a glass plate, so that all was restored excepting a small portion. There, in the ashes, can be read the language of the note, its number and date. This note, which was for ten pounds, the Bank promptly redeemed, and it is now carefully preserved as a great curiosity. There is a case that shows the gradual progress of the Bank in making these notes, by exhibiting specimens. The earliest notes were written with a pen, and it was customary to change their amounts by erasures and interlineations. From these they improved step by step to the almost square white pieces of paper of to-day, printed in bold German text, and whilst being twice the size, yet as unlike the American note as it is possible for two bank-notes to be. Another curious collection contains specimens of attempted forgeries, alterations, and counterfeiting of notes. Some of these are by photographing, others by pasting and raising, some being clever and others poor imitations. But whilst the printing is imitated, there has been no even approximately successful attempt to imitate the water-marked paper, wherein the Bank places its main reliance for the safety of the note. In one case the attempt was made to print upon stolen genuine bank-paper, gotten surreptitiously from the mill, but the checks are so admirable that it was at once detected and the fraud suppressed before the notes had got into circulation.\*

The Bank is a wonderful place, and not the least famous part is the Directors' Room, looking out upon a pretty little garden, for, even in the heart of busy London, land is not so valuable that a little cannot be spared for grass and flowers. In this bank parlor the Directors meet and sit around a large, oblong, circular table every Thursday. Here they raise and lower the discount rate, and thus give official quotation, as it were, to the fluctuations of the London money market, to which all others bear tribute. But, though the enormous money-power concentrates here, the Directors who wield it are, nevertheless, true Englishmen. Whatever else they do, they do not forget the inner man, for here smoked sundry joints of juicy beef and mutton, and other savory viands, showing that, even in the Bank of England, as elsewhere, the stomach still ruled the roast.

---

\* Many tradesmen in England, when they receive a Bank of England note from a customer, require him to write his name on the back. This is done to identify and trace the note, and many notes are in circulation with these endorsements upon them. The author thus had on several occasions to endorse the notes of the Bank of England before the careful tradesmen would consent to receive them.

## THE TIMES OFFICE.

To the journalist the London *Times* office is always a curiosity, and I found that ten years had nearly revolutionized it, externally and internally. The old offices have been almost entirely supplanted by new ones, and the changes that have been gradually going on for years will soon be completed, giving the *Times* a new office, with every modern convenience, fronting on Queen Victoria Street, the new highway cut through from the Mansion House to the Thames at the commencement of the Victoria Embankment. The new structure is a fine building, of attractive appearance and imposing elevation, surmounted by the clock, which is the chief feature of the journal's coat of arms. It towers far above all the surrounding structures, and can be seen far over the Thames. Printing-House Square, the famous little court-yard which runs up into the heart of the *Times* buildings, is being preserved in these alterations, but it will be surrounded when they are completed by an entirely new structure, which, in almost every direction, has covered new ground, so that now the office extends over a greatly increased space. In the mechanism of the *Times* there have been wonderful changes wrought during the past ten years. Then, the machinists were secretly constructing the first Walter Perfecting Press, and had got it into satisfactory working order. Now they have removed every other machine from the office, and are printing the *Times* on eight of these Walter Presses, whilst they have built twenty-four others for various newspapers in England and America, and the large machine-shop in the premises is constantly turning out more. It requires a good deal of machinery to print the fourteen tons of white paper, which is the daily edition of the *Times*. In the type-setting as well as the printing there have also been great improvements made. A type-setting-machine has been constructed in the office, which has been put into successful use, and a half-dozen of these machines now set up the greater part of the type. The compositors still work upon the advertisements, but the machines compose the chief part of the reading matter, an average night's work for each machine being a page of the newspaper. Direct wires, under its own control and leading direct into its office, bring the *Times* most of its telegraphic news, and its telegrams are measured by pages. Pneumatic tubes for transmitting copy and proofs, and electric signals connect different parts of the building, and to save exorbitant gas-bills it is now being provided with the electric light.* These changes, with the adaptation of every possible improvement, are making the *Times* the best-appointed newspaper office in the world. Besides manufacturing its own presses and type-setting-machines it also casts its own type. I have never seen anywhere better or more comfortable quarters for the editors and writers who work in the office. There, if anywhere, the thunderbolts can be successfully forged. The entire new structure is also thoroughly fire-proof. Ten years is a good deal in the life of a newspaper, and in that period great improvements have been wrought in the *Times*. Its then system of making the telegraph secondary to the post has been superseded, and its progress has kept pace with every improvement in newsgetting. It has also, through the inexorable law of change, experienced a change of interior management, though the same master-hand of John Walter guides its successful career. The former editor and manager, overborne with cares, have retired, and one of them has since died. Younger men have stepped into their places to wield the enormous power of the *Times*, and they wield it with all the skill of their predecessors, with the added improvements of these later years. Printing-House Square is, however, always a sealed book to the uninitiated, and whilst the public may wonder and guess at its methods and motors, their source is never revealed. Its provision of comforts for the printers is also a prominent feature in the organization of the *Times*' establishment. It provides all the hands with their meals, cooking their food on the premises and having a restaurant for them, where they get wholesome food well served at cost. It has a sick fund and a medical fund, to which all the employés contribute, and which provides for their support and medical attendance when ill. It also has a saving fund where they all lay by a portion of their earnings. And once every year the entire establishment goes to the country home of the proprietor at Bearwood, near Reading, England, and partakes of the *Times*' annual anniversary dinner. This festival occurred this year on August 11.

---

* The electric light has, since October, 1878, been successfully used in the composing- and machine-rooms of the *Times* office.

## LETTER XXI.

LONDON TAXATION.

LONDON, August 19.

The general impression in America seems to be that the taxation in England is very heavy, and, fully impressed with this idea, I made an examination into the matter, and was astonished to find that London real estate is not taxed at anything like the rate that Philadelphia pays. To all outward appearance the service London gets for its taxes is good,—that is, the police and fire service, the street pavements, lighting, sewerage, cleaning, and everything of that kind are of the best character. We are accustomed to good police and fire service in Philadelphia; to street-cleaning that is good in some parts and bad in others; and to street pavements that, except in a few of our principal streets, London would not tolerate. Public municipal taxation in London provides for about the same things that it does with us, but a very much larger proportion of the taxes collected are poor-rates. A gentleman here was kind enough to show me all his tax-bills, and his case I am about to quote. He occupies in the heart of London, not very far from the Bank of England, a large building, recently erected in substantial style, which fronts about thirty-eight feet on St. Bartholomew's Close, and is about forty feet in depth. In London the tenant and not the landlord pays the taxes, but they are assessed, as with us, on the real estate. This building has a rental value of three hundred and fifty pounds, or seventeen hundred and fifty dollars, and if it could be bought at all,—which it could not,—he said he would be willing to give forty-five or fifty thousand dollars for it. The rentals, he said, were usually estimated at three to three and one-half per cent. of the freehold value of the property, the tenant, in addition, paying the taxes. Were this property located in Philadelphia, and valued, as most buildings now are, at an approximation to their value at a public sale, the tax on it would be eight hundred to nine hundred dollars for municipal purposes. This gentleman paid for his entire municipal tax one hundred and twenty-five dollars, of which sixty-nine dollars was the poor-rate, and the remainder, of about fifty-four dollars, supplied every municipal charge, including about everything for which we pay taxes in Philadelphia. This sum was the aggregate of all his real-estate taxes for every purpose. He paid, in addition, the income tax due the general government on the profits of his business, but that was the only other tax he paid. Now, it impressed me so strongly that this London merchant got so much better return for so much less money invested in municipal taxes, that it would do good to tell the story. It certainly disabused my mind of the impression that London was taxed more heavily than Philadelphia. He paid his taxes at different periods, and not all in one annual bill as is customary with us. The poor-rate, which was more than half the total tax, was collected quarterly; some of the others half-yearly. The valuation on which the tax was based was not the valuation of the property, but a valuation based upon the rental, from which various deductions were allowed. Thus, he being the holder of a long lease, had recently put up a fine new building on the land, and, instead of increasing the valuation for this reason, a deduction had been allowed on account of the improvement,—in other words, the municipality offered this premium for public improvements.

It would, of course, be impossible for London to support its costly city and metropolitan government upon such a tax as this, if the real estate were solely taxed. But it, on the contrary, looks elsewhere for a portion of the burden, and the taxes on real estate are, therefore, lightened. It gets a magnificent revenue, in addition to paying for the cleansing, from the street dirt, from the cabs and omnibuses, the railways and steamers. Everything that here enjoys a corporate privilege, from which money can be made in the city, pays tribute proportioned to the income derived. The markets yield a handsome revenue. The franchises that with us are given away, in London pay a large portion of the taxes; and the men of property impose the taxes, collect them, and see that they are properly spent. They do not delegate these important functions to politicians. The millionaires of London conduct the Boards of Works and Municipal government, and they do it on sound business principles. I asked how much of the public money was squandered here. The reply was that some may be, but if they suspect that as much as a shilling in the pound is wrongfully spent there is an outcry made about it. How happy Philadelphia would be were she sure that only five per cent. of her taxation is squandered!

## A LONDON MARKET.

London has a great meat market and a great poultry market,—both at Smithfield,—and a great fish market at Billingsgate; but other cities have great markets of this kind where there are large transactions, and they are no novelty. London, however, has a market, the like of which, in its entirety, probably nowhere else exists,—the "Old Clothes Market" of Houndsditch. Houndsditch is a noted street in the East End of London, the most populous quarter of the city, but that rarely visited by travellers. Fronting one end of this street is the great slop-clothing establishment of Moses, whose fame and fortune were years ago made by his originally inventing what many have since imitated, poetical newspaper advertising. On one side of Houndsditch there runs off a narrow passage called "Phil's Buildings," which widens into a court-yard covering nearly an acre, whilst adjacent, and communicating with it, are buildings, passage-ways, shops, court-yards, and various purlieus, covering probably eight or ten acres more. This is the "Old Clothes Market," the open court-yard being the Exchange, whilst the adjacent places are the storehouses and offices of the dealers. Signs over the entrance announced that hawkers and peddlers paid one half-penny a day tax on entering the market, whilst country dealers and wholesalers paid threepence. These taxes supported the market. Visitors and casual purchasers paid one penny. Investing that coin I entered. The court-yard was arranged much like an ordinary market, with rows of square spaces separated by low partitions, and a half-dozen alley-ways running through to give access. The dealers sat in their spaces and the purchasers passed through the alley-ways. There were probably five hundred people, of both sexes and all nationalities, bargaining in the liveliest style. No great market or stock exchange on its busiest day ever showed more animation or made much more noise. Each dealer had his wares in front of and around him, and the chaffering and bargaining went on with the greatest earnestness. Each dealer also had his special line of trade.

One dealt in men's cast-off clothing; another in women's; another had old hats for sale; another old shoes; and each class of these articles was allotted a special portion of the market. I never looked upon anything in my life that exceeded in its kind of attractiveness a row of about ten dealers in old hats, who had piled up in all their glory the dilapidated headgear of every fashion since the days of George the First. The old-shoe display was varied and extraordinary, and it had as an appendage several dealers in the old cast-off and partly worn-out soles of shoes. These soles were neatly tied up in dozens, and thus dealt in.

This market is said to represent a vast amount of business and a considerable amount of money. Here have been started some of the great fortunes of London. The old-clothes dealer has amassed some wealth and then gone into other pursuits, in which, carefully concealing his origin, he has grown in fame. The market acts upon the principle of furnishing a place where all the old-clothes collectors of the kingdom can bring and dispose of their gatherings. They go about the country exchanging trimmings, images, and trinkets for old clothes, then bring their collections to London to this market, where the dealers— like any other commission men—sell them, and then, laying in another stock of trinkets and trumpery in Houndsditch, they go out again on their rounds. The pawnbrokers' old-clothes pledges are also disposed of here, and in the adjacent purlieus may be seen the result of some of the purchases for sale—the old clothes, hats, and shoes, furbished up. There are plenty of buyers in the market,—buyers of all kinds,—slop-clothing and second-hand dealers of all grades, and people who buy for their own use. There were quite as many women as men there, and the place had its gin-palace, to which all classes resorted to close good bargains, by the usual potations. This market, certainly the most extraordinary I ever saw, would make a strong impression on every visitor, and shows that there is no business which does not prosper from having its exchange. The same rule which holds good in corn, or cotton, or stocks, is potential in old clothes, hats, and boots. The one is as likely to produce fortunes as the other.

## LETTER XXII.

#### THE AMERICAN MINISTER.

LONDON, August 21.

At a recent dinner-party in Paris, Governor Noyes, the American Minister there, proposed a toast to the health of the two American Ministers in Europe who had not been overhauled by the Potter committee. The point was so well taken that it brought down the house, and the toast was heartily drunk, being responded to by Bayard Taylor, the Minister to Berlin, who had just arrived in Europe, and by John Welsh, the Minister to London. In both of these gentlemen Philadelphia takes much interest,—in Mr. Taylor, on account of his Chester County nativity, and in Mr. Welsh, because the whole of his life is interwoven with the history of the Quaker City. It will be of interest, therefore, to write home something of the American Minister and of the Legation. The Legation occupies the best apartments in one of the finest buildings on one of the greatest streets of London,—Victoria Street, the grand avenue that leads from the Thames Embankment and the Parliament Houses, up past Westminster Abbey to Victoria Station and the West End. This fine new street has great edifices on both sides, some not yet completed, for the street is a comparatively new one, and the Legation is located in the "Members' Buildings," an imposing structure not yet, however, finished throughout. Here, on the first floor, fronted by fine bow windows, ornamented by the window-gardens that are such an attraction in almost all the English cities, the Minister attends daily to receive American visitors and conduct the Legation business. The office is commodious and convenient, and the Minister is as accessible to all comers as he was in his Philadelphia office on Walnut Street. In this respect he has changed considerably the custom of some of his predecessors, who were rather exclusive in their ideas, and he is almost as faithful in attendance at the Legation during office hours as the secretaries. In fact, business is conducted upon the true American system of throwing open the door to every American whom business or courtesy may lead to visit the Legation, the Minister being as accessible as the secretaries. The visitors are consequently very numerous, and pages of the Legation book, which records their calls, are filled every day with American autographs. To these visitors the Minister acts the part of counsellor, friend, adviser, and general guide in a way that is marvellous, doing things for them that diplomacy never contemplated, and, in fact, devoting himself to their service to an extent that few men would be willing to undergo the task of doing. This has made the post a laborious one, but it has also made Mr. Welsh a very popular Minister. His sterling good sense and eminent business qualifications have also commended him to Englishmen, and I have found, in moving about London, that he is held in high estimation in influential circles, and that he probably has greater weight with her Majesty's government than any Minister sent here for a long time from the United States. The active affairs of the British Government are conducted by experienced business men, and they strongly appreciate the advantage of having in the diplomatic corps a business man who is thoroughly conversant with the laws of trade, which are the paramount interests in transatlantic affairs, and who can, at the same time, give a judgment that is unbiased by some supposed interest in the tiresome Eastern question. Mr. Welsh also stands well socially, and, domiciled in one of the finest mansions in London, on Queen's Gate, opposite the South Kensington Museum, his receptions have been prominent features of the London season just closed. His diplomatic career thus far has not been marked by any very stirring question, but there nevertheless are many that he has attended to with fidelity and success, and his marked business qualifications will in the long run tell pointedly in favor of our country, should any important question arise. It is gratifying to know in Philadelphia, that, she having sent abroad the chief American Minister of President Hayes' administration, his excellent character and qualifications are thoroughly appreciated in the country to which he is accredited.

LONDON POPULAR RECREATION.

There is no more marked feature of London than the grand scale on which are got up cheap and wholesome recreations

SOUTH KENSINGTON MUSEUM.

for the people. The Londoner, however poor, need never be at a loss for healthful and instructive entertainments, and there is provided every convenience for reaching them by cheap conveyances. The fares on the cheap trains are not over one cent per mile, and by buying return-tickets even this rate can be cheapened. Then fares are scarcely higher on the enormously costly Underground Railways, that cost an average of three million two hundred and fifty thousand dollars per mile to construct. Then in the outskirts of the city, and also in populous sections where the Underground Railways do not run, there are several "tram-car" companies,—analogous to our horse-cars,—whilst omnibuses run everywhere. For recreation there are provided parks, gardens, museums, and other resorts maintained at the public expense in endless profusion. Every one has heard of that branch of the British Government known as the Privy Council, the chief function of which is to conduct the Civil Service Examinations and look after Education. The Council Committee on Education provides these great museums, which are maintained at public expense, and are officered and governed by this committee. Months could be spent in the task and yet these museums be not half examined. What single individual has yet explored all the treasures of the British Museum? And yet it is a free museum that any one may visit without cost. The South Kensington Museum, which is one of the greatest institutions of the kind in the world, covering several acres with its halls, to which newer and even larger ones are still being added, is accessible without charge three days in the week, and on the other three for sixpence. There nowhere exists a more splendid collection of gems and curiosities than this great exhibition discloses. Here they are from all parts of the world, exhibited by the acre, and rivalling the splendor of our Centennial Main Building, the great halls showing as much, and most of it of more value. The Crystal Palace and the Alexandra Palace, each enormous structures, devoted to art and entertainment, are accessible for a shilling. The former is now a series of grand courts illustrating life in various countries and at different epochs, with reproductions of many famous things. For a shilling the Zoological Garden may be seen, which, whilst on a much larger scale than our own, and containing many more animals, yet does not contain of some species anything like as good specimens as we have in Fairmount Park. This is especially the case with seals and sealions, whilst there are no chimpanzees, and several other animals that we have are missing. But they have about a dozen elephants, which spend their time in riding the little boys and girls around the grounds. For lovers of horticulture and botany there are a half-dozen free gardens provided, the chief being at Kew, the most famous garden in the world. This extraordinary exhibition of what can be done with trees, bushes, shrubs, and flowers is worth going many miles to see; but their greatest hot-house, the "palm house," although it contains palm-trees sixty feet high, can bear no comparison to our magnificent Horticultural Hall in Fairmount Park. There, in a special house, is another Victoria Regia, in full bloom,— an offshoot, I think, from the one at Chatsworth. Fourteen of its enormous leaves, exactly circular and each about five feet in circumference, looking like so many gigantic green dinner-plates, were placidly floating on the surface of the water, whilst one large flower was opening at the centre of the tank. This garden could be explored by days together, and is the great achievement of what may be called popularized botany,—the plants being tastefully arranged to please the eye, and the entire garden laid out with a view to the best artistic effect. Then there are at least a dozen parks, most of them with water scenery, to add to the attractions. Many millions have been spent in thus providing recreation for London. If Philadelphia or New York had one-fourth part of what has been done here at public cost for the public amusement, both cities would be greatly the gainers. And though London, especially on a Sunday afternoon, streams out to these attractive places in crowds, yet I doubt if one-half the population derives any benefit from them. There is a numerous class, especially at the East End, who will not go, but prefer to linger in the noisome purlieus that make up that extraordinary region, and never take any recreation. I can readily believe that there are thousands in London who have never seen grass growing in the green fields, as they can neither be coaxed nor driven to go out and look at them.

These museums and gardens of which I have written are got up on the most extensive scale. There cannot be imagined a more fatiguing task than to go over one of them. Each has grown in all these years, by constant additions, to prodigious size. The succession of novelties is endless. It is like looking at ten thousand most fascinating show-windows. One sees so much of so varied character that the mind fails to grasp it, and the legs and eyes give out before the task is one-third over. What a task it was to go to the Centennial and attempt to see it as it should be looked at! and yet here are a dozen Centennials challenging observation, each a complete representation of its special kind of exhibition. If London wants to be instructed there is abundant provision for it, and the Londoner should not be uneducated if museums and free public exhibitions of all sorts can accomplish it. It is idle to suppose that this great city can be seen in a week, or in a year, —seen as it should be. There are gray-headed men who have passed all their lives in London who still are ignorant of large portions of it, and, in fact, never were in some parts of the city. I know one who has never been to the Tower, and another who had never been through the Thames Tunnel. What can you do with such people? They are as great curiosities as any London has in her wonderful museums, and would be as remarkable beings as a Philadelphian who had never seen Independence Hall.

One great sight of London, in the season, is to go to Hyde Park on a fine afternoon about five o'clock and see the carriages and equestrians on "Rotten Row." There are two roads, one for carriage-riding, and the other devoted exclusively to horseback-riding. No hired vehicle is allowed to enter Hyde Park, and here, at the height of the season, may be seen "everybody who is anybody" in coach or on horseback, turning out for an airing. Crowded with carriages and equestrians, the liveries and badges of the nobility passing in procession before you, the sight of its kind is unequalled in Europe. Each turnout is got up so as to outrival the other in Park equipage, and the ladies in full dress present an attractive array. On a fine day in the height of the season, Rotten Row will thus exhibit pretty much all the nobility and the wealthy and distinguished people of the kingdom, spread out, as it were, for the public, who go there in large numbers, to look at. And then as the liveries go by, and you recognize from them and from the armorial bearings on the coach-panels that the distinguished equipage belongs to the "Lord Knows Who" or the "Count No Account," or some other nobleman of greater or less fame, you can count up just what it costs milord in taxes to make the display. In the first place, he pays two guineas annual tax to the government for using the carriage. Then he pays two guineas more tax for the privilege of putting his armorial bearings on the panels of the carriage, and one guinea more if he exhibits them anywhere else. For the privileges of having a coachman he pays sixteen shillings, and thirty-two shillings more for the two footmen, whilst if a dog runs with the carriage, as many of them have to increase the impression, there is paid five shillings more. Thus, to drive along Rotten Row in style costs about forty dollars tax, so that it may be an open question whether the glory always pays.

## LETTER XXIII.

### SOME ENGLISH IMPRESSIONS.

LONDON, August 23.

The American traveller in Great Britain is naturally impressed by a multitude of experiences which are unlike what he is accustomed to in his own country. Of some of these I have already written. The hotels of England will compare favorably with those of our own country in many respects, but in some matters they appear to have ways that are very odd. There is no such thing as a hotel "office" in the American sense, or that being maligned by so many, but whom I have generally found to be gentlemanly and painstaking,—the American hotel clerk. Young ladies keep the accounts and manage the office-business of the hotel, but the guests are not expected to interview them, and, in fact, that great American institution, the hotel-counter, whereon lies the register, and over which the guests may lounge and ask questions, and get pens and paper and toothpicks, and look at the "Directory," and do the thousand and one things the American expects to do at the hotel-counters, is an unknown article in this kingdom. The porter at the hotel door is the man here who answers questions, and the head waiter is the person who "takes the bill,"—that is, the person to whom the guest pays his board. If you have the temerity to pay your bill yourself, the waiter lets you know it, as it is his prerogative to carry the money to the book-keeper, bring back the receipt and change on a silver waiter,—and get the douceur from the guest which is intended to be extracted by all this ceremony. There is very good service at the hotels, and I have been in probably twenty in different cities in the kingdom. The bedding, linens, and table and room furniture are usually of excellent quality,—better than many American hotels furnish, for the English guest is very exacting in these respects, and his country produces the best linens and bedding in the world. In magnificence of decoration some of these hotels are remarkable, whilst everything is constructed in the most substantial manner. But unlike the American, the English traveller rarely writes his name on a hotel register, so that many of the hotels here do not have such a book. The eating is good and the preparation of food excellent. England is famous for her meats and their good cooking, but very weak in vegetables. The visitor misses that almost endless profusion of vegetables he gets in America, and has to be content at this season with potatoes and string-beans, with an occasional dish of peas, cauliflower, and "vegetable marrow," under which imposing title is introduced our well-known American friend, the squash. The cabbage, of which so much is made with us, is not considered good enough for a first-class hotel table, whilst the tomato is too great a luxury for ordinary people to aspire to. When the Queen wishes to particularly favor a guest at dinner, he is treated to baked tomatoes. Green corn is unknown, and practically the meal is made of soup, fish, meat, potatoes, and beans, on which the variations are played day in and day out. Then the American misses the desserts. If you ask for pie in this country, you are brought the remains of yesterday's dinner hashed up into a meat-pie. The English of pie is "tart," and an English tart, whilst it may be popular among those to the manner born, will never satisfy the great American pie-biter. There is no "dessert" at meals, but they hand around "sweets," but some of the "sweets," which are concoctions of plums, gooseberries, rhubarb, etc., are horribly sour. That grand American solace in hot weather, "ice-cream," is unknown in England. John Bull has attempted to manufacture what he calls "ices," but the attempt is a miserable failure. I can imagine how Burns, or Bruna, or Augustine, or Bauer, or Slocum, or some other of our ice-cream Bismarcks, would look awry at these mixtures, which the untutored Briton endeavors to impose on the American at triple the cost as a substitute for ice-cream. There is a fortune for the Yankee who comes over here and introduces the genuine article.

The great mystery to an American in British home arrangements is how England has managed to get tea ahead of dinner. You breakfast in the morning, lunch at mid-day, and take tea in the afternoon. Then afterwards, at seven or eight o'clock at night, you take dinner, and after spending hours at it—go to bed. The dinner is the grave and ponderous and important event of the day,—never lightly or hastily taken by the true Englishman,—and the dinner is, in fact, an essential part of every transaction. To become a lawyer in England there must be a certain number of dinners certified as eaten in the Temple, and if you visit an Englishman on business, a dinner or two is necessary before it can be consummated. Then your thorough Briton has got himself into the proper state of mind to attend to ordinary affairs. The nation is rarely in a hurry. An Englishman may run to catch a railway train, but he is neither in a hurry to get up in the morning or to go to bed at night. It is nine o'clock before the stores open, and much later when business men appear at their offices. The morning newspapers are issued very late, and, in fact, although the sun gets up very early in summer-time, a large portion of his morning shining is upon a race that has not yet begun the work of the day.

One of the British anomalies is the absence of available water. They have plenty of streams and plenty of rain-storms, and most elaborate systems of water-supply; but their use of water is as if it was not abundant. London would be aghast at the deluge that overflows Philadelphia on Saturday mornings. House-fronts, steps, and sidewalks are innocent of cleansing, and a Londoner told me that he did not believe there was a hundred feet of garden-hose in the city. Therefore one can walk about without being splashed or squirted on, or having a long brush-handle run into his ribs. But they don't have white marble and red bricks in London,—everything is dingy, dark, and dirty,—in fact, the city could not be kept clean if the Thames ran through every street. Your true Englishman, too, is not a water-drinker, and hence very little attention is paid to furnishing water for this purpose. It is seldom put on hotel tables, and when it is asked for is brought in very small quantities. "Water-coolers" are unknown, and ice a scarce article. There is nothing that seems so odd to an American as his difficulty in getting a drink of water. With a single exception, the railways have scarcely any water furnished in cars or stations, and that railway makes a great glorification over having begun the giving of water to passengers, advertising the fact extensively as a reason for patronage, and when the passenger goes on the line he finds that the water is occasionally brought around when the train stops, and is poured out in small quantities from a receptacle that looks like a superannuated watering-pot into a mug, from which you have to drink then and there, or else go without. Thus the passengers are, at stated intervals, watered like so many horses.*

---

* On August 19, 1878, the London *Times* printed the following communication, under the title of "The Water Supply":

'To the Editor of the Times:
"Sir,—I am an American, who has been travelling for about a month past in the United Kingdom. During that period I have crossed many streams of water, and been frequently deluged by rain, and gazed on fountains and lakes, and seen most elaborate machinery and constructions for supplying water to cities, and have passed frequent drinking-fountains in the streets; but have, nevertheless, with all this abundance of water on every hand, been frequently put to sad straits to get a drink of it. With the ability everywhere to get wine, beer, and spirits, I have nevertheless found that most of the hotels I have stopped at do not think it necessary to supply water. In America we are accustomed to having water supplied in every public place, every hotel, railway station, public building, store, shop,—in fact, everywhere that men may congregate. The 'ice-water' reservoir stands in a convenient place, with drinking-cups provided, and all who are thirsty go and help themselves. I do not mean to say that Americans exclusively drink water, but such of them as desire to drink it have the convenience everywhere provided in public places,—not only drinking-fountains along the streets, but especially in hotels and railway stations. The Americans, who are a travelling people, notice the want of this convenience more than anything else on coming to Europe. An American can get a drink of water, of course, if he asks for it; but he is accustomed to helping himself to it at home, and finding the means at hand. Water is always put upon the table at every meal in every American hotel, and is considered as much an essential of table furniture as the knives or dishes. There is not a railway carriage that

I have already mentioned the proneness of our English cousin to exclusiveness. He builds high walls to keep gazers from looking into his grounds, and charters an entire compartment in a railway carriage so as to exclude all his fellows. He wants to be snug in his home and to enjoy his family society, or his club or his "set," without outside interference. I am told that the Pullman parlor-cars which have been introduced at

---

carries passengers on American railways that is without its copious supply of water, besides ample supplies in the stations. I asked for water at the table in a Liverpool hotel upon first landing, and the waiters looked at me and at each other as if I were an Ashantee or red Indian. I asked for water again in the ancient town of Chester,—not at the table, to be sure,—and it took three persons and ten minutes' time to get a drink. One servant, after some delay, told a second to get it, and then, after more delay, a third brought it. In Dublin, for six persons, I was served, after asking at the table, with about one pint, with one glass for the six to drink from. In Glasgow and Edinburgh, I am happy to say, the water was actually placed on the table without being asked for. Here in London, however, there was again difficulty in getting it; but now, since I have been six days at the hotel, I have at length succeeded to-day in getting the waiter to place, without asking, the water and the glasses on the table. It was such a victory for American principles in the British metropolis that I at once determined to write you about it.

"It is estimated that there are this year at least fifty thousand Americans travelling in Europe, and nearly every one of them is at some time a visitor to England. I have noticed that the peculiar characteristics of Continental visitors are amply provided for in England, and would certainly think that those who serve the travelling public would be equally anxious to provide for the Americans, who make up a very large proportion of the guests at hotels and the passengers on railways. Now, an American may drink beer, wine, and spirits without stint, and occasionally 'treat' every one who may happen to be within call, but he still wants his drink of water. It would be a very little boon for the railway management or the hotel proprietor to place this convenience within his reach, so that the free-born American could go and help himself without stint and without hindrance. I can imagine my countrymen flocking to an hotel that set up a free 'water-cooler' for the guests, while of the competing lines of railway from Liverpool to London the one that had drinking-water easily accessible in the stations and in the carriages would attract the most American travellers. It is a subject of such vital importance that it might even avert another Alabama or Fishery controversy between the two nations. Who knows? But, at all events, when I go into my English hotel, gorgeous with all that the builder's and decorator's arts can supply, with its elaborate furnishing, its tiling, its mirrors, its fine linens and grand table service, let me not longer look in vain for water. I would at any time at dinner exchange any half-dozen of the multitude of knives, forks, spoons, plates, and wine-glasses set before me for a good, honest drink of old-fashioned American ice-water.

"AN AMERICAN TRAVELLER.

"LONDON, August 17."

great cost on some of the English railways, will, from this cause, probably fail. The race is not gregarious. They will not ride together in the large American style of car. They want to shut themselves up in the little compartments, and hence the Pullman coach runs comparatively empty. But perseverance is a good Yankee trick, and Mr. Pullman may yet win. In railway arrangements we can teach the English very little, but we can learn from them a great deal. Railroading, as exhibited in and around London, is a science to which few of our railways approach. There is a general impression, too, that our system of baggage expresses in the large cities could be successfully introduced into England, but I doubt it. In Philadelphia we get the local transfer company to take our trunks to and from railway stations, because we cannot manage it in any other way except at considerable cost for hack hire. In London the passenger and his trunk go in a cab, and at a cost not greater than our express charge. The railway porter receives you at the station and takes your baggage to or from the cab as the case may be. There are plenty of porters, no delays, and scarcely any trouble. Your baggage travels with you in the same train. My impression before coming to England was that there was a chance for the Yankee to introduce the conveniences in England that we have about baggage, but my impression now is, that the Yankee who tries it will get his labor for his pains. The baggage-express system, which is founded upon the costliness and defects of the hack system in America, would not work in England, because the same service and more is performed cheaper. So long as a cab carries the passenger for twenty-five cents and his trunk for four cents, the express would have no advantage. Other things being even, a passenger prefers to have his baggage always with him. It saves delays and trouble. This advantage the cab gives, and it is the rule throughout the entire kingdom. In fact, carriage charges of all kinds are very cheap here, and they are so well regulated by laws (which are enforced) that the visitor gets the full benefit of them. I have known five persons (one with the driver) to ride in a coach with two seats three miles between railway station and hotel, the coach also carrying a half-dozen pieces of baggage on top, and the charge to be equivalent to seventy-five cents. The perfection and cheapness of this service—and it is true of costlier vehicles also—is astonishing to an American, who is accustomed only to the hack systems of his own country.

The "cabbies" are a cheerful set, always good-humored, always ready to impart their knowledge for the public benefit. They are too well controlled to take advantage of strangers. In fact, for an extra shilling the cabby's heart can be won for almost any service. He will carefully take home an obliviously drunken man and tenderly deposit him, with all his valuables intact, at his own door, and see that he is securely placed inside it. But still, it does not do to depend too much on his abilities in this respect. Sad experience has proved that it does not do to trust cabby with two such persons, consigned to different places, unless the aforesaid persons are conspicuously labelled. Cabby is sure to deposit the wrong man at the wrong house. They gear the cab-shafts high over the horse's back, and this to one accustomed to our low-down gearing looks very odd. But it is a plan that some of our drivers may find to their advantage. Cabby was asked why it was done, and answered, "So the 'os won't break the shafts when he falls down, you know."

The most striking English impression made on the visitor is, that the country is a garden. It is cultivated, wherever possible, in the highest degree. The green lanes, the hedges and smiling fields, and flower gardens and artistic little cottages are, outside the cities, a rich attraction. A railway ride through the country is a succession of beautiful rural views. Agriculture is studied and carried to the highest point. The crops grown are generally much heavier than ours. Wheat yields thirty-five to forty bushels, and sometimes more, to the acre, and is now being generally harvested around London. On the larger farms steam-plows drawn by traction-engines are common. A very large portion of the fields are thoroughly underdrained. The richness of the agricultural evidences are pleasant to see, though we are now seeing England at her best, for she has better crops this summer than have been gathered for several years. Still, however, she looks across the ocean for food, as, do her best, her wheat growth is always far short of the demand.

## LETTER XXIV.

ENGLAND'S GREAT WATERING-PLACE.

BRIGHTON, August 26.

All England is proud of Brighton,—of its fine situation, great size, grand buildings, decorations, and its glories in the season. Taken altogether it is probably the greatest watering-place in the world, and everything that art and wealth can do to add to its attractions is lavished upon this city by the sea. It is within about ninety minutes' railway ride of London, on the southern coast of England, and the city stretches for over three miles along the English Channel upon a comparatively low shore, though in some places the cliff rises thirty or forty feet above the beach. Almost the entire front is protected by a sea-wall of greater or less height, which supports a broad terrace, or rather a succession of terraces on the same level. In front of these the sea rolls up over a rather steep pebbly beach whereon are bathing-machines and fishing- and pleasure-boats and a few pedestrians, but the walking is rough and unsteady. The bathing is not very good, and in fact is only one of the smaller attractions of Brighton, being but partially indulged in by the visitors. It has none of the comforts or pleasures of our New Jersey coast watering-places in this respect, for no one can take a dip in the sea to his entire satisfaction when his feet are tortured by such rough and unsteady pebbles as compose this beach. But Brighton has along the beach and behind the sea-walls what no other watering-place in the world possesses,—a grand drive, at least sixty feet wide, extending over three miles along the coast, with a broad promenade frequently ornamented with lawns, gardens, and flower-beds in front, and on the land side a succession of palaces and great buildings of most imposing construction, which look as if the Boulevards of Paris had been brought here, and their buildings of ornate cream-colored stone ranged along the sea. The city extends far back on the hill-sides and along the valleys into the land, and has a population of one hundred thousand, which is frequently doubled during the season. And

F*

the greater part of this population crowd out upon the broad terraces in front known as the Marine Parade, where they ride or promenade, to see and be seen, and give the city a life and attractiveness that are all its own. When London empties Brighton fills up, and here come the equipages that have made Rotten Row famous. No ocean-border scene ever equalled in my eyes what the Brighton Parade last night presented, and yet the season is only beginning, and will not be at its height for some weeks yet. Before dark the crowds moved along between the succession of palaces and great hotels and fine houses, with beautifully-ornamented public squares on the land side, and the beach, with its terraced edge and gardens and flower-beds, on the other. As the night came on and the lights were lit, the scene gradually assumed the form of an illumination, whilst far out over the water were the hundreds of colored lights on piers and vessels, making it look like a Parisian festival. In fact, Brighton seems as if a portion of Paris had been brought to England, for it is not dingy and dark like most English towns, but light and attractive, and when the sun shines more of it seems to come here than to most English cities. It is in the season the gayest of all places in the kingdom, and manages to concentrate a very large portion of the wealth, fashion, and aristocracy of the realm. Its hotels are of large size, and one of them towers nine stories high, and covers a large square. There are rows of similarly-constructed buildings, fronting the sea, hundreds of feet long. In one case a splendid structure surrounds a square, and fronts the sea, extending probably fifteen hundred feet in frontage. Scores of new buildings of the largest size are going up, showing that the building trades have plenty to do. Millions upon millions of money have been laid out upon the decoration, construction, and ornamentation of the Marine Parade, over which will probably promenade during the next three months a large proportion of the "fast" life of England.

The affairs of England, like those of the Romans, I am told, are regulated by the flight of birds. In other lands the summer drives fashionable life out of the cities to the watering-places, whilst the winter brings it back again. But not so with England. The summer is spent in London, and the winter in the country. Fashion decrees that when the grouse begin to fly in August the London season must terminate, and

ENGLAND'S GREAT WATERING-PLACE. 131

it must not begin until winter has bade good-by to the last pheasant. Hence Parliament opens in February and ends in August, and this marks the duration of the London season. The thermometer does not regulate it as with us. The hot weather is spent in town and the cold weather out of it. Therefore, in August and September, when Americans are getting back to the cities, the English are leaving them, and when we are coddling around our hottest fires in town, about Christmas-time, the true Englishman will still be in the country and endeavoring to enjoy himself. "It is awfully absurd," said a distinguished Londoner to me last week, "but the flight of the birds decrees it." Over two hundred thousand people shut up their houses and left London during the week that followed the close of the session, August 17. Belgravia looked as if it had suffered a terrible collapse. Thus Brighton is growing at the expense of its great neighbor, and all that money and art can accomplish are lavished upon it to attract the visitor.

Two piers extend out from the Parade, each for a thousand feet over the sea, and are used for promenades. At their ends they widen to broad platforms, sixty feet square, where bands play, and where at night there are, as all along the piers and Parade, beautiful illuminations. The older one is the famous Chain Pier, built as a suspension bridge and supported on piles. The new pier, ten years old, is grander than the other, and is a most spacious and ornamental structure of iron. Both are strong, and to either, to enjoy music and all, the admission charge is but twopence. George IV., when Prince of Wales, built at Brighton a royal pavilion, in imitation of the Kremlin at Moscow, or, as others hold, of an East Indian pagoda, and embosomed in trees and surrounded by gardens, its curiously-knobbed, turreted, and peaked roofs present a remarkable appearance. But it is surplusage in a city of such beautiful structures to describe any. The methods of transportation are varied from those in use elsewhere, by both coaches and goat-wagons. In the former, round-shouldered men laboriously drag ancient dowagers, whilst in the latter the children gladly ride, being furnished double as well as single teams. In fact, goat-power, as a means of juvenile transportation, is as conspicuous at Brighton as donkey-power was at Scarborough; and a Brighton goat-team, with youthful coachman and footmen, can be engaged for a juvenile ride for threepence. The coachman and footmen walk, however, so that the goats are not overladen. Brighton has regularly established fire-engine stations, which are not very numerous in English cities, and in large letters on the outside is the announcement that for every alarm of fire two shillings and sixpence will be paid. But, with the caution that is proverbial among Englishmen, this is supplemented by the further announcement that "no reward is paid for a false alarm."

#### THE BRIGHTON AQUARIUM.

Perhaps the feature of Brighton which has most worldwide fame is the Aquarium, and yet the stranger without a guide has difficulty in finding it. This comes from its peculiar location. I was consigned to a hotel "opposite the Aquarium." I looked out to find it, and saw across the grand esplanade in front, the open sea, and no Aquarium. Then, walking over towards the sea-wall, it suddenly opened, sunken below the level of the roadway, covered in and hidden by the sea-walls on both sides, yet stretching almost eight hundred feet on either hand, and a hundred feet in breadth, and surmounted by gardens and footwalks. The Aquarium, to facilitate the movement of the sea-water, is set at as low a level as is consistent with safety, and its top presents a strange appearance, with its variegated roof of foot-paths, flowers, trap-doors, and skylights. This Aquarium is worthy all the fame it has, for it far exceeds the feebler attempts at imitation elsewhere, and in its interior decorations is superb. The design is to represent the fishes, as far as possible, in their native haunts and habits, and, as the presence of visitors might interfere with this if known, the visitors go through darkened passages, and are thus concealed from the fish. This makes their actions much more natural, and, in fact, they seem to move about with perfect freedom. Some of the tanks are of great size, one of them wherein the porpoise disports being one hundred feet long. Schools of herring and mackerel swim through the waters as they do on the Grand Bank. The octopus gyrates his fearful-looking arms, and gives an idea of what he may be when he becomes a full-grown devil fish, for these specimens are only about a foot long. The codfish circulates, and the whiting, bass, and pretty much every fish we know of, either in England or America, is exhibited as in its native haunts. Here are those extraordinary little fellows, the sea-horses of the Mediterranean, which are horses' heads driven forward through the water by little propeller-like fins in the tail and clinging curiously to the coral spurs. The Aquarium is full of all sorts of aquatic curiosities, having American alligators, of whom an entire family—gentleman, lady, and two children—bask in the mud ; seals and sea-lions, which, like those at Fairmount Park, are blessed with good appetites, and a particular favorite is the lively little " Prince," the baby sea-lion, born last year, who has an especial tank devoted to his own use, because he has got so big that, as they told me, he occasionally " whips his daddy." The preparation of the tanks for the fish has been conducted on the most perfect and expensive scale. The seals and sea-lions have extensive ranges of rocks to climb upon. The alligators can bask in savannas and crawl through expanded grottos. The porpoises and larger fish are given a range of a hundred feet. The visitor walks through groined and vaulted passages, artistically decorated with colored marbles and polished granite, and the entire structure is prepared in the costliest manner, whilst music during the day and concerts in the evening add to the attractions. This is the land of cheap amusements. A shilling is all that is charged for admission to the Aquarium, whilst in London the South Kensington Museum, which when entirely completed will cover fifty-six acres, is opened half the week free and the other half for sixpence. And all the other public institutions of the kind in England are on a similar basis. The Brighton Aquarium is also made use of to show the process of hatching trout and salmon, and for experiments which have greatly increased the world's stock of knowledge as to the habits of fish. Its tanks hold an aggregate of five hundred thousand gallons of sea and fresh water, and its many thousands of specimens embrace almost the entire range of the fish kingdom.

Brighton stands almost on the line of one of the routes of travel between London and Paris, that by New Haven and Dieppe. It is fifteen miles from New Haven, and stopover tickets are issued by the railway, which runs south from London through a most picturesque country, with frequent tunnels piercing the hills and viaducts over the valleys. As the south coast is approached we get into the region of windmills, their broad sail-like arms surmounting almost every hilltop. Here graze the sheep that provide that famous English meat, the Southdown mutton. Here feed the black cows that in this country seem to outnumber those of all other colors. Here are the broad acres of grass land, underdrained and cultivated as carefully as possible, which feed these famous meats, and which are valued in some cases as high as two thousand and two thousand five hundred dollars an acre. Bordering them the chalk cliffs slope down to the English Channel, across which is this year's Mecca for the American traveller—the Paris Exhibition. But the crossing is a treacherous one, and, though there have been many attempts made to improve the means of transportation, none as yet have driven off the Channel malady of sea-sickness. Both the Dover and New Haven routes, however, are provided with better steamers than those of ten years ago, and the terrors of the Channel passage are therefore to some extent mitigated.

## LETTER XXV.

### CROSSING THE CHANNEL.

PARIS, August 29.

As one approaches Paris he is reminded of the Centennial times, of the overloading of railway trains, and the frantic zeal of transportation people to compress humanity into contracted spaces; of the ability to pay much for little, and the natural weakness of mankind in business affairs to make hay while the sun shines. All that we did in Philadelphia at this sort of thing in 1876, and more, they have been doing in and on the road to Paris,—I say, " have been," for the public have been finding them out, and thus making the evil work its own cure in many respects. The visitor from England first strikes the Exhibition influence at the Channel, and the American visitor, with his experience of the Centennial, is at once impressed with the inability of some of the railway and steamboat people to handle vast crowds when suddenly cast upon them. They do it with skill at London, where the crowds are steady and the traffic enormous but uniform; but they sadly need an American lesson in transportation, in getting visitors across the Channel from London to Paris. Here are the two great cities of the world, and yet no American travels between them without feeling that the railway managers of his country could teach a lesson in transportation if their own clever ideas were only adapted to the purpose. There are three routes,— by Dover and Calais, Folkestone and Boulogne, and New Haven and Dieppe. The first two are practically the same. Ten years ago the service across the Channel was simply disgraceful. Now they have better steamers, but they cannot properly manage the increased traffic. It has poured in upon them in such streams as to overwhelm them. Therefore the journey is as miserable as ever, but in a different way. In the course of this correspondence, I have been generally a sincere admirer of the great abilities displayed throughout the British dominions, both in land and sea navigation, but the nation that has made the wonderful railways centring at London, and has dug out the Clyde as the Scotch have done, are nonplussed by the Channel. They say they cannot remedy it except by a tunnel, and although they have improved the steamers, yet they have not much improved the passage. Here is certainly a case in which Americans could teach a lesson, and either President Scott or President Gowen could send a score of men of railroad genius over here from their staffs who could work out a solution of the problem.

The best route to cross is by Calais and Dover, simply because it is the shortest Channel-passage, and the company, knowing this, extracts nearly twice as much fare. The New Haven and Dieppe route, aware of the competition, has this year tried to meet it, by putting on two new steamers,—described as the largest, most powerfully constructed and best-appointed vessels that cross the Channel. They are the largest, but still are small, and they are swift and strong, as the Clyde build of steamers usually are,—but they are no nearer meeting the Channel problem in Exhibition times than were the old, miserable, little craft that formerly crossed the Channel with passengers, and which we would not tolerate for the Smith's Island ferry. The Dover route, after having failed with the ship which had a suspended saloon, is now trying the steamer Calais-Douvres with twin hulls, but which does not seem to do much better. None of these things, however, can be learnt in the advertisements, for their adjectives are all of the other kind, and the poor mortal who ventures on the boats learns to his sorrow that printer's ink sometimes don't tell the truth. The Channel-crossing accommodations are only provided for a certain amount of traffic, and there is no elasticity in them to accommodate a rush. It is the rush that the management are unable to deal with. All the methods of making the transportation better seem to be directed to the single point of endeavoring to avoid sea-sickness. Instead of recognizing sea-sickness as a fact, and endeavoring to ameliorate the condition of the passenger, they go on experimenting with hulls that won't work, instead of trying to make the passenger comfortable. What is wanted is comfort and cleanliness and more room, but these things are as sadly neglected in the new steamers as in the old. A little Yankee invention would do a world of good, if applied to the methods of crossing the Channel.

On the night I crossed the Channel from New Haven to Dieppe by the line of direct travel, but the longest sea-route, there was an excursion taken over. This, which was one of the regular excursions made weekly by the railway from London, and could be anticipated and measured by the management, probably doubled the number of passengers, and transportation had to be provided for about twelve hundred persons. An American railway manager does not fear any such number as this even on ordinary trains, but it seems to have been too much for the people managing this line. They got four steamers in readiness to carry them over the Channel, and were telegraphing all the evening between London and New Haven about the arrangements. I naturally supposed from the glowing advertisements that state-room accommodations were easy to obtain, but was amazed at the discovery that the steamers on this line had only two state-rooms apiece, —one holding two and the other four persons, and that one cost five dollars and the other eight dollars for the night in addition to the fare. Thus twenty-four persons could get special accommodations, whilst the remainder had to pass the night in the saloons or on deck. The train came down from London in sections, and there was a rush on board the steamers at midnight, and a scramble for the chance of lying on the sofas. All classes took part in the scramble, and evidently seemed accustomed to it. There were not sofa accommodations for one-fourth the people, and the others had to lie on the floors or take refuge on the decks, without cover, and these were ultimately driven into the companion-ways by the rain. Women with first-class tickets thus passed the night partly on deck and partly crouching or standing in the companion-ways. Then there was all sorts of trouble in getting the steamers off, for the task seemed too much to cope with. Finally, long after midnight, one after another, they sailed, and crossed the Channel. But such a crossing! Four out of five passengers got sick, and the discomforts were appalling. Herded together like cattle, the scene, when dawn came over the saloon and disclosed the confused mixture of passengers, wash-basins, portmanteaus, sofa-cushions, bags, beer-bottles, and boxes, was saddening. If it had been an American enterprise the captain would have run the risk of lynching. But not being American, the passengers growled and threatened to make complaints, and that ended it. With the peculiar pertinacity of John Bull in any cause which he espouses, the solitary waiter allotted to the saloon persisted in serving out beer as long as there was any stomach left in condition to hold it, and then even the English could stand it no longer, but drove him and his bottles out with a volley of curses. The ladies' saloon in the morning produced a woe-begone party, who had tried to crowd in a place only half large enough to hold them. Thus passed a miserable night in a good sea-boat, swift and strong, but with wretched accommodations, entirely unfit for passengers who were expected to be sea-sick, and redolent with the questionable perfumes that aggravate the disorder, yet could be readily removed if there were proper attention to cleanliness. Then, in the morning, the passengers, tired, worn out, and anxious for rest and a particularly good breakfast, were poured upon the landing at Dieppe, with very little accommodations for breakfast and no waiting-rooms to speak of. They overflowed the "buffet," as the meagre restaurant is called, and swarmed out into the cafés of the neighborhood. They could get little to eat but cold ham. That was almost the sum total of the larder, and it would have been a rare treat to a student of physiognomy to have watched the countenances of those sea-sick passengers as the broad slices of fat ham were placed before them, flanked by coffee that ought to have been good, but had suffered sadly by dilution. Imagine such a meal for the delicate stomach of the convalescing victim of *mal de mer*. It was their first introduction to that art praised throughout the world—French *cuisine;* and as it was, there was not room in the buffet for half of them, or comfortable places for any. There were few satisfactory breakfasts taken that morning, even though they were served in *la belle* France, and by French servants—in soiled clothing. So long as the sun shone, however, the situation could be endured, because it had to be, and the demoralized passengers could saunter along the dock and watch the stevedores unload the cargo from the steamers. But it began to rain, and then there was flight for shelter. There was little room and no accommodations in the station, and most of the people fled into the freight-sheds, where they perched themselves upon boxes and casks, and sat up in empty fish-baskets, endeavoring to overcome the perfume by vigorous applications of hartshorn. Then could be heard, in all the tongues which originated at the Tower of Babel, expressions of very decided opinion about the character of that route to Paris. The necessity of getting language sufficiently strong to meet the case did good to the sick, however, for it started the blood into circulation and revived their spirits. It was amusing to see how the railway officials and the steamboat people kept away from the station. Even the woman who had been charging the passengers ten cents apiece for the doubtful privilege of washing their faces in a lot of dirty wash-basins, disappeared before this tempest. The rain poured down; the passengers huddled together among the freight packages, and thus wore away hours,—for the Western Railway of France, as much nonplussed as the steamers by the crowd thrust upon them, was unable to get up a railway train sufficiently capacious to carry it. I have read about Job and how he triumphed over many tests of patience, but doubt if that extraordinary man's reputation would have successfully survived a journey across the English Channel. Be that as it may, however, there was not one in all that crowd who was in condition to assume the *rôle* of Job. There they waited, each passing the time according to the fashion of his nationality when supremely disgusted. The sick women tried to get rest by reclining over fish-baskets; whilst the Americans, with that spirit which is characteristic of the race, discussed with a very liberal sprinkling of "cuss-words" the bad characters of the steamboat and railway corporations, and the feasibility either of tarring and feathering the management, or else of establishing (on borrowed money) a rival line. Finally, after three hours of waiting, the long-delayed train appeared. Then there was a rush for seats. No Cossack horde or Indian foray ever swooped down upon their prey with greater vigor than that crowd of worn-out, draggled, and disgusted passengers rushed through the rain for the railway train. It was about one minute of scrambling, shouting, scuffling, and quarrelling, and then it was settled that the train was not big enough to hold them all, and as it was, many of the first-class passengers had to be content with second- and third-class accommodations. One robust Englishman, who was too dignified to enter into the scuffle, was endeavoring to expound his rights, but a drenching shower came along and he rushed for shelter into a third-class carriage. Then there was more delay before the train got started, for accommodation had to be found for the people who could not get in, and every available carriage was scoured out of the yard to give it. Then it was discovered that the train was too heavy for the engines, and after more delay it was cut into sections. Finally we got off,—late and behind time,—but the sun came out and somewhat cheered the drooping spirits. But such a getting to the Exposition I do not think any of the passengers would like to experience again. I am quite sure that if there was anything like the American ingenuity of 1876 devoted to this purpose, these railways and steamers could get their excursions from London to Paris in comfort. Here is a case where the Exposition has been opened nearly four months, with this kind of extra demand for transportation recurring at regular intervals, and yet they do not seem to be able to cope with it, though the excursion-party was comparatively only a small one, and but a fraction compared with those that our transportation managers handled daily and with ease in 1876. What these people want is better attention to the comfort of the passengers. They could, with a small part of the ingenuity shown at Dublin, Glasgow, or Belfast, make the landing-places on the Channel capacious enough for large steamers. These steamers, with an adaptation of the same methods employed elsewhere, could be made comfortable for the passengers. No American would think of putting day-boats on a night-line; and yet this is practically what is done. Nor would an American steamboatman think of putting passengers on decks unprotected even by awnings,—yet these boats do not always have awnings, and when they do, the allowance is almost too meagre to speak of.

### FROM DIEPPE TO PARIS.

The railway journey from Dieppe through Rouen and up the Seine to Paris is by far the most picturesque of the routes from the Channel, passing through a succession of attractive landscapes, all peculiarly French, in the chateaus, cottages, and rows of trees along the roads and field hedges. Here the women go about in white caps and wooden shoes, and the men in blue smock frocks. The railway discloses many beautiful scenes along the Seine, and finally comes in through the partially dismantled fortifications on the northern border of Paris to the station at St. Lazare. Here the Customs and Octroi, as at Dieppe, have an examination, which is, probably, the most incomplete examination ever made by customs officer. He approaches, dressed like a field-marshal, with waxed moustache and pointed goatee, and saying something which you don't understand, you answer something which he don't understand, and then, with a grunt and a shrug, he puts a hieroglyphic in chalk upon the trunk (without looking into it) and the performance is over. I saw those huge Saratoga trunks, which only Americans indulge in, thus passed without being opened, for in France the influence of an American countenance and the American style of talking French is magical. But the customs revenue might, nevertheless, suffer from such laxity. Thus ended the journey across the Channel,—taken, as I knew, by the least comfortable, but most picturesque route of the three,—but what should not an American sacrifice to get to that city where it is said all good Americans hope to go when they die? To some, however, the crossing of the Channel may even then be too great a price to pay for it.

PARIS AND THE SEVEN BRIDGES.

## LETTER XXVI.

### SOME PARISIAN IMPRESSIONS.

PARIS, August 30.

Two prominent impressions are this year made upon the visitor to Paris. One that a very large portion of the population of the city are Americans, and the other that the gay appearance of the city has suffered from the downfall of the Imperial régime. Whilst all races are represented just now in Paris, for its attractions, permanent and special, are designed to and always do draw visitors from all lands, yet this year it is the general remark that Americans have come to Paris in greater numbers than any other people. They have heard that everything has risen to enormous prices, and, being of an inquiring turn of mind, have come to investigate the matter, and in order to make the investigation more thorough, and to get evidence on the subject that is the more complete, they are paying these high prices in all directions. Everywhere one goes in Paris Americans are met, and the universality of their presence is shown by the shops putting up American signs. It used to be the English that were thus catered to, but the French draw a distinction now between the English and the Americans, and, having a keen appreciation of the value of American money, and of the proneness of the race to lavish expenditure, they endeavor to attract them as much as possible. In fact, our countrymen have this year overrun the whole of western Europe, and scores of hotels are flying the American flag because the majority of their guests come from across the Atlantic.

But Paris does not exhibit the gayety that was the rule before the downfall of Napoleon. In the heyday of Imperialism the magnificent equipages that crowded the streets and the Bois de Boulogne were one of the great attractions of the city. The Champs Elysées was then an almost endless panorama of grand turnouts, and, so far as stylish horseflesh, and grand trappings, and gorgeous liveries and equipages could do it, the visitor was impressed with the splendor of the Court.

Now all this is ended. The nobles have put away their grandeur and ride about, when they do ride, in simpler style. There are no more four-horse teams, excepting occasionally in omnibuses. The footmen and lackeys have mostly disappeared. The streets are as full of life as ever, and are crowded sometimes to repletion, but there is not that flavor of overpowering rank and aristocracy that formerly almost overwhelmed the visitor to the Champs Elysées and the Bois de Boulogne. The American can pay as much for his coach now as ever, but he cannot get such stunning turnouts as were formerly available for our petroleum and bonanza princes, whose well-filled purses are always open and gladdening the hearts of impecunious Frenchmen. The American goes to the Bois now, generally in a "one-hoss shay," and finds that most others do likewise. In nothing has the advent of the French Republic made a more marked change in French customs than in the enforced moderation of equipage. Even the President hesitates about getting into a four-horse coach, and no one, be he of high or low degree, ventures upon trappings or gaudy display. The revulsion from the lavish exuberance of the Imperial Court is marked indeed.

### THE CHAMPS ELYSÉES.

But whilst it has lost its grand equipages, the Avenue of the Champs Elysées still stands without a rival as the finest street in the world. It has lost no other attraction, but has gained vastly by the application of the electric light, which will soon be in full operation all along the avenue, from the Tuileries Gardens to the Arch of Triumph. There is no more splendid scene than that presented by this great street when fully illuminated. The Frenchman loves display, and on this street are provided every possible appliance, by gas-lamp, electric light, or other device, which can in any way be permanently fixed, that will illuminate it. A broad avenue gradually sloping up to the Arch, with gardens on either hand, fountains playing, myriads of rows of lamps, illuminated concert-gardens blazing with light, thousands of carriages with their brilliant lamps, flitting about like so many fireflies; the piercingly radiant stars of the electric light interspersed among the others, and shining in clusters from afar around the Arch; this scene, when one stands in the Place de la

Concorde and looks along the street towards the Arch, is unequalled anywhere. Here in times of festival concentrates all the splendor of Paris. Here is the artistic centre of the city, and here flock the people when on holidays and fête days they wish to make a celebration. Along it the dazzled American loves to ramble and wonder, if Paris can put street-lamps in rows twenty feet apart, why something like it cannot be done in some parts of his own dimly-lighted cities. Here, in picturesque costume, are seen the people of all lands, like a greatly enlarged stage setting for an opera chorus, in their clothes of many colors. Here wanders the bicycle with its red and green lights of warning; and sometimes the patient peasants, men and women, slowly dragging wagon-loads that would do credit to a horse. The scene at night is one of enchantment almost, and it goes on far into the morning hours before the cafés close and the lights go out and Paris goes to bed. This great street is the personification of the French idea; for all the beauties of trees and flowers, fountains, statues, gardens, and illumination, are combined to make it as attractive and as beautiful as such a street can be made. The object has certainly been accomplished, and there could have been no more thorough badge of submission than the German conqueror imposed, when, on the surrender of Paris, he marched his victorious troops under the Arch of Triumph and along this great street. It was practically the occupation of Paris, and was so intended.

### THE PARISIAN RECEPTION.

But admiring Parisian beauty and endeavoring to get along in Paris are two different things. The American discovers, as soon as he lands at the railway station, that he is practically deaf and dumb. He can speak and he can hear, but it avails not. He may be a graduate of a French academy, but American-taught French is not the kind spoken here. The earliest encounter is with the railway porter, who overwhelms with a perfect Niagara of gibberish the unfortunate traveller who, in the polished language taught at French schools at home, politely requests that his trunk be taken to a carriage. The porter evidently does not understand French; neither does the cab-driver. You tell him in your best accent the destination, and the result, after a long parley, is a consultation with a half-dozen other cabbies, each wearing a shiny high hat that almost dazzles in the sunlight, and their combined knowledge of French is at last sufficient to designate you in somewhat contemptuous tones as an "Anglais." Everybody that the Frenchman does not like, seems to be an "Anglais." This insinuation of English nativity you repel with scorn. You casually mention the word "American," and the problem is solved. Cabby seizes your trunk and thrusts you into the coach. Americans are proverbially good pay,—lavish pay in fact. He is sure of his money, and knowing where you want to go is a comparatively small matter. He will willingly drive you all over town whilst you search over the "phrase-book" to talk to him, and endeavor to unravel the mystery of where you are going; it will swell up the fare that he knows will be paid. And he knows further that whilst his foe, the "Anglais," has spent weeks previously in calculating how low cab-fares can be got, and will not only abuse him, but probably take him to a police court, if he mistakes the distance, the American will as probably pay an extra franc for every mistake made, and let him keep all the change into the bargain. "American" is a cabalistic word in France. It opens the hearts of customs officials, railway employés, and cabmen; it smooths over probably more bad French in a day than any other race utters in a month; and it puts up prices fifty per cent. for every polite shop-keeper. How they smile as the untutored American visitor enters their doors to examine the apparently very cheap wares, which the high tariff makes so dear when imported into his own home! and you pay well in Paris for all the politeness.

### THE PARISIAN HOME.

If you go to a hotel, there you find English spoken, and get a very small room, very high up both in location and price. If you go into lodgings money is saved in Paris, but it requires experience to learn how to do it. The hotel gives an idea of hotel life as it is everywhere seen, but the lodgings show the true Parisian life. There is rarely such a thing in Paris as a family having a house to itself, so that the method of living here is as completely the opposite of the Philadelphia method as it is possible to be. The families live on "flats"; that is, each has a suite of rooms on one floor. There may in this way be twenty families in one house, yet each will be provided with parlor, chambers, dining-room, kitchen, and front door. The idea of twenty front doors to one house is amusing, yet the house I live in has about that number, for it has twenty suites of apartments and would accommodate as many families. First, is the great door at the street, which is more like a gateway than a door, and inside which presides the "concierge," that important Parisian being who guards the safety and keeps the keys, and endeavors to pry into the letters of all the families in the house. From her apartments there ascends a winding stair, which leads on its way to the roof to a succession of front doors, each with a door-bell. Get admission inside one, and it will be seen how cosily the Parisians live and how completely isolated each family is from every other in the house. The servants come in the morning and go away when the work is done at night. The cooking is done with charcoal, easily ignited and as easily put out when no longer needed. The food that is wanted is bought from meal to meal; and the care with which Mademoiselle, who takes the contract to provide the meals, counts noses in furnishing the same would win admiration anywhere. There is one piece of beefsteak, or one chop, or one egg, or one roll, as the case may be, for each person. The French have discovered in the metrical system the true principle of measure, and it is the most exact and geometrically accurate system that can be devised. They do nothing by halves, but, with the zealous nature of their race, they apply the system throughout. Therefore, exactly four accurately square lumps of sugar are allotted to each person for tea or coffee, and the cognac bottle, if you indulge in it, has a gauge cut into the glass to disclose the amount imbibed. One teaspoon, one knife, one fork, one everything, for each individual is the table setting, and if you borrow a spoon to give jam after meals to the children, Mademoiselle organizes a Congressional investigating committee to inquire its whereabouts. We requested fried potatoes, and got exactly five slices apiece; tomatoes, and were given one uncut whole one each. The same veneration for the tomato which I observed in England prevails in France. It is evidently a royal dish, to be partaken of sparingly by the unanointed. If the Frenchman eats them, he buys probably one or two, and gives one slice to each of his family. To want a quarter of a peck for a single meal, as in an unguarded moment we ventured to suggest, was an evidence of American extravagance that almost overcame Mademoiselle's weak nerves. This accurate system of providing meals is the universal rule of the French in their own households, and it promotes the thrift for which this great people are so noted. They get just what they want to use and no more. There is no waste. Everything is consumed. The lavishness of supply which promotes unthrift in so many American households is the exact opposite of the French idea ; and herein is the secret of the ability of the French to live well and yet to spend so little. It would do good if some of these ideas were taught at home.

But, after all, the paramount idea impressed upon the visitor to Paris is, that the greatest misfortune which befell mankind was what happened at the Tower of Babel. If these people, thinks the visitor, could only talk something that we understand how much better it would be. I have seen the utterly demoralized American expatiate on street-corners in the purest and most energetic English ; but in vain. What a glorious thing it would be if all mankind spoke the same language! How much trouble it would save ; how much anxiety ; how much time spent in study! How easy it would make the traveller's path! Yet such a millennium will probably never come ; and until the end of time Paris will witness the linguistic struggle of French-speaking Americans who have learned the language perfectly at home, yet who when they get here are so unfortunate as to continually fall in with a class of people who persist in not understanding French as it ought to be spoken.

## LETTER XXVII.

### A SUNDAY IN PARIS.

PARIS, September 2.

A Sunday in Paris is as thoroughly unlike a Sunday in Philadelphia as it is possible to be. Work goes on here the same as on a week-day; the shops are almost all open; the wagons, laden with goods, go about the streets; people attend to nearly all their avocations, and until noon they work just the same as if it were a week-day. After mid-day, however, everything closes, excepting the cafés and the newspaper offices, —for the evening papers all come out on Sunday with their raciest editions,—and the city takes a holiday. I suppose that some of the Parisians go to church on Sunday, but it really seems as if church-going was the least matter thought of by most of the people. They have their horse-races and their elections on Sunday; their theatres and operas give the best performances in the evening; and the Exposition on Sunday draws its largest crowds. In fact, the day is treated as a day for extra merry-making, and as a holiday which is to be made the best use of for the public amusement. This is the French idea of Sunday, and it is as entirely unlike our idea as two dissimilar things can possibly be. All the great French festivals are celebrated on Sunday; and it is the day when the largest crowds can be attracted, and when the public, by turning out in the largest numbers, make those great displays for which Paris is famous.

All the shops being open on Sunday morning in Paris, this peculiar people, who live only from hand to mouth, first bought their breakfasts, and then went out to buy their dinners. They first invested in a little bunch of kindling-wood to start the fire with, and then in a little bag of charcoal to keep it going. The person who bought more than a day or two's supply of fuel, would be looked upon as a foe to the State, so fixed is the public habit of buying only enough for the day. The kindling-wood and charcoal-shops are as prominent and numerous along the streets as any others, and they display their goods in the windows as attractively as possible, the kindling-wood neatly tied in small bundles sold at one and a half cents apiece, the coal, in square blocks, and the charcoal, in bags, varying from ten to fifty cents apiece. If firewood is wanted by some aristocrat, who is bold enough to establish a fireplace, he pays for it at the rate of about two cents a stick, and he buys just enough to last till the dinner is over and the company bids farewell in the evening. In food the range is somewhat restricted, the Parisian buying almost everything by weight, at so much for the kilogramme, which corresponds to nearly two and one-third pounds. Reducing the prices paid to American money, and the purchases to pounds, it is found that Parisians pay about forty-two cents per pound for veal, thirty-six cents for ordinary rump-steak, and forty to sixty cents for beef-steak; thirty-five to forty cents for mutton-chops, thirty-eight cents for leg of mutton, sixty-four cents for coffee, one dollar to one dollar and twenty cents for ordinary tea, four and a half cents for bread, fifty cents for butter, forty-eight cents for ordinary ham, and seventy cents for boiled ham sold in slices at the shops (the usual way in which it is bought); fifteen cents for loaf-sugar broken into the accurately square lumps universally used here; about eight cents a quart for milk, four cents each for tomatoes, and twelve cents a half-peck for potatoes. These are the usual prices now paid for these articles, and although the list does not include all, it shows the high prices at which most articles of food are sold in Paris. This is due not only to the increased charges consequent upon the Exhibition, but also to the "octroi," or city customs, Paris levying a heavy duty upon almost everything brought into the city, in order to raise revenue. But, with these very high prices, the Parisians can still live more cheaply than in most other places, owing to the small value of the articles of food they subsist upon, and the absence of wastefulness. I do not suppose there was a dinner, outside of a hotel, served in Paris yesterday (Sunday), of which the food that composed it was not bought at the shops and markets on Sunday morning. This important business over, the populace started for the day's amusement,—to the Exposition, to the theatres and cafés, to the Boulevards or to Versailles. It being the great fête day at Versailles, the first Sunday in the month, at least two hundred thousand people directed their steps to that famous city and palace, but Paris could readily spare them, for, including the strangers attracted by the Exposition, there are probably three million population here now.

THE PALACE AND GARDENS OF VERSAILLES.

On the first Sunday of the month the great fountains are set in motion at Versailles, and, as these are the most famous fountains in the world, the event naturally attracts a vast concourse. This grand palace, built by the great monarch of France, Louis XIV., to eclipse every other in Europe, is about twelve miles west of Paris. There are many means of access to it, and the railways have to provide for an enormous travel on the fête days, for the crowds that go out from Paris on these occasions are extraordinary. We are told that the palace, gardens, park, fountains, and ornamentation which were nearly forty years in construction after 1650, cost the enormous sum of two hundred million dollars, and that the heavy taxes thus imposed upon France were the original cause of the first French revolution, which came a century after. These structures certainly are one of the greatest sights of Europe, and when overflowed by the Parisian population, as was the case yesterday, present a scene of most wonderful character. From noon until sunset the people poured into the park in droves. Every avenue was a mass of humanity, which swarmed through the palace and gardens, and filled up the accessible portions of the enormous park, yet still maintained the best order. The railways despatched their huge trains as fast as they could be made up, and vast crowds besieged the ticket-offices and entrances all the afternoon. The fête culminated at five in the afternoon, when all the great fountains were set in motion, throwing enormous amounts of water, and doing it in the most unique, fantastic, and attractive ways. All the scenery on the broad terraces and spreading lawns of Versailles culminates in fountains, which appear in all directions, and throw out their spray in great clouds to leeward. Imagine a broad palace, fronting over sixteen hundred feet, with terraces spreading out in front and on either hand; the terraces bordered by beautiful gardens with embowered walks and ornamental shade-trees; the gardens running down to lovely sheets of water; and in every vista view, as well as on every broad terrace, a fountain, most of them being of large size and very elaborate design.

13*

Then fill up all the palace, and the terraces, gardens, and walks with a dense mass of humanity, and there can be some idea formed of yesterday at Versailles. It was like the Pennsylvania day at the Philadelphia Exhibition; and the getting home at night was one of those problems of transportation that only great railway-men on great occasions know how to cope with.

The palace is a wondrous structure, with its miles of galleries of paintings and sculpture; its great ornamented halls, some of them hundreds of feet long; its outward ornaments of statuary, vases, and bronzes; its orangery, with acres covered with orange-trees in boxes, ready for removal if frost threatens; its grand avenues of approach through columns of tall poplars, or the arched coverings of more spreading trees; its path-borders of closely-trimmed yew and box; its lakes, canals, flower-beds, and the great surrounding expanse of forest where the deer still roam, ready for the huntsmen. Days could be spent in wandering through this palace, gardens, and park, and in viewing the Trianons, the smaller palaces in the park built by the kings of France for their mistresses, but which later became the embodiment of the warmest remembrances of Napoleon and Josephine, and the unfortunate Marie Antoinette; or in examining the huge, gilded carriages of state, gaudily ornamented, which cost millions of dollars, and which were the carriers of royalty in the days of both Napoleons. These carriages, with the gay harness and caparisons of the horses hung up in glass cases near them, are considered precious by the French. But though they go to Versailles to admire them, woe to the official who now dares ride in them! They are not for these days of republican simplicity, and the Parisian who goes to Versailles to worship these gilded coaches would probably stone the President if he were caught riding in them.

The journey to Versailles is not only picturesque, but full of historical interest. If by the railway on the north side of the Seine, it goes through a country that was the battle-ground between France and Germany, and afterwards between France and the Commune. The railway, after leaving St. Lazare Station, rises to high ground and makes a long semi-circular sweep around the western portion of Paris, with all its great structures in full view. There rise up against the sky the three objects which are prominent from whatever direction Paris may be approached, if the visitor gets on elevated ground,—the Arch of Triumph, the Dome of the Invalides, where Napoleon I. is buried, and the towering columns of the Trocadero Palace of the Exposition. Far away across the valley of the Seine, which winds among the most carefully-cultivated gardens, these three great structures are seen, and to the east of them the heights of Montmartre, and to the west, the great hill on which stands Mont St. Valerien, the strongest fortress of Paris. It was this fortress that poured iron hail all along the line of the railway, and that, with the counter-fire of the Communists, so badly devastated all the western and northwestern suburbs of Paris. Yet almost every trace of the havoc of war is obliterated, and the only vestige remaining is the patch, here and there, seen upon some building that was riddled by cannon-shot. Then the railway takes a turn, and going through Courbevoie, west of Paris, where there was fierce fighting, passes close to the foot of Mont St. Valerien, and thence on past St. Cloud to Versailles. I suppose this railway, which is only one of the lines to that city, yesterday carried one hundred thousand people, making up and despatching trains as fast as they could be filled and started. Its capacity was greatly increased by having two-storied cars, taking as many passengers on the roof as inside, both men and women climbing cheerfully up to that altitude, and filling up the cars almost as quickly as they got into the station. The French, like the Americans, very easily adapt themselves to circumstances, and accept the situation with cheerfulness. Easily pleased, they thus went in droves to see the Versailles fountains play. Yet there was no overcrowding. Every car and omnibus had its exact complement fixed by law, and no one attempted to exceed it. No one stood up, or, when the vehicle was legally "full," attempted to thrust in. Five hundred people may have waited at a street corner for an omnibus, but each on getting there took from the omnibus office a number, so that the first that came had the best numbers and got the first seats, without pushing, crowding, and quarrelling. It was not a grand American rush, in which the active and muscular triumphed and the women and children were sent to the rear.

In the evening the Exposition and Versailles sent their

crowds back to Paris, and then there was a general flocking to the brilliantly-lighted Champs Elysées. Here, with cafés in full operation, carriages moving, thousands promenading, Sunday evening was spent. There was general liveliness, and some hilarity, but no drunkenness. The Frenchman cannot get intoxicated on thin and sour claret at twenty cents per quart-bottle, which is his great drink; neither can he upon the five or six cent "bock" of very weak beer, with which he usually winds up the evening. He may sing and make merry, but he never loses his steadiness or good humor. The more he imbibes the more intensely republican become his sentiments, and the more anxious he is to pay off certain scores against Germany. But his politeness remains as polished as ever, and when he goes to bed he sleeps peacefully, with a thorough confidence in his own ability to match the world.

## LETTER XXVIII.

### A FRENCH CEMETERY.

PARIS, September 4.

The 3d of September was the anniversary of the death of M. Thiers, and it was marked by a solemn ceremony in the Cathedral of Notre Dame at noon for the repose of his soul, whence a funeral procession afterwards escorted Madame Thiers to his tomb. The great church was magnificently decorated and crowded to repletion by thousands of people, including all the strangers in Paris who could possibly get tickets of admission. A solemn high mass for the dead, with the impressive ceremonial of the Church, when celebrated for the repose of the soul of so great a man, is no ordinary service, and it attracted a crowd outside of probably a hundred thousand persons, but the police arrangements were perfect, and they kept the crowd fully a square away from the church in all directions, so as to allow the invited persons free movement. I was invited to the church, but preferred to go and see what we do not see in America,—the way in which the French pay homage at a great man's tomb on the anniversary of his death. M. Thiers is buried at Père la Chaise, and thither I went. It seemed, however, as if almost all Paris was going in the same direction judging by the crowds passing into this famous cemetery. The "Cemetery of the East," or of "Père la Chaise," the more popular title which it takes from the old confessor of Louis XIV., who lived there, stands upon the sides and top of a hill in the northeastern part of Paris. It is of great extent, containing over twenty thousand tombs, and from the higher ground there is a fine view of the city. All the streets approaching it seem to be monopolized by the trades which are intimately connected with the cemeteries,—the undertakers, the stonecutters, and the people who provide memorials of the dead. There must be over five hundred shops devoted to this purpose south and west of the cemetery, and they hang out their specimens with all the display for which the French are noted. The dealers in tombs and stone-work do not have their marble-yards, as with us, but are in shops, and display their work in the windows. The dealers in memorials I do not think have any counterpart in America. We put flowers on our graves and get them from the florists. The French do this also, but very sparingly. Their memorials consist chiefly of wreaths of immortelles, of huge constructions of bead-work, representing wreaths, crosses, baskets, etc. ; of representations of leaves, plants, and flowers made of tin and painted in the colors of the plants or flowers ; of mottoes painted on glass with pictures representing tombs with weeping relatives ; of banners announcing that such and such societies or persons pay homage to the dead, which are hung on the tomb, and many similar devices. The idea seems to be to get something durable which the weather cannot destroy, and to provide these things, which are used in great profuseness, is the business of a large number of people in the neighborhood of the cemetery, whose shops display their wares as effectively as possible. The many thousands who went to the cemetery to do homage to the memory of M. Thiers were liberal purchasers of these things, and, in fact, throughout the cemetery the tombs all gave token of the generous grief of relatives and friends who thus piled upon and in them marks of their affection.*

---

* The Parisians have a beautiful and appropriate custom at funerals. As the procession moves through the streets, be the dead never so humble,
G*

Père la Chaise is very unlike a Philadelphia cemetery in appearance. We are accustomed to burial-lots, railed in or surrounded with stone-work, with most of the graves marked by tombstones or monuments, which show generally great artistic skill. This is a cemetery, not of graves, but of vaults. The funeral comes, the stone cover is taken from the vault, the coffin lowered, and men below receive it and push it into a shelf, where it reposes. There may be a dozen of these shelves in the vault, one below the other, and the bottom one be twenty feet or more below the surface. This system makes the burial-lots much smaller than in our cemeteries, and it precludes, in most cases, the erection of separate tombstones or monuments. Over the vault there is generally built a small ornamental house of stone, much like a sentry-box. The public look in through the railings of the door, for they are all left thus partially open so that you can see within, and on the sides and back are inscribed the names of those buried in the vault beneath. At the back is a shelf where there is usually a crucifix and candles, and here are placed memorials of the dead generally of the character above described, but sometimes of a more personal nature, such as displaying children's favorite dolls, etc. Over the door will be inscribed the name of the family owning the tomb, there being sometimes two or three families in common. The cemetery is almost filled with these little stone buildings, in and upon which are placed the memorials. There is thus given plenty of opportunity for the sculptor's art, and it is availed of for the construction of many beautiful tombs. The cemetery, however, is very unlike an American burial-place in appearance, though its situation on the hill-sides is taken full advantage of for attractive horticulture and beautiful foliage.

The tomb of M. Thiers is one of these small stone structures, probably five feet square and eight feet high. It is unpretentious, and belongs to two families. His name is inscribed prominently inside, and there are other persons entombed in

---

every man reverentially takes off his hat when the corpse passes by. Every one does it as a last mark of respect to the dead. I have seen a hearse pass through a crowded boulevard followed by a solitary carriage containing the few relatives of the dead, yet ten thousand people of all degrees, from nobles down to those of the humblest avocation, reverentially removed their hats as the corpse was carried before them.

it, but it was difficult to read the names, from the profusion of offerings thrown in and piled up all around. There was a very liberal supply of gens d'armes (police) around, but every one was orderly; and thither came a constant stream, crowding around, making their offerings, and writing their names in a book that a person who sat inside provided. If they could not write, he wrote the name for them, and this book was to be kept as a remembrance of the occasion. The grave, prior to the arrival of the cortege from Notre Dame, was visited by people of all characters, but chiefly of the lower class,—men in blue blouses, women with wooden shoes,—many of them, of both sexes, bareheaded, but many wearing curious white caps, and strange clothes, indicating the dress of the French provinces. They paid their homage reverentially, and showed in every movement a complete veneration for the great man. Thus the day passed on, the steady stream continuing uninterrupted after the cortege arrived until nightfall, and displaying one of the most marked traits of the French character.

While this was going on a somewhat similar scene transpired near by, at the tomb of Raspail, the Republican Deputy and Communist sympathizer, who died about ten months ago. He, too, was buried in a family vault with many others, and there had been an almost uninterrupted homage paid to him since his burial. This tomb showed how the Communistic spirit still prevails in France. In the first place, on every accessible part of the marble-work devotees have been carving their names and initials. Then they have hung all over it, inside and out, and far above it in pyramids, memorials with inscriptions showing that they came from workingmen's societies of various places, or with cards bearing the names of the donors. Some of these memorials bore a score of cards. Then it seemed as if every visitor had also left his own card. There were ten thousand cards piled up on the floor of the little house surmounting the vault, and thousands more lay trampled and half destroyed on the ground outside. Some were visiting-cards, others business-cards, others bits of paper with people's names written on them, and also containing approving sentiments for Raspail and his cause. This card-leaving had gone on for some time, just as if all these people expected the dead man to return their calls; and it was still going on, for hundreds were there throwing in their cards and showing their Communistic sentiments in that and other ways, for one of them skilfully helped himself to my wife's umbrella while we were looking at the tomb. The gens d'armes were numerously on duty near by, but this strange devotion continued without interference, and certainly showed a curious element of Parisian character. Raspail was one of the earliest Republicans of France and the oldest Deputy in the Assembly when he died. He was a Parisian druggist, and made a fortune through the sale of camphor. He was an earnest advocate of the doctrine that the use of camphor was a sure cure for all diseases; that, in fact, it would cure anything excepting a broken limb, and he made camphor and Communism work together until he won fame and fortune. His admirers are said to continue to be devotees of camphor.

The tomb of Abelard and Heloise is the great object sought in Père la Chaise. It is a sort of Gothic temple, in which effigies of both are laid on top of a catafalque, side by side, with hands folded. The tomb is an old one, but has recently been cleaned, and presents an attractive appearance. This ancient tomb is the Mecca of despairing lovers. The unfortunate of both sexes, whose love-affairs get desperate, go there to lay tin flowers and bead-work leaves on the tomb, to thus invoke the lovers' friendship; but, as it has been railed in since its restoration, they now either toss them on or hang them on the railings. I counted twenty-three such offerings on the tomb and the railings, and whilst there an alleged despairing lover came up and threw on another. But he did not look as if his supposed despair had had much effect on his health. A fat, red-headed youth, with rosy cheeks, a smile on his countenance, and every evidence of a good appetite, he looked just the opposite of what Americans would think his condition ought to be. There are many fine tombs in this cemetery. M. Casimir Perier, the statesman and financier, has one that is particularly noticeable, surmounted by his statue in bronze. Ledru Rollin, the author of universal suffrage in France, who died in 1874, has a modest tomb, but it was almost entirely covered with offerings. The finest tomb I saw was that in memory of Generals Lecompte and Clement Thomas, killed by the Communists, this tomb being erected by the Government, and having magnificent carved work. In Père la Chaise are buried almost all the great men of France,

great in politics, literature, art, war, and science,—and their
names and memorials appear on every side. It fills for France
the place that Westminster Abbey occupies for England.
There are separate enclosures in it for the Jews and the Mohammedans. There are also occasionally seen, in walking
through this cemetery, the tombs of Americans who have
died in Paris.

The routes to the cemetery generally go through a very
poor part of the city,—through streets that modern improvements have not reached, and that thus reproduce, as it were,
the Paris of olden times Narrow, crooked, stuffed full of
little houses, with an overflowing population, here live the
people who foment revolutions and set up Communes. It is
a curious fact that almost the last place in which the defeated
Communists were able to defend themselves was in Père la
Chaise, fighting among the tombs. Through most of the
parts of Paris having this sort of population, boulevards have
been opened, so that the troops can have a clear sweep for artillery. There is a wide boulevard thus opened along the city
side of Père la Chaise, its centre being used as a market, a
large portion of which is occupied by the old clothes, old iron,
bottle, and other second-hand dealers. That section of the
city, however, is very little frequented by foreigners, and they
prefer the wide streets, better buildings, and greater attractions
of the neighborhood of the Arch of Triumph.

## LETTER XXIX.

#### THE PARIS EXPOSITION OF 1878.

PARIS, September 6.

It would hardly be proper to write from Paris without mentioning the Exposition, and yet there can scarcely be imagined
a subject more difficult to encompass in a letter. If I had
never seen the Philadelphia Exhibition the task would be the
easier, for it would involve no comparisons; yet having seen
both one cannot help comparing. They resemble each other,

and still are different. All exhibitions have many points in common. If the visitors to our Centennial were asked what is the most lasting impression made by it, the majority of them would probably answer that it was the recollection of the utter and most desolating fatigue that the task of going over the show involved. In this respect the Paris Exhibition is almost like the Centennial. Its millions of visitors are getting fully as tired as those who wearily wandered through Fairmount Park, though they have not so many acres to go over. They also have quite as much trouble in obtaining a chance to ride home at the close of the day, though the distance from the heart of Paris is not so great as the distance was at Philadelphia. Pedestrianism is a cardinal virtue here as it was with us in 1876. But, excepting these things, which are necessary misfortunes of all exhibitions, this show at Paris loses nothing by comparison with Philadelphia. It gains much by its greater compactness, whilst, from the character of the ground and of the exhibitors and their goods, it is a display that has been made to disclose more concentrated grandeur than we were able to present at Philadelphia. Everything at Paris is brought within one great building and its immediately adjacent annexes. All the structures representing different nations, such as the American House, the Prince of Wales' pavilion, etc., are within this grand building, which is not a single structure like our Main Building, but rather a series of courts, passages, and galleries, enclosed within a rectangular-shaped building, which forms a sort of ornamental border for them. It is as if our Main Building were enlarged to three or four times its size, with the interior divided into passages and courts, with other intervening passages and spaces open to the sky. Within this is the Exhibition,—not scattered as at Philadelphia in scores of buildings spread over many acres of ground, but compactly placed within one great structure a half-mile long and nearly a quarter of a mile broad. This condensation of space, if it may be so described, saves pedestrianism, whilst the excellent classification of articles keeps the species as distinctly separate as if they were in entirely different buildings. But at the same time the French have nothing like our attractive Horticultural Building to show, though in their display of horticulture, which is made in the open air, they have produced a garden along the Seine far exceeding anything we had at the Centennial. The French are great in everything pertaining to flowers and plants, and in the space of about one thousand feet square in front of their building, and bordering the Seine, they have produced a horticultural and aquatic display which is unrivalled.

SCENERY OF THE EXPOSITION.

Sloping down to the Seine, from the Exhibition building to the south bank, is a scene of floral loveliness, enhanced by fountains, statues, pretty little cafés nestling among the vines, and the greenest and smoothest lawns that only the balmy climate of Paris could produce, and sloping up from the north bank to the Trocadero Palace is its counterpart on a smaller scale, but with the grand cataract as a centre-piece flowing over one cascade after another down to the river, and disappearing, as it were, under the broad Bridge of Jena, which connects the two parts. This scene, with the palace on the hill circling around on either hand, its airy towers rising above the rounded centre pavilion, and the whole structure dazzling the eye in the sunlight, for it is built of light cream-colored stone, is the triumph of the Exhibition. The formation of the ground, sloping on either hand towards the river, greatly favors the view; so that whether looked at from one side or the other,—from the palace towards the dome-crowned Exhibition building, or from the building towards the palace,—it is a scene of enchanting loveliness. The two structures are probably fifteen hundred feet apart, and within the intervening space the French have put everything that could be adapted to the creation of an open-air scene of rural beauty. It is an art they know as much of as any race in the world, and they have exerted themselves to the utmost here. This is the crowning feature of the Exhibition, and it has so charmed every beholder that it is to be maintained permanently after the Exhibition shall have passed away. It has only been within a few weeks that it has been finished. The earlier visitors did not see it as it exists now. Curiously enough, this view is only obtainable *inside* the Exhibition. None of the *outside* views, excepting that of the Trocadero Palace from the Bridge of the Alma over the Seine below, are at all impressive. The approach to the palace from the city side does not compare in beauty to the views of our

Memorial Hall, for the architect sacrificed everything to obtain the grand impression made on the interior and river sides. Likewise the long, low walls of the Exhibition building, with its annexes, as one approaches them from the Alma Bridge, on what may be called the north side, in coming that way, as most visitors do, from the city, are not nearly so impressive as the grand sweep of our two great Centennial buildings as seen along Elm Avenue. This structure has enormous length, and its surmounting domes relieve it, but there is no good view obtainable, and it has not the massive solidity of the two great buildings in Fairmount Park. When it comes to the combined barn and railway station style of architecture necessary for this kind of building, which is to be measured by half-miles, and is to be constructed at the rate of I don't know how many acres per day, the Parisian must take off his hat to the Philadelphian.

A PARISIAN "SHANTYTOWN."

There is another matter in connection with the outside of the Exhibition in which Paris is a close imitator of Philadelphia, however. That grand aggregation of remarkable structures which, in West Philadelphia, sprang up into the mushroom growth of "Shantytown," has its thorough counterpart on the outskirts of the Paris Exposition. It flourishes chiefly on the Porte Rapp side, along the Avenue Rapp, which leads from the Alma Bridge, over the Seine, and in the adjacent streets, and also appears to a moderate extent in the neighborhood of the Trocadero Palace. There are hundreds of cafés, booths for selling Exhibition tickets, minor theatres and show-shops, and, as at Philadelphia, most of them are light, tinder-box structures of wood, liable to ignite at any moment. They include, however, one feature that was missing at Philadelphia. This is the establishment of booths by the Bible and Tract Societies for the free distribution of sacred writings. Almost every visitor to the Exhibition, from whatever direction he may come, is freely supplied with these by a large corps of colporteurs, who environ the entire place. The cafés in these regions have their rows of tables, and here thousands breakfast and dine, avoiding the higher charges inside the enclosure. There are, of course, restaurants inside, but there does not seem the bountiful supply that Philadelphia had, and hence these outside establishments may have a chance to thrive better than most of them did with us.

## INSIDE THE EXHIBITION.

Inside the Exhibition, the visitor is impressed with the skill the French display in the art of decoration, shown in the adornments of the buildings and grounds. Whatever painting, gilding, bunting, gardening, or artistic construction can do is availed of to give beauty to the inside views, to the fronts of the various structures, to the roofs and walls of the courts, and to the many open-air passage-ways. Gardens are numerous. The odd corners and little waste pieces of ground are made gems of floral beauty. There are also little beds of flowers and foliage inside the buildings at many places. Everything that is intended to have any permanence is built solidly, with stone floors, and this is the nature of the construction of the entire Trocadero Palace, and also of the western end of the Exhibition building, which fronts the Seine. The building itself is divided longitudinally into what may be called six sections, of which, counting from the north, the first is devoted to French machinery; the second to French exhibits; the third is a series of buildings in the open air, surrounded by uncovered passage-ways, and may be described as the central court of the Exhibition building; the fourth contains exhibits, not French; the fifth, machinery, not French, and the sixth is the foreign annexes. By this system very nearly one-half the Exhibition is French, and the remainder foreign. The central court contains the fine art galleries, and the special building exhibited by the city of Paris, whilst on the south side of this central court is what is called the Avenue of the Nations. This avenue has along it a row of buildings characteristic of each nation exhibiting, and these buildings front the special sections of each nation, each of which sections crosses from the centre to the south side of the enclosure. Thus each foreign nation has its exhibit of goods, of machinery, and outside of all, its annexes. The system is a very good one, for it keeps in the longitudinal passage-ways all the goods of the same character, no matter what nation exhibits them. Of the foreign space, Great Britain occupies one-fourth. The plan, whilst it has its advantages, also, however, has its drawbacks. Thus it prevents the showing of what most visitors thought the greatest success of the Exhibition at Philadelphia, —all the machinery in motion in one grand hall, with the great Corliss engine in the centre furnishing the power. The machinery is divided into two widely-separated parts at Paris, and the power is furnished by scores of small engines, many of them provided with the familiar Corliss cut-off. If all the machinery, French and foreign, were put together, it would be as much as at Philadelphia, and show some excellent machines, but the system of division loses the grand effect of the whole in one scene, such as we had it.

MERITS OF THE FRENCH DISPLAY.

But the Exhibition, to American eyes, has other merits which must be conceded. Every one at Philadelphia was charmed with the view presented at the centre of our Main Building, where the finest gems of the United States, France, England, and Germany were clustered, in and near the central court, whilst proceeding westward we had on the front avenues similar gems from other nations. This exhibit was beautiful but limited in extent at Philadelphia, for it is the kind of thing that foreign nations chiefly deal in, though we were too far away for them to send much of such goods across the ocean. Here it is, however, multiplied a hundred-fold, and gems of art in the precious metals, porcelain, silks, and the myriads of fabrics so effectually wrought in Europe line miles of passage-ways, and are displayed in almost endless profusion. The eye is almost dazed with the sight of acres covered with the most splendid things that human hands produce. Thus, there is at least an acre covered with diamonds and jewelry; another filled with India shawls; another of the finest glassware, with chandeliers and huge constructions of glass that dazzle the eyes; several acres of the finest porcelain; with silks and stuffs of all sorts spread over extensive spaces, and dresses and bonnets sufficient in number, it seemed, to clothe almost half the ladies in Philadelphia. There also seemed to be at least five thousand French dolls on exhibition, with their wardrobes and appurtenances, and enough toys to fill fifty large toy-shops. As France is the greatest of nations at all this sort of thing, so her exhibit exceeds that of any, though the others come very well to the front in fancy goods, and all of them show far more and much better than they did at Philadelphia. Prices too are less than were asked with us. These people say they had to ask high rates at Philadelphia on account of the import duty; but they have to pay a high duty on their goods brought into Paris. The truth is, they thought, as all foreigners do, that there was no limit to American pocket-books. Thus, I saw several familiar objects of the Japanese collection at Philadelphia in the Exhibition here, ticketed at one-third to one-half the prices asked, but not obtained, in Fairmount Park. Buyers here are accustomed to fancy goods and will not tolerate fancy prices. There seems to be a great amount of buying going on, and, as a general rule, the attendance is very good, every case having its representative, generally capable of speaking at least two languages.

We had nothing at Philadelphia that equalled the Avenue of the Nations, with its row of representative houses of each nation. Running from one end to the other of the great building, this broad avenue gives nearly a half-mile of these representative houses, each artistically constructed, and the whole combining, as it were, the world's present system of small house and cottage architecture. Then on the other side of the avenue are the pretty buildings containing the fine art exhibits, which exceed greatly the amount displayed at Philadelphia, and are particularly strong in the representation of European art of all schools, as may naturally be expected.

## THE AMERICAN DISPLAY.

Of the United States section at Paris the part which first arrested attention, because it had, from absence from home, become an unwonted sight, was the colored messenger at the stairway leading to Commissioner Richard C. McCormick's office. I have been two months away from home and do not think I have seen six colored people in Europe. Therefore this messenger, with his fancy hat, naturally attracted attention, as he did that of people from all parts of the world, who wonder what he can be, and who come and bring their friends to peep at him and guess where he came from. He is, however, a true American exhibit, born on the soil, and like most Americans in this foreign land longing for something to eat,—not that he could not get enough to eat, such as it was,—but wanting something to eat that he was accustomed to,—anxious for watermelon and pumpkin-pie, ice-cream and tomatoes, hoe-cake and squashes, and several other dishes, the value of which France as yet knows not. He had been six months away from home, and hadn't seen a short-cake or a slapper since he left dear old Philadelphia. This colored man and his wants, I think any American knowing Europe will admit, were among the very best exhibits of American peculiar institutions that could have been sent to Paris.

The United States labored under disadvantages in going to Paris, in having too little money and having the law passed ordering the display at too late a period. But tardiness was made up by prodigious energy and Congressional parsimony by private individuals going down into their own pockets. We filled our space and more; and we sent the useful rather than the showy goods, thus making not the more splendid appearance of our European cousins, but certainly giving them ideas of Yankee useful notions that they did not have before. To American eyes the exhibit of the United States does not compare to that of other countries, because our eyes are used to it, and are not used to the endless profusion of magnificence elsewhere displayed in the Exhibition. But to foreign eyes it is just the opposite. They are tired of magnificence and want something useful. They crowd the American passages, and look at American manufactures, and wonder at their simplicity, cheapness, and utility. The boards of judges have yielded the palm of superiority to the United States by giving us, in proportion to exhibits, more awards than have been given any other country, the proportion being, in fact, very much larger; whilst we have carried off seven of the best prizes out of twelve of all classes offered for agricultural implements. In fact, in several branches we have secured the best prizes, and these against keen foreign competition. As the test of the pudding is the eating, so is this opinion of judges and this gazing of foreign eyes the test of the excellence of the American exhibit. When Congress has to provide for another exhibition it is to be hoped the matter will be looked at earlier and more liberally than in this case.

A Babel of all tongues crowd the American passages and chatter about the American goods; and these people seem to have bought nearly everything in the American department that was for sale. The entire Waltham watch exhibit is sold, and the orders for agricultural machines and sewing-machines are reaching a large total. The signs denoting sales are liberally sprinkled over the cases. The French look with wonder on Tiffany's display of art in the precious metals, which was an attack on their stronghold, and carried off several prizes. Mr. Samuel S. White's display of artificial teeth has no counterpart in any other department. Disston's saws and Blaben's oilcloths, Gutekunst's photographs, Lewis's cotton fabrics, the many displays of Philadelphia tools, rivets, etc., and other useful things, arrest attention. I saw a thousand people struggling to get a look into the Pullman palace-car, and the crowds that could not get in were wondering what the huge Reading Railroad locomotive alongside could possibly be. It is about five times the size of the locomotives used here, and, excepting that it has wheels and a smoke-pipe, looks as much unlike the French locomotives as can possibly be. A surprised visitor who had endeavored for several minutes to comprehend what the machine was, finally was told that it weighed forty-two tons and was an American locomotive. He looked at it again and in broken English answered, " Mon Dieu, she not pretty, but Amerique grand country, plus grand country." Likewise our European cousins do not know what to make of that American institution, the jig-saw. They crowd around it, and watch its performances with pleasure, and invest their sous in puzzles and rocking-chairs, but they cannot comprehend the combination of Yankee skill and nimble fingers with a swift-moving saw that does it all. And as the French vocabulary does not contain words sufficiently strong or comprehensive to translate "jig-saw" into the Parisian vernacular, it is probable that the nation will suffer for some time for want of this comprehension. There are in fact many Yankee institutions and names that cannot be translated into French, and some of the French signs displayed in the American part of the Exhibition that attempt this show very remarkable combinations of words. Most of the exhibitors, after struggling with their French dictionaries, have evidently given it up as a bad job, and put up their signs only in English. This is the case with our friends who work the jig-saws. In one place an energetic Irishman talks doubtful American to a French boy, who makes his speech by bits to the attendant crowd. The threshing-machines and other agricultural implements are, however, presented by men who are not afraid to air their French in its stronghold. Thus the Empire thresher became "L'Empire Machine à battre le Blé," and the Champion mower startles us under the prodigious name of "Faucheuses-Moissonneuses de Champion," whilst the Buckeye implements are "Machines Agricoles de Buckeye," and Wood's Binder is the "Lieux de Wood." The French look at these signs and others like them with puzzled amazement. They can read the front names, but it is the other end that bothers them, for the words Buckeye, and Champion, and Empire, etc., used in that sense, are beyond their comprehension. It will probably be another century before the average Frenchman can be made to comprehend the American use of this class of words. What they think is the truth, however, seems to be dawning upon them, for occasionally there is a polite request at the railing for an interview with "*Monsieur* Buckeye."

### THE SYSTEM OF ADMISSION.

The French keep their Exhibition open every day in the week, Sundays included, and they charge only one franc (about nineteen cents) admission. They have tickets which are bought at booths outside, and are taken to the entrances, where one man punches them and another, collecting them, finally admits the visitor. These tickets are also sold at thousands of places about Paris, and in fact any one may sell them who chooses, upon permission being granted by the authorities, for a bonus of two tickets is given with every one hundred purchased for re-sale. The French count the admissions by the tickets, and hence there are no counting-machines interposed at the entrances to batter the ribs and test the temper. The only obstacle is the omnipresent gen d'arme, who watches that all goes right. The Exhibition is the largest yet held in the space covered by exhibits, but the foreigners who were at Philadelphia all deplore the absence of the splendid inside views made by our great buildings, which the system of construction here precludes excepting in a few cases, and they also say there is too much sameness in the show, the splendor being, as it were, without relief. It was the unique character of the Philadelphia Exhibition—its dissimilarity to previous ones— that made it attractive to them.

## LETTER XXX.

### STORES AND STREET COSTUMES IN PARIS.

PARIS, September 8.

There are one hundred and fifty thousand American and English strangers in Paris, and one runs against them wherever he goes. They are all sight-seeing, and they fill up the show-places, and are furnishing a harvest of gain to the keen Parisians, who leave no stone unturned to reap the profit. The active representatives of the chief stores watch the newspapers and the registry lists, and quickly follow the Americans, who they know will spend their money if they are tempted. Hence you are deluged soon after arrival with circulars announcing bargains, and are waited upon by polite callers about mealtime, who, after anxious inquiries as to your state of health, offer for sale specimens of jewelry or perfumery, dresses, bonnets, etc. People wonder how they are so quickly found out, but the American's weakness on coming to Paris is to get his name into the published lists of arrivals, and this, as the address is always given, is sufficient introduction for the Parisian shopkeeper. The insinuating politeness of the Gallic race is expected to do the rest. Paris is a glorious place for an American to shop. Rows of shops are found on almost every street, and some of the stores cover acres, there being two or three here like the "Bon Marché," the "Belle Jardiniere," and the stores of the "Louvre," that are enormous establishments, exceeding in size anything that we have in America, Stewart's stores in New York not excepted. It was from these great Parisian bazaars that Mr. Wanamaker got the design of his, and the extent of these, especially of the "Bon Marché," is something astonishing, covering a large surface. But with its many thousands of shops, and its rows of show-windows, and its miles of magnificent streets devoted to business purposes, there does not exist in Paris anything in the way of show-window displays that equals the scene on Chestnut Street, from the *Ledger* Building for a mile west beyond Broad Street. There are at least a hundred show-windows in the great stores on Chestnut and Eighth, and Second Streets, in Philadelphia, that excel anything Paris can produce in this line. Paris can show the Philadelphian big stores, but the Philadelphian can teach Paris how to get up large and attractive show-windows. Likewise as to the shoppers. Thousands of ladies are making purchases in Paris and moving about the streets, but it is the marvel of all Americans that, whilst every American woman is constantly excited on the subject of the latest Paris fashions for dress, those magnificent dresses and bonnets, which are the gems of the promenade at home, are rarely seen on the street here, and if they are worn, it is not by the French. The Parisian *modistes* have plenty of magnificent dresses in their establishments, but the elaborate and beautiful costumes with which American women adorn themselves for the promenade, albeit they may be "the latest Paris styles," are not seen on the streets here. The ladies in Paris go about in ordinary clothing, and reserve their fine dresses for balls and parties, rarely showing them outside the house. Hence every American female visitor is disappointed in *not* seeing in Paris what was fully expected, crowds of gayly-dressed ladies in the street. The scenes on the Philadelphia promenades on a fine afternoon on Chestnut and on Eighth Streets, in the way of a brilliant array of pretty women in elaborate and stylish toilettes, no street in Europe can produce.

But the American in Paris cannot go sight-seeing and shopping all the time. Purses will get low, and eight hours per day of a continued round of palaces, churches, picture-galleries, tombs, and museums is too much for human nerves to long stand. Even the Exhibition, with all its magnificence, when taken in too strong doses has an effect upon the sight-seer the very reverse of beneficial. By the time you are ten days in Paris, and find that, after having labored most industriously, only a portion of the regulation "sights" have been seen, you begin to wish that the Commune had destroyed all the rest. You want above all things *not* to go sight-seeing and to have a day of relief; to roam about and avoid palaces, etc., and not be compelled to quarrel with cabmen or attendants about their "tips" and "pourboires." Such a day of wandering, starting out in the morning, really gives more actual enjoyment than a regulation sight-seeing day, wherein every half-hour has its palace to be visited and hurried through, and you come home so mixed up that you hardly know where you live.

#### FRENCH BREAKFASTS AND BARBERS.

The French "first breakfast," of a roll and coffee, is taken, say at eight in the morning. You do it because the rest of Paris does it, and it is therefore the thing, though there is a lingering idea as you put the allotment of four lumps of sugar into the mixture of coffee and boiled milk, that the beverage is not quite as good as your mother makes, and that the roll, which may be six inches or six feet long, according to your appetite, would slip down easier if it were buttered. But you take it nevertheless, because Paris does so, and try to be satisfied, or else, after a quarter of an hour's halting practice of the French language, are able to convince the waiter that next day he is to bring you butter, whereupon he leaves an order overnight at the shop for two cents' worth of butter, which is duly served (without salt) next morning. There is nothing extra served in this economical country, not even salt in butter, unless specially ordered.

The breakfast over, but a yawning abyss still left in the American stomach for the lack of something more substantial, you hand over your key to the concierge who guards the lower door, and start on the day's wandering. And first to the barber's for the toilet. Here the American is consoled by finding prices much lower than in his own country, but his heart sinks when he is set bolt upright in an ordinary chair to be shaved, whilst the "tonsorial artist" bends back his head till the neck almost breaks, so as to get the razor under the chin; and the victim is unable to find words (in French) strong enough to express his feelings. Then, the rasping over, the "artist" makes a speech which, after much explanation, you ascertain to mean that you must get up and wash your own face. But all things, sooner or later, have an end; and, after the barber has several times used your nose as a handle to move the head around, the toilet is complete. There is an excellent chance in Europe to introduce American barbers' chairs.

#### PARISIAN STREET-SCENES.

Next, the walk begins with that valuable companion in England and France, the umbrella, for it rains whenever the opportunity arises, and the man who ventures out without one gets into trouble. You move about the streets, and look into windows, and watch the men who do the street-watering, using long jointed sections of pipe, which they haul about on little wheels, for there are few water-carts here; try to interpret the cries of the street-peddlers; wonder why it is that on that great low-wheeled, but carefully-balanced vehicle, the tumbril, one horse can draw what would be a four-horse load at home; watch the hacks driving quickly about at rates not over forty cents an hour; look in at the kiosks along the boulevards where the widows and orphans of soldiers sell newspapers, or at the tobacco-shops, where these deserving women, or else the wounded soldiers themselves also conduct the sale, and in addition frequently act as deputy postmasters; or go up on the Arch of Triumph, and at its great height look down over Paris, laid out like a map, with the twelve broad boulevards starting out towards all points of the compass, from the circular space within which the Arch stands, and see the towering fortress of Mont Valerien on the one horizon, and that of Montmartre on the other; or go to the Seine and watch the swift and pretty steamboats that are bringing tens of thousands to the Exposition at four cents apiece; or else enjoy a ride for miles on top of an omnibus for three cents. You mount to the second story of this big machine and watch the buildings, gardens, and palaces as they go by, and the thousands of people, and talk American-French to your neighbors, who reply that they "no speak English"; and then, as if a second Commune had broken loose, you are startled by the commotion all hands make if any one dares to get on the omnibus after it has the legally-limited number of passengers. When it is full, the fact is displayed on a sign, and the man who dares attempt to get on then gets berated by everybody on the vehicle and everybody on the sidewalk, and seems in danger of the guillotine. What a marked contrast this is to an American street-car!

THE AMERICAN LEGATION.

But the American does not want to move about aimlessly all day, so, to give point to the occasion, he performs the duty all Americans owe their country, by calling on the American Minister. General Edward F. Noyes and his accomplished secretary, Mr. William Hitz, are found in their offices on the Rue Chaillot, not far from the Champs Elysées, and give all callers a cheerful welcome. They are there seven or eight hours a day, and the latch-string always hangs out in the true American fashion. Here they give advice, and attend to every one's wants, and, as is the fashion with American envoys abroad, look after all sorts of things that would be scouted at in other Embassies, but which the American exacts. General Noyes has made a very popular Minister, and has gone through the trying ordeal of an Exhibition season with high credit to his hospitality, but I fear with sad havoc to his pocketbook. But he is going to continue as he has begun, for the credit of his country, and when his means are exhausted he says he will return home. Like Mr. Welsh, in London, his salary does not begin to meet expenses, and heavy drafts have to be made on his private resources. The American Legation at Paris is expected to cope with Lord Lyons, the British Minister, who has fifty thousand dollars salary, a palace to live in, and an extra allowance for entertainments. And yet, representing the most exacting race in the world, for the Americans expect their foreign Ministers to spend more and do more than any other people do, there are continued attempts to cut down the present salary of seventeen thousand five hundred dollars, with no allowances.

The American, by this time, prompted by the yearning abyss within, feels the need of that "second breakfast" which the French take in the neighborhood of noon. To get this, he has choice of ten thousand cafés, and dropping into the nearest, eats his chop or steak with a relish, and drinks his sour wine as if he also liked it,—though he generally don't. Then he pays the bill, after an argument about the price, in which the café always wins, for the American is the last man to haggle long about prices in an unknown tongue, and it is quickly learned that all Paris prices are raised on account of the Exposition. And next he thinks he would like to hear from home. So he goes down into the heart of the city along any of the streets leading to the new Avenue of the Opera, and in the neighborhood of that great Academy of Music, which is the largest and finest in the world, and has cost France over ten million dollars in its building and decoration, whilst the opening of new streets to show its magnificent fronts has cost as much more, he seeks his reading-room and bank.

### THE "HERALD" READING-ROOM.

The reading-room is that of the *New York Herald*, which great and enterprising journal has established in Paris one of the most popular, convenient, and useful offices for Americans that can be devised. The office registers American visitors, and telegraphs by cable their arrivals to the *Herald* in New York, where they are published for the benefit of friends at home. It gives the visitors access to the news by posting up the latest telegrams, and it furnishes a newspaper reading-room containing four or five hundred newspapers, embracing almost all that any one wants to see, that are published on either continent; and the files are carefully kept up, so that the visitor is pretty sure to find, from wherever he may come, his favorite home journal. It is one of those conveniences of Paris to the Americans that they all appreciate, and do so with warm recognition of the princely liberality of the proprietor of the *New York Herald*.

### AN AMERICAN BANKING-HOUSE.

From the *Herald* office to the Bank is but a short distance. It has come to pass in the progress of American financial events that the solidly-anchored bank of Drexel, Harjes & Co. has become the chief American bank in Paris. Almost all Philadelphia, and a very large portion of the rest of the United States, bank there, both for travelling and commercial credits when abroad; and their circular letters, available at hundreds of the best banks in all parts of the world, are one of the travelling conveniences of the day. The tourist now has no risk of losing money; he simply carries his circular letter, and wherever he may be, in near or remote parts of the world, he can find a bank which will honor it and pay him what he wants. With this system travelling, especially for Americans, is made easy. The Paris house has grown to large proportions since I first saw it ten years ago, and its central location, on the Boulevard Haussmann, near the Academy of Music, is one of the American headquarters in Paris. It is an European bank conducted on the American system, giving its clients reading, writing, and conversation rooms, taking care of their parcels and conducting their business for them, receiving and forwarding their letters, and in every way aiding their business and pleasure whilst abroad. Over its affairs Mr. Harjes and Mr. Winthrop preside with skill and amiability. Mr. Harjes has very successfully conducted this popular house since its first establishment, and has become a leading Parisian financier. Its operations in managing travellers' and commercial business have grown to large figures, and it is this year taking care of the money and affairs of a great number of Americans abroad.

## THE GREAT BALLOON.

Having read his letters from home, and possibly drawn some of that essential motive-power in all parts of the world —especially Paris—money, the American again starts out to lounge about and finish the afternoon. He wanders along the Avenue of the Opera and down towards the Seine. He may make a few little purchases from the small-sized but loud-voiced merchants who sell knick-knacks on the avenue, but his steps are naturally directed to the chief out-door sight of Paris in this locality, which is in full view before him—the great balloon. This is in fact, as well as in name, a *great* balloon, by far the greatest the world has yet produced. The Commune, it will be remembered, almost entirely destroyed the Palace of the Tuileries. It is now being slowly rebuilt. A portion of the large court-yard which it formerly enclosed, is used for the preparation of materials for the new buildings, whilst the remainder is an enclosure used for the balloon. The Parisian never does anything without calculating its dramatic effect; therefore this balloon is so placed as to be in an exact line with the Champs Elysées, and thus visible for miles. It is a captive balloon, held by an enormous cable. You enter the enclosure and see it go up for a fee of twenty cents, or you can go up in it for four dollars. My finances admitted of the first expenditure, but not of the latter. To send it up and pull it down takes about fifteen minutes, and a steam-engine does the work, the cable being wound around a large horizontal drum, such as is seen at our coal mines. This balloon is big enough to take up fifty people, and it raises them to about two thousand feet height, from which altitude those who do not get frightened or sick, as many do, have a fine view  I saw thirty-eight ascend at one time and forty-two at one time afterwards. Three or four aeronauts ascend with them. When this balloon has its car resting on the ground it stands about one hundred and seventy feet high, and almost all Paris can see it towering above the surrounding buildings. It is one hundred and twenty feet in diameter, nearly four hundred feet in circumference, has nearly four thousand square yards of surface, and contains about two hundred and forty-nine thousand cubic feet of gas. Huge cables—a half-dozen of them—anchor it when the wind blows hard. It is the most enormous thing of the kind ever produced, and, as it sways backward and forward in the wind, shows prodigious power. I do not think any balloon has previously been attempted that has anything like the lifting power of this one, which, with car, passengers, cables, sandbags, and all, will raise nearly five tons.

### THE CHAMPS ELYSÉES.

From the balloon, which is certainly one of the present wonders of Paris, the American will naturally wander to that great street, the Champs Elysées, which is not far off, and amid the beautiful gardens sit down for a little while to watch the carriages that in streams are going out to the Bois de Boulogne or else are coming home from the Exposition. He is scarcely comfortably seated when a tidily-dressed woman will demand a penny for the use of the chair. He pays, and then, having watched the unending panorama before him for awhile, continues sauntering along the beautiful street, past the concert-gardens preparing for the evening, and the circular horse-revolving machines set up for the children, until he reaches the theatres. There are five of them, and they give performances every afternoon. He thinks he will go to one, and walks in and takes a seat. They are little open-air theatres, where puppets play and attract audiences, not only of children, but also of grown men and women. The admission is two cents, which gives a reserved seat under the trees, but you are politely requested to take a back seat, that the children may sit in front. The orchestra is an accordeon, the player of which takes up a collection to pay his expenses. On important occasions the accordeon is reinforced by a violin. You go to the oldest, and the best, of these five theatres, which are all in full operation every afternoon and attract crowded houses.

The Theatre Guignolet was established in 1818, and has been in operation ever since. This little puppet-show has been going on for sixty years, and antedates any theatre we have in Philadelphia. It has a stage seven feet wide, and the proscenium is about four feet high. Fully five hundred people, more grown ones than children, look at the very funny show, part pantomime and part comedy, that goes on for a half-hour. The French are clever at this, and their two-cent show is equal to the funniest bit of nonsense ever put on the stage at more pretentious houses.

A FRENCH DINNER.

Then it is necessary towards dusk to eat dinner,—a French dinner, with a dozen courses, in which the toothsome viands are given incomprehensible names on the bill of fare, and are cut up into the smallest pieces consistent with handing them around. The plates are changed every few minutes, and the wines about as often, the waiters going round and round the table serving one morsel after another with machine-like precision, so that you have nothing to do but lift the food to the mouth. The little mouthfuls are eaten, and the eater gradually gets full, he knows not exactly how or what of, and he thus partakes of that great accomplishment of cuisine, a French dinner, whereof every dish has an almost national history and every sauce is the product of as much brain-work and culinary ingenuity as can possibly be put to the service. The French can in their cooking make more out of less than any other nation in the world, and they do it better; but how they do it seems to be a secret confined to the nation, and to be intended to remain a French attribute forever.

PARIS BY NIGHT.

The dinner over, for it takes a long time, and night has fallen in the interval, the American will again start out to see Paris by gaslight, and view it at its best and worst phases,— the worst, if he is inclined to vice, and I am sorry to find that it is the stranger in Paris who chiefly supports all its vices,—but the best phase, if the beauty of illumination and the brilliant scenes the busy and brightly-lighted streets afford are to be taken as the test. He will wander along miles of boulevards and arcades all made as brilliant and showy as gas and electricity can do it. He will go into the Palais Royal, and, as the fountain plashes and the band plays in the garden, walk with thousands along the ranges of shops around it, and wonder how two hundred jewelry and diamond stores can possibly thrive alongside each other, and how many millions of capital they display in their shop-windows, in the diamonds and precious stones they expose by tens of thousands, and the brilliant jewelry in the shapes of lizards and scorpions which in Paris is now all the rage. He looks in at Chevet's restaurant, the Napoleon of French cuisine, who furnishes the great men their greatest dinners, and he marvels at the excellence of the viands and vegetables there exhibited. He goes into the Avenue of the Opera, blazing with light from one end to the other, and rivalling the noonday sun in the brilliancy produced by hundreds of electric lights. He goes to the Place de la Concorde, and, with electric lights behind and alongside of him, he looks far up along the Champs Elysées, a mile and a quarter to the Arch of Triumph, sees the grand display of electric lights there, and the many thousands of lamps and lights in long glittering rows between, and in fact stretching out in myriads in all directions, with the carriages, like a torchlight parade, moving up and down the broad avenue. Then he looks at the grand illuminations on either hand, fronting the rows of open-air concert gardens, which are the places of the first *début* of many of the great singers of the opera and the actors and actresses of France; and, entering one of these dazzlingly brilliant places, he sits down to drink his beer and watch the performance. A thousand people will attend, and he will be astonished to find that more than half speak the English language; for it is true that if it were not for the stranger the Paris amusements, like its vices, could scarcely be sustained. And then the day over and the night half spent, the American will leave the enchanting scene, and, going home, ring the concierge's bell, and have a sleepy fellow in a bed, put into a recess half-way up the hall, poke his head out, pull a string that opens the door, and, letting him in, request him to shut the door again. "Bob swore," or something like it, will say the American, as he takes his key and climbs the stair to his apartment; "Bon soir" will reply the sleepy fellow from his little bed, and the day in Paris is over.

PALAIS ROYAL GARDEN.

## LETTER XXXI.

### THE FÊTE OF ST. CLOUD.

PARIS, September 10.

Every town and village of France has a patron saint, who guards its welfare, and when in the course of the year the saint's day comes around, there is a fête in honor of the occasion. The village thus has its Fourth of July, as it were, and continues the festivity for a week and sometimes for two weeks. But our idea of Fourth of July gives but a slight indication of a first-class village fête in France, which generally combines all the American pranks and oddities of Fourth of July, Christmas-Eve, All-Hallow-Eve, and several more annual merry-makings, together with a large amount of other goings-on so peculiarly French that the combination thus produced is something that America has never yet seen. St. Cloud is a thriving village on the Seine, several miles west of Paris. Here are the famous palace, park, and gardens of St. Cloud,—the palace, once so attractive, being now a ruin, having been destroyed during the Franco-Prussian war by the guns of Mont Valerien. But the gardens and park continue to be gems of loveliness, covering the hill-sides for a long distance as they run down towards the Seine, and from their tops give a glorious view of the city of Paris. Here are beautiful fountains and a wonderful cascade, constructed with all the ingenuity for which the Frenchman is so noted in his management of waterfalls. St. Cloud was a favorite residence of both the elder and the younger Napoleon, and here, until Sedan changed the course of events, the Prince Imperial, who is now in England, held his court, passing his time amid magnificent playthings, with a corps of generals and field-marshals to help him play tenpins and leap-frog.

It so happened that on Sunday, September 8, the fête day of the patron saint of St. Cloud came around, and then began a fête that is to continue two weeks. Thither, therefore, went the peripatetic dealers in gingerbread, fruit, nuts, candy, toys, pop-guns, chinaware, dolls, gewgaws, and knick-knacks of every kind in this part of France. There went out to St. Cloud several hundred of these, and taking possession of a grand avenue in the Park, running for over a half-mile along the level ground near the Seine, they filled it and the adjacent avenues with rows of booths. To these there were added all the wandering theatrical and opera troops in this part of France; also all the great swings, circulating wooden horse machines, blowing-machines, weighing-chairs, telescopes, velocipedes, and, in fact, everything calculated to secure investments of French sous, the whole forming an aggregation of novelties spread over a large surface such as only the French could get together. With three exceptions they had there everything that America can congregate for similar occasions, and about five hundred more outlandish things that we unsophisticated Americans do not dream of. There were no itinerant venders of acidulous tooth-wash, or hot-corn, or my old American friend,—the peanut.

On Sunday afternoon the fête began. The villagers dressed themselves in their best, and went out into the great avenue where all these booths, theatres, etc., were placed, and people poured in from the surrounding country. There came by railway, and omnibus, and coach, and on foot from Paris, many thousands. By four o'clock, when the fête had fairly got underway, there were a hundred thousand people crowding the broad avenue and the hill-sides of the Park,—dancing, singing, decking themselves with ribbons, flowers, and badges,—riding on the circulating horses, going up and down in the immense gyrating swings, buying things at the booths, and enjoying themselves as best they could. Every vender who had booth or basket was shouting at the top of his voice what he had for sale, whilst the more pretentious had hand-organs, and the opulent, who could afford it, bands of music. These organs and bands, of which there were at least fifty always within earshot, played their liveliest tunes without any reference to each other, and the din of shouting, singing, hand-organ music, and altogether, had become by half-past five as if twenty Bedlams had been let loose.

Then the theatres, opera, circus, and other shows began their performances. There were nine of these, each having a little temporary theatre erected, in front of which was a platform open to public view. As nine shows thus had to attract audiences, it may be supposed there was a good deal of rivalry. Each show, therefore, paraded its company on the platform in front of its house each performer dressed in the most attractive costume, and whilst the bands played their noisiest tunes, the public walked about in front, inspected the actors and actresses thus displayed, and, by the look of their clothes, selected the theatre to be attended. In a little while all the performances began. The acrobatic and circus shows were in the open air, the audience sitting within railed enclosures, whilst the public could get a free view outside. The opera company sang the "Chimes of Normandy."

At the "Grand Theatre Becker," the most pretentious of all these establishments, there were accommodations for an audience of about four hundred. Orchestra chairs were sold at ten cents, the parquet seats at six cents, and the circle at four cents. Such of the aristocracy as attended were given seats in private boxes at fifteen cents, these boxes being arranged along one side of the house, whilst the other side was the platform on which the actors, when not on the stage, exhibited themselves to the public in the street outside. The play was the "Knights of Liberty," in which appeared fifty performers. It was a high-pressure drama, in two acts and four tableaux, the costumes, as the play-bill announced, being furnished by one of the celebrated *modistes* of Paris. The orchestra of five powerful horns was placed in a little box under the roof, and the play, which turned out to be a forty-horse-power tragedy, resulted in the murder of about eighty-five persons whilst it was going on. The stage fights were numerous, and whilst they went on the five horns played their liveliest tunes, so that each killed man died in a hurry to quick music. The curious part of the play was, that every time a man was thus killed on the stage, he appeared in a twinkling on the platform outside, and either harangued the crowd to come in and see the show, or else leaned over a railing that separated this platform from the audience and watched the progress of the play. By this system the entire company kept up a healthy circulation between the stage and the outer street, and at least a dozen of them were killed four times over in the course of an hour. The audience too* a most lively interest in what was going on, applauding the stage speeches and welcoming the mowing down of platoons of men with a hurrah. I can imagine that if Mrs.

Drew or Mr. Gemmill were to import this play to Philadelphia, and give it in the exact French fashion, with all the gore, and all the circulation of murdered artists between the stage and the street, it would be a theatrical novelty that would have a wonderful run.

All Sunday afternoon and evening the din at the fête was kept up, the crowds increasing and becoming more hilarious, the people buying chances in two- and three-cent lotteries, in which all drew prizes of little fancy china images,—or taking chances in shooting-galleries, for similar rewards; or singing and dancing as well as the crowds would permit; or watching the illuminations and fire-works that came with the darkness; or else trying to get home, and finding that every vehicle was overloaded, and that pedestrianism was the best reliance. Occasionally, in the uncertain weather of this season, a shower came down, and there was a rush for shelter. The cafés did a thriving business; the booths gathered in many stray coins; and general cheerfulness and hilarity prevailed. The immense crowd was in thorough good humor and the enjoyment seemed complete. Thus began the fête of St. Cloud, which I am told is one of the great fêtes of this part of France, and at which the merry-making will continue for two weeks, although with nothing like the intensity and large attendance of the opening day.

### THE BOIS DE BOULOGNE.

Paris has, in the woods at the village of Boulogne, west of the city, a park that bears much the same relation to it as Fairmount Park does to Philadelphia. Here go the Parisians, on foot, on horseback, or in carriages, to breathe the fresh air and enjoy themselves. It is the particular Mecca, especially on Saturdays, of bridal parties. They get married in the morning and have a picnic in the Bois de Boulogne throughout the day, all hands wearing the bridal costumes. Then they go home; hire a hall, and have a ball in the evening. The Park has a lake and a cascade, both artificially constructed, and these give beautiful water-views, but as the land is mostly flat, I do not think its views can compare to those in Fairmount Park. Neither can the equipages. There are a great number of carriages every afternoon on the road around the lake, which is the principal drive of the Bois, but they are mostly one-horse vehicles, and the display, taken altogether, can hardly compare to a fine afternoon in Fairmount Park, where the handsome drive, and, in fact, the entire road from Green Street to George's Hill and back through the East Park is full of magnificent turnouts. Parisian horseflesh is generally poor, and this spoils the effect. The horses' ribs show economical feeding. The vehicles are heavy and lumbering, and are not the light and handsome coaches and other road wagons that we are accustomed to. Hence, although it has more fame, no Philadelphian need wish to exchange Fairmount Park for the Bois de Boulogne, either for extent, for views, or for the display of carriages and people. Now that our Horticultural Building has been surrounded with acres of flower-beds, and there are at George's Hill and Lemon Hill also beautiful flower-gardens, these will give a good idea of the French peculiarity of putting gardens in their parks, though there is very little of it done at the Bois, excepting at the nurseries, and there the chief attention is paid to the growth of trees. The wars around Paris having so recently devastated this Park, its timber, which is now mostly very young, is disappointing, and very little of it can compare to our acres of fine old trees along the Schuylkill. The Bois, however, has what we have not, and that is a fine, broad avenue from the Champs Elysées that gives easy access for carriages. It is unfortunate that Fairmount Park is not better provided, and that some street like Fairmount Avenue is not put in proper condition to enable carriages to get easy access over a good wide roadway to the Park, with enough room for the passing crowd of vehicles to easily move. From the Arch of Triumph the French have opened a magnificent street called the Avenue of the Bois de Boulogne, direct to their Park, and here the procession moves between the city and the Bois.

I have seen all the great Parks of all the great European cities, and there is not one that for original beauty can equal Fairmount Park. This is conceded by all the European visitors who have seen it, and yet they all—as they are racked over cobble-stones and tortured by their vehicles being wrenched into and out of car-tracks, and frightened by fear of collision in narrow streets—express astonishment that Philadelphia does not open up such a gem by giving a fine avenue of access from Broad Street. Possibly, some day we may have it.

And, now, good-by to Paris, which has this summer seen her greatest crowds, and put on her best appearance. But, through all the crowding, there comes for me the elements of another comparison with Philadelphia, in which our city has the greater advantage. Paris is the best and the worst place for an exhibition. The best, because, being the most attractive city, there is so much to please the eye outside the Exhibition grounds. The worst, because the city has very little power of expansion to accommodate a crowd. Paris has many hotels and apartments that are let, but when these (which every other city also has) are filled, there is no power of expansion, by which the excess of the inflow of visitors can be accommodated. I have seen people wandering about offering any price, but unable to obtain beds. Paris has not that great Philadelphia home institution, the "spare-room," or guest-chamber. The Frenchman in Paris has only just as much room as is necessary for his family to live in. The idea of accommodating a guest in his own apartments is almost unheard of; and when a new baby arrives in the family it generally has to be sent out into the country to nurse. Therefore Paris is unable to provide adequate accommodations for the crowd of Exhibition visitors, and this has caused prices to go up, and given the internal economy of the city a strain that it cannot bear. There was more comfort in Philadelphia for half the cost than Paris gives its visitors; and this interferes greatly with the enjoyment of a visit to the Exhibition. Then the means of getting to and from the show in cheap public conveyances are entirely inadequate, and the French law preventing overcrowding has its inconvenience in compelling crowds of tired people to walk home. Carriages are abundant and cheap, four people being able to ride for fifty cents almost anywhere within Paris in one of these vehicles; but it is not according to American ideas to force people to hire coaches when omnibus and car lines run over the same route. Were it not for these carriages I do not know how people would get from the Exhibition, and as it is, for two hours at least at the close of the day it is next to impossible to get a carriage. The omnibus and car lines seem to have no expansive abilities for the crowd, having no extra vehicles to put on, and not expediting their time or increasing their trips to accommodate the increased travel. They give out numbers, it is true, and thus prevent a scramble, but this compels long waits. Our home management, even with the crowding, is much better,—for the india-rubber principle on which all American accommodations are based, provides for crowds, and the people, unlike many here, good-humoredly share their comforts with each other

LETTER XXXII.

A RIDE INTO BELGIUM.

BRUSSELS, September 11.

It is a problem which has probably puzzled all travellers, why it is necessary for railway companies to start their through trains so very early in the morning; why, for instance, if it takes five or six hours to accomplish a railway journey, the train must always be started just after daylight, when a few hours later would do just as well, and enable the traveller to prepare for the start with less haste and more comfort. As it is, the earlier the train starts the farther off the station usually is from where you live, and the more vexatious are the delays in breakfast, coach, or other preparations. How many travellers, since railways were invented, have laid awake all night so as to be sure to be in time in the morning, and as they tossed in bed have wished all sorts of unpleasant fates for the railway managers who get up these early-bird time-tables? Why must a train start, for instance, at 6 A.M. from a station three or four miles away, when eight or nine o'clock would do quite as well, and compel travellers to bolt their breakfasts and ruin digestion for fear they will be too late! This sort of thing is what the Northern Railway of France condemns its patrons to do, for it gives them, on the road to Brussels, no choice of a daylight train, except it be a very early one or a very slow one. And then this very early train, when it starts, runs to the first station, and there waits a half-hour before the journey is continued.

But being an American, and educated in our rapid country to be equal to the occasion, I made the train, though part of the breakfast had to go into my pocket, and, almost before the Paris population were astir, was whirling along on the road through Northern France towards Brussels. Passing through the Paris fortifications, and out over the wide expanse of gently-rolling garden-land, which almost all this part of France is, we soon came to Chantilly, where the great race-course is at which the French Derby is run, and where quite a colony of English horse-jockeys live, who thrive upon the three or four races that take place there every year. Chantilly is in a valley, the richest possible agricultural wealth being displayed in its green fields, but nothing save the difference in the kind of crops seems to mark the boundary between the little farms, out to which the people go from the little low-tiled cottages that cluster together in frequent villages. It was here that the great Condé lived and built the famous stables at the race-course, that are said to be the finest in France. The forest belonging to the estate, which can be seen from the railway, covers seven thousand acres. Then the train passed Compiègne, with its grand forest of thirty thousand acres and its equally grand palace, which for many years was one of the royal residences of France, whither the Court went to hunt, and where Napoleon I. magnificently welcomed his new wife, Maria Louisa, after he committed the fatal mistake at the zenith of his power, of divorce from Josephine. Here, also, in the olden time, Joan of Arc was treacherously captured and delivered up to her foes, who ultimately executed her. Next we pass Noyon, where John Calvin was born, and not far from which is the celebrated fortress and State prison of Ham, where Louis Napoleon was so long confined, but from which he managed to escape, although the walls are thirty-six feet thick; and then the thriving city of St. Quentin, with its great cathedral and its canal, uniting the waters of the Scheldt, in Holland, by passing through several other rivers, with the Atlantic by finally going down the Seine. Here is a region thick with relics of the late Franco-Prussian war, and containing many a sad remembrance in battle-field and ruin of the German invasion. The flat, highly-cultivated country, with its long stretches of woodland for miles and the villages of tiled and thatched houses, were pretty to look upon, when you could see them through the clouds of dirt and smoke raised by the train; for this part of the ride through beautiful France was as dirty as any American railway could get up, and sent the rich, finely-powdered soil whirling into the car-windows. Then we came to a region where almost every little eminence had its gyrating windmill, and beyond this the land gradually flattened into an almost treeless country, that seemed a nearly exact reproduction of the prairies of the West. Thus, past windmills and through dust and among little detached villages, we journeyed, passing at a distance Cambrai, whence comes the name of "cambric," so familiar to your lady readers, until finally we reached the great fortress of Mauberge, one of Vauban's construction, and part of the French line of frontier defence towards Belgium. As we approached the Sambre River, on which this fortress stands, the country became more rolling, and we gradually got into the coal regions of Northeastern France, which adjoin the coal-fields of Belgium, and make their presence shown by the great iron-works of this section, and the long trains of cars, laden with the brightly shining coal, much of which, unlike ours in appearance, is of a shining gray color, and resembles little lumps of zinc. Here Paris gets her coal, which is sent by the canal past St. Quentin and along the Seine to that city.

Crossing the frontier into Belgium, the train was stopped for fifteen minutes whilst the passengers went through the Custom-House examination. This was as superficial and as merely formal as such an examination could be, yet it was made most uncomfortable for the passengers. They had to leave the train and carry all their bags and boxes into the station, where the officers chalked them. Then the passengers carried them all back. Of course nobody had anything to pay duty on, and if he had he would not acknowledge it, so they were put to all the trouble of lugging their bags in and out for no good to the Belgian Government, but great discomfort to themselves. In all tongues the passengers were expressing their very decided opinion of the unnecessary nuisance of these examinations,—which are practically no examinations at all,—yet annoy the traveller almost every day in journeying on the Continent. Having entered Belgium, the evidences of coal-mining were multiplied, and the train soon reached Mons, in the centre of the coal region, and gave a fine sight of its beautiful yet strange-looking (being so unlike French architecture) Church of St. Waudra. At Mons was cast the famous old gun "Mons Meg," now at Edinburgh Castle. From Mons to Brussels, by way of Halle, the railway passed through a rich country, where the women were harvesting a second crop of hay, and scattering fertilizers over the soil, and finally we were trundled into the station of the Southern Belgian State Railway,—for the Government conducts all the railways in this country,—and landed in the city which is fond of being called a miniature Paris, which Brussels, especially the new parts, resembles in no small degree.

### BRUSSELS LACE.

Brussels is chiefly known in America from being the source of product of that article which the ladies are fond of describing as " real lace." Lace, in these modern days, makes its presence known in Brussels by appearing in myriads of shop-windows, and tempting the eye and threatening the pocketbook on every side. It is a great sight to visit a lace-factory and see the patient workers fashioning this lace, which looks so fine but involves such terrible labor. The girls begin work at six years of age, and gradually acquire proficiency in handling the bobbins or plying the needle, until death or worn-out eyesight ends their toil. The fineness of the work is only equal to its tediousness. I was shown one piece of lace that an old woman was working at, which covered a breadth of but three inches, yet in this space there were over four hundred threads, each attached to its bobbin, all of which she was skilfully twisting, turning, and fastening among the thousand or more pins stuck into a cushion, on which was fastened the parchment with the plan of the work. This looked difficult enough, yet I was told that only the coarser laces were made in this way, and that the finer ones had all to be made with the needle and by hand, and there were other patient toilers using their needles with thread as fine as a hair, to work out the gossamer fabric, the veritable "point-lace," that has such an electric influence over the female mind. Talk of the ' Song of the Shirt," that "stitch, stitch, stitch," though hard enough, is nothing to this. There they worked, twenty-five women, of all ages, in a room, some of them bent almost double, others with magnifying-glasses; some with

## PUBLIC BUILDINGS IN BRUSSELS.

strange, nervous twitches, that convulsed their entire bodies every time they took a stitch; yet all patient and plodding, and hoping that some day the slow weaving of the tedious web would end. Near them hung the medals of all the International Exhibitions to attest their proficiency, including the medal and diploma from Philadelphia in 1876. These were the workers in the house, but there were besides nearly three thousand others outside who did the work at their homes. In the warerooms the sight of carrying about these almost priceless laces by the armloads, and tossing them over counters regardless of their great value, was calculated to create the same impression on the mind as the sight of men shovelling gold about in the Bank of England. It was certainly unique. The thread of which the costliest Brussels lace is made is spun from the finest flax, and the best grows just outside of Brussels, near Halle.*

Brussels is the only city I have yet visited that knows how to make use of its dogs. No curs run wild in the streets, but all are made to do useful work. The little fellows turn spits, whilst the big ones draw wagons through the streets. All the bakers' carts, milk-wagons, and hand-carts are moved about by dog-power, and dog-teams are as frequent in the streets as horses.

### PUBLIC BUILDINGS IN BRUSSELS.

Brussels has in the new part several fine streets and some noble boulevards. It also has many magnificent buildings, all placed in good situations to show their attractive architecture, as the new town is built upon a hill, and overlooks the old portions. I looked with admiration upon the new Palace of Justice, which is nearly finished, and which is as large as our Public Buildings at Broad and Market Streets. This palace has been nine years building, and will be completed in

---

* The mystery of what is "real lace" which had long puzzled me was cleared up in Brussels. "Real lace," whether made of linen or cotton, or both, is made by hand, as above described, whilst "imitation" lace is machine-made. I found out also in Brussels that a man pays for experience in this world. I came out of the lace-factory considerably poorer than I went in, but my wife was that much happier. The gossamer-like thread of which the finest Brussels lace is made is most carefully prepared, and some of it costs one thousand dollars a pound.

two years more, at a cost of thirteen million dollars. Another magnificent building, intended for a Museum of the Fine Arts, is going up near by, on a scale almost as large, and is to be surrounded by eighty-five columns of polished granite, several being already in position. It would take pages, however, to describe the many beautiful palaces and other buildings, parks, monuments, and fountains of this attractive city. Its picture-galleries are also famous, and here one begins to see the paintings of Peter Paul Rubens, the German artist whose pencil was so prolific that he is said to have turned out paintings by the acre, whilst others only could do it by the yard. The Brussels Cathedral, which is nearly nine hundred years old, is a fine building, with magnificent stained glass, and has one of the grandest carved pulpits in Europe.

### WATERLOO.

Brussels is also famous as being on the road to the battle-field of Waterloo, which is but a few miles off. For several centuries it has been the habit of the great European nations when they get into quarrels to go into Belgium to fight it out, and the most conspicuous instance of this was at Waterloo. Hence Belgium is popularly known as the "cock-pit of Europe," and, although Waterloo was fought over sixty years ago, troops of sight-seeing visitors, including many Americans, are still going to that place, and ascending to the top of the monumental mound, built two hundred feet high to commemorate the event, to look down over the almost level grain- and grass-fields and endeavor to understand how the battle was fought. They listen with credulity to the tales of guides who describe the contest in accordance with the supposed sympathies of the listener, and then pay high prices for ancient-looking bullets, and old bits of muskets and trappings that have been dug up on the field,—a day or two after their importation from Birmingham to be buried there.

## LETTER XXXIII.

### THE JOURNEY TO THE RHINE.

Cologne, September 12.

"Get in your carriages, if you please," said the polite railway guard at Brussels, which speech corresponds to the sharp "all aboard!" without the "if you please," of the American railway conductor, as the latter whisks off his train without further ceremony. But here, on the Belgian and German railways, they do not start in such a hurry, but ring a bell, blow a whistle, and then these signals indicating that the ticket-office and baggage department had completed their business, the guard having personally looked into every carriage and seen that the passengers are rightly bestowed, blows his little whistle, the engineer gives three sonorous blasts on the locomotive whistle, and the train moves off. The system is deliberate and careful to the last degree, and just the opposite of what we are accustomed to at home; but we did not have, as is often the case at home, a portion of the passengers chasing after the fleeing train, and we still managed to get off on time. We were bound for the Fatherland and the Rhine; the land of castles, legends, and churches; of famous baths, of thrift, and true politeness; the land that has sent America millions of her best people, and has a sincere admiration for most things that emanate from America, especially petroleum and tobacco. The land of the Rhine has been fought for and about more than probably any other, and the varying fortunes of the great river have been entwined into Europe's chief history for centuries. Not eighty years ago the Rhine was almost all in French possession; now, in the wonderful recent growth and prowess of the German Empire, it has all been conquered by the Fatherland. Napoleon III. was ambitious to make the Rhine again the French frontier, and this ambition precipitated the war which overthrew him.

The railway from Brussels to the Rhine, at Cologne, runs almost eastward through the level garden-land of Belgium, and passes several famous places. Every town has its church, many of them large and imposing, with their towers and spires reaching far above the surrounding buildings, and seen from afar as the railway enters and leaves them. Liege, with its coal-mines, iron-mills, and overhanging streams of smoke, looked like a sort of Pittsburg. But cannon and firearms, cutlery, rails, and metal-work are not the only things to be seen in this fine old city. It has its Cathedral and its historical buildings; and here was the house of William de la Marck, of whom Sir Walter Scott wrote, whilst the principal scenes of his novel of "Quentin Durward" are laid in Liege. The city is beautifully situated, the almost prairie-like appearance of the country west of Liege suddenly changing to a rolling surface as the city is approached, and giving it, despite the smoke, an attractive look. Crossing the river Meuse, the railway continues eastward through a beautiful country, winding in and out among the hills, rushing through tunnels and over and along pebbly brooks, and among the iron-mills and coal-mines that in scenery and surroundings make this portion of Belgium resemble portions of Westmoreland County in Pennsylvania. Among the bold rocks and precipitous hills there nestled frequent pretty valleys, where little villages and green fields set off the rugged hill-sides. In this sort of a country is located the famous watering-place of Spa, where eight different mineral springs are reputed to be a cure for almost all diseases, and attract crowds of invalids and idlers who want to drink or bathe in the waters, or else make believe they do. Here in former days were famous gambling establishments, carried on by the sanction of the Government and giving it half their profits, but public opinion six years ago forced their suppression. Then we passed Verviers, beyond which the Belgian Railway control ceases and the German trains take us with their luxurious carriages, and thus as we go along the French gradually dissolves into the German, and the quick, restless speech and movement of the Gaul is changed for the slower and more ceremonious manners of the Teuton. At Herbesthal, on the frontier, the German Custom-House is located, but the revenue officers, instead of compelling everybody to get out of the train with their bags, adopted the more comfortable system of visiting the passengers in the carriages. This formal ceremony over, the train was started by blowing a horn and ringing a bell, and sounding with due deliberation several whistles, on the road to (Aix-la-Chapelle, as I was taught it at school, but as the people themselves call it) Aachen.

## AIX-LA-CHAPELLE.

Aix-la-Chapelle is, historically, one of the most famous cities in Germany. Here the founder of the Empire, Charlemagne, was born and died, and he gave it, more than a thousand years ago, its first great eminence. Here, his successors, for centuries, on the throne of Germany, were crowned, and took the oaths of office, not, as with us, by swearing upon the Bible, or as in England by sitting upon the old stone of Scone in the high-backed coronation chair in Westminster Abbey, but by swearing upon the famous Charlemagne relics,—the lock of the Virgin's hair and a piece of the true cross, which he wore round his neck, the leathern girdle of Christ, the bones of St. Stephen, the cord which bound the rod which smote the Saviour, the fragment of Aaron's rod, and the bone of Charlemagne's arm,—all of which are now kept with jealous care in the Cathedral, and exhibited for an adequate " tip." Here, also, the Cathedral contains other precious relics, but they are only exhibited once in seven years, and as the next period will not come around until 1881, when hundreds of thousands of pious pilgrims will journey thither to see them, I was debarred the pleasure. These relics were presented to Charlemagne in the days of the Crusades, by the Grand Patriarch of Jerusalem, and they include the swaddling-clothes in which the Saviour was wrapped, the scarf he wore at the Crucifixion, the robe worn by the Virgin at the Nativity, and the cloth on which the head of John the Baptist was laid. These, with some costly gems, are deposited in a silver vase of great value, and are only exposed to view, as I have said, once in seven years, and then with great ceremony. The Cathedral is one of the great churches of Germany, but the fame of its relics almost eclipses the fame of the church. Charlemagne's tomb is under the centre of the dome, a simple slab of marble bearing his name marking the spot. Aix-la-Chapelle, like Spa, is also a watering-place, its springs, which are strongly impregnated with sulphur, attracting many visitors, but it has not in this respect secured the great fame of its neighbor Spa. The surrounding country is of great beauty, not so rugged as that near Liege, but rich in agricultural wealth, and having here and there a round-topped hill raised up generally with a church or a chateau on top, to vary the attractions of the landscape. As we passed the neat little German railway stations, the servants came out with their glasses and we were greeted with the familiar sound of "Swei lager." The women went about in wooden shoes and carried their baggage on their heads. The little girls with their three-cornered neckerchiefs and ponderous gowns looked like reduced *fac-similes* of their grandmothers. The villages, around which so many legends clustered, had become the location of matter-of-fact factories and iron-works, giving evidence of busy industry, some of these establishments being of great size, with small mountains of slag outlying them. Then the country again flattened into an almost treeless prairie, and for miles before reaching Cologne was more like a section of Illinois than anything else it can be compared to. There was not a hedge or a fence to mar the symmetry of the broad expanse of agricultural land which both men and women were busily cultivating, gathering in and stacking their ripened crops, or else ploughing and harrowing the ground for new ones. Finally, as we approached Cologne, the tall Cathedral could be seen for miles away, reaching far above the houses; and passing through the massive fortifications and over the drawbridge we entered the station, and I found that the school lesson must again be unlearned, for all the people who lived in Cologne were writing it " Coln."

### VIRGINS' BONES AND COLOGNE WATER.

The visitor to the ancient city of Cologne, as he tries to travel its crooked streets of variable width, and to keep a footing on its remarkable sidewalks, that frequently narrow to six inches and often disappear altogether, soon finds that whilst its great possession is the bones of the Eleven Thousand Virgins, its great puzzle is to determine who makes the genuine Cologne water. The people of Cologne themselves do not seem to be able to settle this question, as there are some thirty establishments, the owner of each claiming to be the *only* genuine maker of the famous fluid. It seems that one Jean Maria Farina, who lived in former times, was in his day the veritable maker. In this they are all agreed; but unfortunately he could not live forever, and each of the thirty now claims to be his only direct descendant and successor. The old fellow either had a very large family, or else somebody hangs out false lights; and as nearly every druggist in the United States is also a maker of "genuine" Cologne water, which he compounds in his little back office, Jean Maria Fariua's mantle must have been divided into many pieces. But, be this as it may, the Cologne puzzle is still unsolved, and the more one tries to solve it the more mysterious it becomes. The chief occupation of the townspeople seems to be to tout for these Cologne water makers. The waiters in the hotels and people on the street are all imploring you to buy Cologne, and when your coffee and eggs come to the hotel table in the morning, a neat specimen Cologne bottle is delicately laid alongside as a reminder of the visitor's duty to buy. If an American can get out of Cologne without buying a bottle he will possess much more endurance than the race usually has.

The Virgins' bones are a greater curiosity of Cologne than the Cathedral, and yet we rarely hear of them in America. Among thousands of legends of the Rhine is that of the pious St. Ursula and the eleven thousand virgins, who fourteen hundred years ago went up the river on a pilgrimage to Rome, and returning were all murdered by the Huns. Their bones were gathered together, and, in some way unexplained, were brought to Cologne and buried in a common tomb, over which, after many years, was erected the present Church of St. Ursula, which is eight hundred and fifty years old. Subsequently the bones were exhumed from beneath the church, brought up into it, and placed around it, forming one of the most extraordinary displays that the eyes of man ever witnessed. The church is not very large, and its heavy walls, low ceilings, and ancient style of construction show its antiquity. All around this church are encased the skulls and bones, large stone receptacles being filled with them, with apertures in the sides through which the bones can be seen, and the skulls being put on rows of little shelves divided off like pigeon-holes. All the skulls have the part below the forehead covered with needle-work and embroidery, and some of them are inlaid with pearls and precious stones. The collection is certainly a remarkable one, there being, besides the collections of bones, eighteen hundred of these skulls arranged in cases around the church, whilst in an apartment known as the Treasury, which is about thirty feet square, there are seven hundred and thirty-two more skulls on the walls, and the entire upper portion is covered with bones, which are arranged everywhere, excepting where the windows let in light. Here, under special glass cases, are the skulls of St. Ursula herself, her lover, and several of the principal virgins, together with the bones of her right and left arm and one foot. There are also other relics, including one of the alabaster vases wherein the Saviour turned the water into wine. This vase would hold about four gallons; but part of the mouth and one handle are gone, and it is so cracked and dilapidated that it probably will hold very little now. It bears evidence of great antiquity, being worn quite thin in some places, and is partially transparent, whilst the edges show the wearing caused by pouring out a fluid.

The Cologne Cathedral is as grand as ever, and the means being furnished by the German Government, its great towers, which are to be five hundred feet high, are gradually rising, and before long will be capped with the admirable spires that will make it the finest church in Northern Europe. This Cathedral of St. Peter's is, next to St. Peter's at Rome, the largest church in the world, and its builders, who have been laboring for six hundred years, begin to anticipate its completion. The masons can be heard among the scaffolding away up aloft, chipping the stone, and steam-hoists busily raise the materials that are being gradually converted into the delicate tracery of the spires. This church is, inside, the most impressive I ever saw. The narrow nave and transepts seem to lift the roof away above you, and the length of over five hundred feet makes all the inside distances very great. The stained glass of this grand church is very fine, and the work upon it seems to be in every way complete, excepting that upon the towers, which, it is said, will take five million dollars to finish. The great relic in this Cathedral is the fine silver vase which contains the skulls of the "Three Kings of Cologne," who were believed to be the three wise men who came from the East with presents for the infant Saviour. This treasure originally came from Milan, and it is highly prized. The choir is rich in statues, frescoes, and fine carvings, and, in fact, this church is one of the most wonderful constructions in the world. The ancient city which contains it has not belied the odorous reputation given it by Coleridge, for, despite the liberal supplies of Cologne water with which it abounds, there still are localities in it that evidently need more. Said Coleridge:

> "Ye nymphs who reign o'er sewers and sinks,
> The river Rhine, it is well known,
> Doth wash your city of Cologne;
> But tell me, nymphs, what power divine
> Shall henceforth wash the river Rhine?"

---

## LETTER XXXIV.

### THE RHINE AND SOME OF ITS LEGENDS.

MAYENCE, September 13.

The river Rhine, the most famous and the finest river in Europe, flows eight hundred miles from the Alps to the sea. Its vine-clad, castellated banks are renowned in song and story, and from Cologne up to Mayence, for that is the portion of the river which is most attractive, there is not a town, or hill, or rock, or island that has not its tradition. From Cologne up to above Bonn the pretty little steamer, which is built with a saloon deck, like a miniature of our Delaware River steamboats, takes the traveller between low green banks, which remind one very much of a trip on the Delaware between Wilmington and Philadelphia, excepting that the Rhine is much narrower, and we do not see at home the picturesque little windmills that are frequent near the banks or the dykes that occasionally run out from the shores to improve the depth of water in the channel. The river current runs swiftly down, and bears on its bosom all sorts of craft, which the boatmen steer with long, oar-like rudders, ahead and astern. There are rafts of timber in profusion, for the forests of the Upper Rhine contribute nearly all the timber used below; and there are sail-vessels laden with empty petroleum barrels, going back to the seaport for shipment to America. Steamboats with long lines of barges and other vessels laden with coal and supplies that come from the sea, slowly toil up-stream against the current, and at Cologne make them take out a portion of their curious bridge of boats so as to give a passage through. Cologne, with its powerful defensive works of stone and brick, and grassy slope and moat, and its loop-holed round towers and conical-peaked church steeples, is left early in the morning. For miles away, as the steamboat courses along between the winding but low banks of the crooked river, the tall Cathedral and the scaffolding around its unfinished towers can be seen. Its origin is shrouded in mystery, and the legend tells us that the first architect, perplexed by myriads of plans from which he could not select one to suit him, finally dreamed of one which his Satanic Majesty opportunely presented, and, after considerable negotiation, sold his own soul and that of the first person who was to enter the church in return for it. When the consecration came, however, the Archbishop, although he could not save the architect, endeavored to prevent the sacrifice of another soul, and got a female malefactor condemned to die to agree to enter the Cathedral first. She was brought out with solemn ceremonies in a covered box, which was taken to the church door and the box being opened, crept into the church, and Satan, who was waiting inside, quickly seized her and broke her neck, and then rushing to the architect's house, inflicted a like fate upon him. But lo! when he had gone out of the church, the woman suddenly emerged from the box alive and well, and was given her freedom. His Majesty had been fooled by a pig clad in a woman's gown, and there was great rejoicing in Cologne.

Bonn, with its University, which attracts students from all parts of the world, and its paved levees and stone-protected river-banks, is touched at for a moment, and its ancient-looking houses are very pretty with their round and conical towers and their little gardens; and then the ranges of hills of the famous Siebenbierge—the seven mountains—begin to loom up in the distance. As we approach them the lofty peak of the Drachenfels is seen, with the top an almost precipitous cliff, on which are perched the gaunt gray ruins of the old castle, nearly fifteen hundred feet above the river, in which the robber chieftains of this part of the Rhine formerly had their stronghold, and spying out the vessels as they sailed along the river, came down to levy toll from the poor mariner. The upper part of the mountain is covered with trees below the cliff, and the lower with grape-vines, whilst along the river's edge the railway runs and pretty cottages stand em-

## RHINE WINES.

bosomed in trees. The seven mountains raise up their lofty heads in a sort of curved line running diagonally back from the river. Here is the cave wherein the famous Siegfried killed the dragon and released the maid, who afterwards dutifully married her deliverer, as she ought, and they founded the castle on top of the Drachenfels, the highest mountain of the seven. People, looking like little specks, were wandering among its ruins, and a white tent was set up near by as their abiding-place. Just above this ruin, on an island in the river, is the former convent of St. Ursula, whilst high up on the hills of the opposite shore are the ruins of the Rolandseck, where Charlemagne's nephew, Roland, lived to watch the convent wherein his intended bride had immured herself on hearing a false report of his death. Trees above and vines below cover the hill-sides, and at least a score of pretty cottages and miniature castles are seen along the river-bank.

### RHINE WINES.

Now we come into the land of the "heims" and the "steins,"—well known in America by the names on imported Rhine wine-bottles,—where the hills on both banks run down steeply to the river, giving charming scenery, and from the vines which cover them furnishing the famous wines of this region,—each hill growing a different flavor, and each flavor being recognized by those practised in their use by a different name,—the beginning of which it is hard to recollect, whilst the end generally terminates with the affix "heim" or "stein." Hills so steep that they would be rejected by cultivators in America, are here made enormously valuable by being terraced for vine-growing, the soil being sometimes carried up in baskets, whilst the people who till them seem literally to hold on by the eyelids. Wherever it is possible for human hands to hold on, or for human feet to tread, the grape is cultivated, and some of the vineyards are esteemed so sacred that even the bruised fruit that falls to the ground is preserved for the wine-press. Railways run along the river-bank on both sides, and the frequently passing trains take some of the romance from the "vine-clad hills" and "fields which promise corn and wine," of which Byron has sung so sweetly.

It must not be inferred, however, that the Rhine is throughout the romantic stream that steep hills and narrow valleys make, for there are long reaches where the hills, falling far back from the river, leave broad stretches of level land. Here are frequent villages, large mills, and in several places most extensive iron-works. But among them all appear the occasional ruins of old castles, and the square- and conical-topped towers of the middle ages, to recall the former days when this river was the constant scene of feudal robberies and quarrels. After passing through a protracted stretch of almost level country, which is availed of to take dinner, which meal the polyglot assemblage of passengers, though hailing from all parts of the world, wash down with copious draughts of Rhine wine, of a great variety of vintages, the steamer in the afternoon approaches the magnificent scenery in the neighborhood of Coblentz, which was the Confluenza of the Romans, standing at the confluence of the Rhine and the Moselle.

### THE WACHT AM RHEIN.

The river, sweeping grandly around to the right, discloses on the left hand the towering rock of Ehrenbreitstein, one of the greatest fortresses of Europe. This fort is on a broad-topped and almost isolated rock, four hundred feet high, whose precipitous sides are covered with a maze of batteries and fortifications, towers, drawbridges, and galleries, the prominent feature being a long flight of steps running up the river side of the rock, and a gradually-ascending roadway which passes around it and enters the top on the land side. It presents every outward indication of the impregnability for which it is so famous; and, though often besieged, it has only been captured twice, first by stratagem and afterwards by starvation, never by actual force. Over it floats the German flag, in token of the Kaiser's mastery of the Rhine, which skill and Ehrenbreitstein give him. Five thousand men are sufficient to man this great fortress, but it will accommodate one hundred thousand, and can store ten years' provisions for eight thousand men in its capacious magazines, which at present contain fifty thousand needle-guns. The Rhine and Moselle at this point fairly bristle with fortifications. All the hills near the great work are covered with batteries, whilst the row of hotels on the river-bank, which is what the traveller first sees of Coblentz, is protected by water-batteries and towers, and on back, front, sides, and far away in the inland hills cannon bristle and the gray stone facings of the earthworks show that the place is to be held with a strong hand. In fact, this is the key to the great river, and Germany carefully keeps " Wacht am Rhein."

The Coblentz bridge of boats is taken apart to let us through; we pass under the pretty railway bridge, and farther along go beneath the airy suspension bridge which is building above the city, and journey on to the Upper Rhine. Here come successively in sight castle after castle on the passing hill-tops, all of them the scenes of legends, and most of them reconstructed by their owners of the present day and made into attractive residences. From their lofty perches, three hundred to five hundred feet above us, these lordly castles seem to look down upon the passing traveller in disdain. They have been there for centuries; we but a moment in a single day. Here we pass the romantic river Lahn, which comes in on the eastern side; the Königstuhl, where the old Electors of the Rhine held their meetings, with its dark-gray tower, at the water's edge, with the seat on top where they deliberated; the picturesque Lahneck, where an Irish gentleman has made out of an old Electoral castle a beautiful modern home; Marksburg, five hundred feet above the river, where the Counts of Katzanellenbogen once lived to furnish materials for any number of tales, and from its square-topped towers on the conical hill came down to the river to fight their foes, and if they caught them put them into the horrible dungeons beneath the castle, where they were tortured; Leibeneck, which appears more like a church than a castle, with its peaked spire, and which looks down upon the great dyke that is constructed in mid-river for a long distance here as the stream sweeps around to the east, so as to throw the bulk of the current into the channel on the outer side of the curve. The Rhine, as it approaches Boppard from the north, sweeps grandly around first one way and then the other among the hills, and is a strong reminder of much similar scenery on the Upper Allegheny River, in Western Pennsylvania. The Allegheny has not the castles or the vines, but it has almost everything else in the way of fine river scenery that is visible on this part of the Rhine. It only needs to be more thickly peopled and to be more talked about to aspire to popularity.

### BOPPARD, THE CAT, AND THE LURELIE.

Boppard, with its ancient walls, and its old convent turned into a modern water-cure establishment, and its double-spired church, is passed, and recalls the tale of Conrad and Heinrich von Boppard, who loved the same lady, and the older yielding to the younger the idol's hand, both went to the crusades; but the younger, forgetting his German love, returned with a Grecian bride. Then the jilted lady shut herself up in a lonely chamber, and the elder brother, coming back to find that the younger had been perfidious, challenged him to mortal combat. But, instead of one killing the other, as would probably have been the case in these prosaic days, the lady who caused all the trouble appeared at the opportune moment, compelled a reconciliation, and afterwards retired to a convent. Then the brothers each built a castle so as to look at the convent, and the visitor is shown the convent on the bank and up on the top of the hill the ruins of the two castles. I had almost forgotten to mention that the Grecian bride referred to, just at the proper time to make the tale complete, proved faithless to her husband and disappeared. Here, as the river narrows, the hills come even closer to the bank, and castle after castle passes in review. Here is the imposing ruin of the Rheinfels, founded by the Katzanellenbogens, who have had so much to do with the robber history of the Rhine, used by them to collect toll, and finally, becoming a strong fortress famous in many conflicts, abandoned in the last century because superseded by the improvements of modern warfare. Here, also, on the opposite bank, near St. Zoar, is the new Katzanellenbogen castle, called familiarly the "Cat," which was also abandoned about the same time. The German tricolor floats above it. Then rises, almost perpendicularly from the river, to a height of four hundred and fifty feet, the famous Lurelie Rock, where dwelt the beautiful siren who used to lure her lovers by attractive music to her feet and then drown them in the waves that washed the base of the rock. She does not do it any more, however, and the railway has pierced a tunnel through her rock, which is now only famous for its echo, whilst some bold German has planted a flag-staff on its pinnacle. At Oberwesel, near by, where the principal hotel is called the "Golden Corkscrew," are the

RHEINFELS.

ruins of Schomberg Castle, where lived the Seven Sisters. All along this most romantic portion of the Rhine it turns and twists among the precipitous rocks, which in many portions are too steep even for the vine-growers to cultivate, whilst the railway trains on both banks dart in and out of the frequent tunnels that are necessary to get them through the gorge. As the river becomes narrower the current also gets stronger. Churches with difficulty secure a foundation on the hill-sides, whilst ponderous round towers guard the water's edge, the outposts of castles farther inland. Rocks interrupt the channel and make navigation difficult, and thus the Rhine continues its romantic course up to Bacharach, whence come the famous wines; the curious old castle of Pfalz, with its projecting gables, being built on a low island, in mid-river, and washed by the swift current, a short distance below.

Bacharach nestles in a narrow indentation among the hills and along a little verge of level ground on the river-bank. In front of it is the rock in the river from which the town gets its name. This rock marks the depth of water in the Rhine, and when uncovered denotes a dry season. The vine loves a dry season, and, as the rock was uncovered when we passed it, I supposed Bacharach's wine-growers were happy. Their product is one of the famous vintages of the Rhine, prized like the Johannisberger by crowned heads. The town looked well, with its cathedral ruins in the background, and Stahlick Castle on the hill behind it. Fürstenberg Castle, also in ruins, but having a fine round tower standing, is passed above; and then at Lorch, on the eastern bank, almost opposite, comes in the picturesque stream, the Wisper. Up this valley lived any number of fairies, elves, and mountain sprites who played all sorts of pranks with the people and their love-affairs. Next pass in quick review the castles of Heimberg, Sooneck, and Falkenberg, all built by robber knights, and now in ruins. Rheinstein, on the opposite bank, is in good repair, and is maintained to exhibit a feudal castle of the middle ages. The scenery along the Rhine at this part is very much like the Hudson River near West Point. It has the hills, the steep banks, and the beautiful views, and, as the steamer approaches the junction with the river Nahe, the Rhine sweeps grandly around the broad hill that is terraced with vines to the sum-

I*

mit, and is known as the Rudesheimer Berg, and produces that famous brand of wine; and before us in the distance, looking past a strange little tower on an island in mid-stream, is the far-famed town of Bingen,—"Sweet Bingen on the Rhine."

### BINGEN AND THE MOUSE TOWER.

Few towns in the world have a more lovely position than this famous little town of Bingen. Standing at the entrance of the beautiful Nahe Valley, it looks out upon hill and vale and river scenery in all directions, the Rhine broadening before it, whilst opposite is the great hill of Rudesheim, and behind and on either hand are picturesque castles and delicious cottages that fitly set the outlines of the scene. The strange little Mouse Tower, wherein, as Southey's ballad has described, the army of rats from the shore picked Bishop Hatto's bones, is on its little island almost in front, whilst other little islands dot the water. Bingen's glorious situation is a fitting close to the beauties of the Rhine, which began at the towering crag of Drachenfels; and as the day waned and the moon cast a silver sheen over the river, hills, castles, and town, the effect was almost enchanting. Here the Rhine scenery ends, for the banks above Bingen sink to flat land,—pretty with their fringes of trees, but tame compared with the views below. The great Johannisberg Castle and vineyard are passed above Bingen; and a short distance farther the Rhine steamboat journey is ended at Mayence. This is one hundred and eighteen miles from Cologne, and the voyage is accomplished against the swift current of the river in almost twelve hours. Mayence will commend itself to the printing craft as the birthplace of Gutenberg, whose memory is kept green by a handsome statue by Thorwaldsen. Here, where the Main flows into the Rhine, is the heart of the famous Rheingau,— the region that produces the finest wines. The entire country here is a blooming wine-garden, and, as I end my voyage, which is one of the most famous river-voyages that can be taken, so must I end this long letter, jotted down as the journey progressed, in the hope that it may give pleasure to friends at home, and recall to some green memories of one of the brightest regions of the Fatherland.

# LETTER XXXV.

## THE OLD RED SANDSTONE.

BADEN-BADEN, September 15.

We have at length got into the land where the traveller sleeps under the feather bed instead of on top of it, and where the chambermaid bids him good-night before he retires. The Fatherland provides you with every comfort at reasonable prices, treats you the most politely in essential things of any nation of Western Europe, and has better railway carriages at much less fare than either England or France. The landlord receives you at the hotel door on arrival, and when you depart, takes off his hat and shakes you by the hand,— these courtesies being rarely committed to subordinates. The people of all degrees are polite, and what astonished me the most was to find the almost universal knowledge of the English language, not only among the hotel servants, where contact with English-speaking travellers would impart it, but also among the shop-keepers, market-people, and similar classes. Along the entire Rhine and its neighborhood this knowledge of enough English to make themselves understood seemed to be quite general, and it gave token of a culture that I did not expect to find. In fact, without any knowledge of German, I could manage to get on quite well, being sure to find somewhere an English-speaking German who could comprehend my language, this being the rule among the lower as well as the higher classes. This will impress itself upon most visitors, and equally strong will be the impression also made by the old red sandstone which is used for all the great edifices in the Rhine region, from Mayence southward, and which is an entirely different colored stone from that used in most other parts of Europe.

This is also a land of fortresses and battle-fields, full of the marks of war, for it has been fought about for centuries, and has been alternately in possession of French and German for years back. Mayence, where the Main flows into the Rhine, is a strong fortress, surrounded by the most skilfully-constructed defensive works, and has frequently been a bone of contention. In the older parts it is a city of singularly crooked, narrow streets, innocent of sidewalks, and opening into irregular-shaped squares, which are used as market-places. Here come in the women from the country on market days, trudging along, as in all this part of Germany, with their baskets of produce on their heads, or if they are a little better to do in this world's goods, riding on a cart, to which is hitched the family cow, driven with reins like a horse. The people flock to the market-places to gossip and buy, the women with wooden shoes and stiffly-starched handkerchiefs tied over their heads, and judging from the light baskets they carried home most of them gossiped more than they bought. It is astonishing what a very little amount some of these people would buy and what a long time it took to get it. Two eggs, three potatoes, and one apple are not much to feed a family on for a day, yet many of the buyers, after running over the market for an hour, went off with no more, though they probably heard all the news that was afloat.

The red sandstone stands out prominently in the quaint old Cathedral at Mayence, with its strange-looking towers, and in many a house and monument and public fountain about the ancient-looking town. It has a fine effect, and does not seem to be so soft as the stone of Paris or of England, for it does not wear away so quickly. The old Cathedral, which is having a new altar erected, is a fine specimen of pure Romanesque architecture, and though it has been bombarded and burned and battered in the wars that have raged around Mayence, it is again in good repair, and its frescoes and windows and statues are well worth looking at. In it are the monuments of the Electors of Mayence, among which the French troops, during the first Napoleon's time, used to barrack; but the Prussian troops, in their helmets with spikes on top and their soldierly-looking uniforms, are seen all about Mayence now, showing that the Kaiser holds it with a strong hand. The little town and its bridge of boats will amply repay a visit, for it is one of the most ancient cities of this ancient land, and shows every evidence of antiquity. From Mayence a short ride over the almost level plain bordering the Rhine, which in parts resembles a Western prairie, and in other parts is like a section cut out of the New Jersey pines, brings the visitor

THE SHATTERED TOWER, HEIDELBERG.

to Heidelberg. To reach this famous city the railway leaves the level plain, and turning up the valley of the Neckar goes in among the hills and forests of the Odenwald, where Heidelberg is built on a long, narrow strip of land adjoining that swift-flowing stream. Here, in one of the most beautiful spots that could be selected, the famous University, founded five hundred years ago, educates its students, and attracts men who desire culture from the New as well as from the Old World.

## HEIDELBERG.

In America, college education is said to be chiefly directed to learning how to win boat-races, whilst in Heidelberg its object seems to be to teach how to fight. You see the Heidelberg students walking about, and at table, with faces and arms full of scars and wounds, and wonder whether the wars which for years have desolated these frontiers are really ended. On inquiry it is discovered that over one-quarter of the eight hundred and odd students who are in attendance at the University are attached to seven or eight different corps; that this attachment to fighting bodies seems to be a leading part of the collegiate system; and that the jealousy between the corps runs so high, that fighting with swords between the students is continual. This military education and practice is of course natural in a city which in the wars that have been fought around it has been five times bombarded, three times pillaged, and twice burnt; and down upon which from its perch up on the hill look the ruins of the famous Schloss, or Castle, which has itself been battered as badly as any part of the town. Every Friday the students fight their duels in a house over the Neckar, using sharp double-edged swords, which inflict frequent and ugly wounds. If the contest is for the honor of the corps, the students wear bandages for protection, but if it is a duel to resent an insult, they fight to hurt. All the fights are limited to fifteen minutes' duration, and the one having the fewest cuts is declared the victor. The University itself is a modest building, of little pretensions, though it has such great fame, and it is entirely eclipsed by the three greater sights of Heidelberg,—the Schloss, the Tun, and the Church of the Holy Ghost.

The Schloss or Castle stands on the steep hill, back of and

almost overhanging the town, and is about three hundred feet above it. It is built of the old red sandstone, and is one of the finest and most attractive ruins in the world. In its day it was one of the most extensive and famous of the German castles, but bombardment, fire, lightning, and gunpowder explosions have all contributed to its ruin, and now it is as carefully preserved, with its broken walls, roofless apartments, and overthrown towers, all overgrown with ivy, as is possible to do it. It is a much more remarkable ruin than Kenilworth, which has got much more fame; and there is ivy here with stalks resembling the trunks of trees, which has been overrunning the walls for centuries. The amazing strength of construction by the Germans of the middle ages is shown by the walls, fifteen to twenty feet thick, and by the wonderful adhesion of the masonry of the towers, which, when blown up by the French, did not crumble to pieces, but fell over in a solid mass, and now lie far down the hill unbroken. The cement in those days held better than some that we have now. This Castle was evidently built for a fighting race, as every appliance of defence known at the time is provided, whilst the artistic skill shown in the ornamentation of the fronts of the buildings in the interior court is remarkable.

The American reader has probably heard more of the Heidelberg Tun than of the Heidelberg Schloss, though the Schloss contains the Tun. Down in the cellar, under the chapel, and in a vault built especially for it, is this famous Tun, the largest wine-cask in the world, built for the Elector Charles Theodore over one hundred and twenty-five years ago, to hold eight hundred hogsheads of Neckar wine. It lies on its side, and is thirty-two feet long and twenty-three feet in height. Enormous wooden hoops hold it together, and you can go on top and look in at the bung-hole, which is about three inches in diameter. In front of it stands a strange statue of a fat little fellow, all puffed out and swollen, and the German woman who exhibits the Castle, pointing to the Tun, says, " that holds three hundred thousand bottles of wine," and then pointing to the statue, adds, " that held eighteen bottles." The statue is that of Perkeo, the Elector's court-fool, who could drink eighteen bottles of strong wine at one sitting, and never went to bed sober. The Tun, like poor Perkeo, has no wine in now. It has been filled three times, but has been empty for many years.

The Church of the Holy Ghost is another sight of Heidelberg, not that it is architecturally very fine, or is very large, but on account of its curious history. The religious wars of these countries have raged furiously around and in this church. It was at first a Catholic church, then a Protestant church, and then was used by both religions conjointly, and in order to enable both to worship, a dividing wall was constructed in the middle of the church, running across the transept, and effectually cutting off the nave from the choir. This wall was erected in 1705, after the church had been fought about for nearly two hundred years, and the fiercest combats had raged to settle which religion should worship in it. The Catholics afterwards worshipped in the choir and the Protestants in the nave. But building the wall by no means ended the strife. Each party wanted to oust the other and get possession of the whole building. In 1719 the Catholics put out the Protestants and the wall was torn down, but the latter appealing to the Diet of the German Empire, they were restored and the wall was rebuilt. The fighting over the party-wall in this quaint old church at times involved in dispute the whole German Empire. At present the wall is intact, the Lutherans worshipping at one end and the sect known as the Old Catholics at the other. There is very little inside that is attractive, but outside the free-and-easy way in which all sorts of dealers have set up their booths against the church walls is rather noticeable.

To climb up to the Königstuhl, or the "King's seat," on top of the hill behind Heidelberg, is the proper thing to do, for it gives a magnificent view of the valley of the Neckar, of the town, and far away to the left of the level plain bordering the Rhine. This view discloses a picture not unlike that seen from the top of Mount Pisgah, at Mauch Chunk. At your feet the narrow town stretches along the edge of the river, which winds through the steep, thick-wooded hills on both sides. The railway, with its moving trains, is seen far below, and there comes up the distant noise of moving wheels. On the right the river can be traced until it is lost among the hills of the Odenwald, whence it takes its source. On the left it passes out of the hill country and meanders through the plain until it falls into the Rhine, a silver streak far away at Mannheim. This Königstuhl has spread out before it one of the finest landscapes in the Rhine country, and it has been appropriated, as we would do in America with such an attractive place, to a restaurant, probably by some German emigrant, who has been to the new country, and taken back some Yankee notions with him. But he treats his countrymen better than is done at some similar American resorts. Our Königstuhl landlord does not charge for his landscape, or stint his supply of that universal beverage—beer. He sells better beer for less money than in our free country, and is too honest to hold the glass "high down" when he draws it, so as to get his profit from the froth.

The State Railway of the Grand Duchy of Baden carried me from this attractive city south again, over the level plain adjoining the Rhine, among the rich fields and growing vines, and through the fine pastures of Baden, past Carlsruhe, and through the great fortress of Rastadt, one of the chief of the chain of posts controlling the Rhine, until we came to the little village of Oos. The train did not move over-fast in the direction it was going, but it did have a very large amount of motion in every other direction, and most of it unnecessary. After being shaken about almost as much as if I had been riding over Philadelphia cobble-stones, a transfer to a short branch railway leading from Oos took us up the valley of that little stream into the Black Forest, and finally within the edge of that famous region, among its hills, landed us at Baden-Baden, which is probably the best known of the great watering-places with which this minerally impregnated region abounds

## LETTER XXXVI.

#### THE GREAT GERMAN WATERING-PLACE.

BADEN-BADEN, September 16.

At Baden-Baden a perfect fusilade of church-bells waken up the population on Sunday morning, and then they go out to the Trinkhalle to hear the band play and drink that hot, but very thin, decoction of weak pea-soup, which is about what the Baden waters taste like. Then such of the people as wish to do so go shopping, for the stores are all open, and a few of them may go to church, but the majority seem to prefer lounging about the magnificent public rooms and gardens of the Assembly Hall, which make a perfect paradise along the banks of that very little river Oos, which runs through the town. But Baden-Baden, though it is the most famous watering-place in the world, and this is the height of the season, is not happy. The Assembly Hall is not patronized as formerly; the crowds do not come; a sort of languor and want of population seems to overhang the place, though it is as beautiful and as attractive as ever, and though the two spigots of hot water still run steadily in the Trinkhalle for the free supply of weak, salty soup to the public. Baden-Baden lacks the lodestone that formerly drew the crowd, for they wander through the dazzling halls and miss the old familiar form of the croupier and his rake. The rake, the roulette-table, and the croupier have disappeared together. The gold is no longer piled up to be won or lost every few minutes as the ball runs around and seeks a resting-place in the red and black spaces. There are checkers and there are chess, but what are these to the old-time Baden *habitué*, male or female, who wanted a quick turn, and no brain-work excepting the calculation of chances. When the Kaiser defeated the French and consolidated the German Empire, one of the first results of getting control of Baden was to abolish the gaming-tables, and for six years they have been gone, to the detriment possibly of the town, but to the moral vindication of the German Empire. The men who used to rake in and out the coins on the table may have been among those who were raking hay in the fields around the town on Sunday, for agricultural work seems to go on every day in the week in this region, women as well as men being busy in the fields.

I looked with admiration on the gardens around the Hall; the ten thousand dollar Chinese Pagoda where the band plays; the lovely walks and flowers; the suites of magnificent rooms, which formerly contained the gaming-tables, and are as resplendent as mirrors, gilding, painting, and the most elaborate ornamentation can make them, and the thought would force itself upon me that these decorations, which are the most splendid of any watering-place in the world, and which cost many millions of money to construct, were paid for out of a *part* of the profits of gambling, by what are called *fair* games. These *fair* games yielded an enormous profit to the banker, who paid half of it to the State Government, and out of the other half there was enough to satisfy him and at the same time pay the great cost of all this magnificence. What a commentary this is on the *fairness* of gambling, when the banker can always count with certainty on a steady profit made from the fools who venture their money! At Baden-Baden the public law was invoked to make the game as fair as it could be, and still the chance was against the gamester. How much greater, therefore, must be the adverse chances of the illicit gambling of America, where the intention is to fleece the victim! The gardens and great rooms are maintained now as formerly in all their splendor at Baden-Baden, and everything is done that can be devised to attract visitors. There are balls twice a week; music every day, morning and afternoon; a reading-room of great merit is provided, and the other attractions are made most seductive, but the town shows that it misses the tables. It has not now the rush of visitors it used to have, although the number of gouty limbs and shattered constitutions, real or alleged, that need the waters is probably as great as ever. To support the magnificent establishment a small tax is assessed on the visitors. I paid twelve cents. The waters come from seven springs in the side of the hill, and are conducted from the chief springs into the magnificent Trinkhalle, and also into enormous bathing establishments, for the water is used for vapor and other baths, as well as for drinking. These springs are all alkaline salt springs, and they yield the large outflow of over one hundred and seventy-one thousand gallons a day, so that the copious streams always run. The temperature is about 160° Fahrenheit, and the water pours out from the hydrants, in hot, steaming streams, clear and pleasant to look at, and here, in the early morning (for Baden-Baden visitors who lie in bed late at home, get up before seven o'clock, to be out in the magnificent Trinkhalle at the proper time), the people come and take their drinks. There is not much smell to the water, but its taste is repulsive, having a sort of greasy, weak, pea-soupy flavor, as if they had handed you out the contents of the dishpan. In fact, the whole arrangement—the running hot water, the sinks receiving it, the flavor of grease, and the surroundings—remind strongly of the scullery. Yet you drink this water because it is the thing to do, and you take the drink amid flowers and frescoes and magnificence of all sorts, and to the music of one of the best bands in Europe.

The city of Baden-Baden, which has a population of about twenty thousand,—frequently increased during prosperous seasons to seventy thousand,—stands in a valley just within the hills that form this portion of the famous Schwartzwald or Black Forest. The red sandstone and porphyry of the Rhine region crop out in great masses from some of the huge hills that surround it, and are the chief building material. Here, no one knows how long ago, the Romans built the old Schloss or Castle, a thousand feet up one of the hills, and its red sandstone ruins—for it was very unkindly blown up by the French two centuries ago—overlook the town. From their top, where the Prussian tricolor floats, there is a magnificent view over the town, and its pretty gardens and valley with the towering peaks of the Black Forest far away to the left, and the broad plain through which flows the Rhine on the right, and in which the river can be traced away off in the distance to where the tall spire of Strasburg Cathedral stands up a little mark against the sky. This old Castle, with its Roman walls and towers, its fine ivy, and its centuries of recollection of German and Baden history, is now devoted to the peaceful occupation of selling beer. But after climbing up to it, and finding that after the hill is scaled the Castle still stretches up its ponderous towers two hundred feet above, the good beer of Baden is not always an unacceptable beverage. The forests on these hills are magnificent, full of the tallest pine, spruce, and hackmatack, and were our Philadelphia ship-carpenters here they could get out many a vessel's mast over a hundred feet long, to supply which they now have to pay high prices for a very rare article on the Upper Susquehanna. More massive or straighter timber seldom grows than is found in this edge of the Black Forest.

### THE FAVORITE PALACE.

A ride of about five miles out of Baden-Baden, along roads guarded by the statues and crucifixes with which this region abounds, and lined with those low, roomy houses, apparently all roof, eaves, and dormer-windows, that one sees in German pictures, around which play the chubby-faced, flaxen-haired children whose little mouths seem scarcely able to hold the huge German words that roll out of them, brings the visitor to the most celebrated place in the neighborhood, the Favorite Palace. Here the Margravine Sybilla Augusta, of Baden, built in the seclusion of a wood a most gorgeous little palace as a summer retreat. She was a famous voluptuary of her day, and arranged a suite of rooms most highly decorated with embroideries, mirrors, and trappings of every sort. Here is the famous Mirror chamber, twenty feet square, surrounded and ceiled with little mirrors, reflecting and multiplying the image, yet so arranged that in one spot a person can stand and not be reflected in any mirror. Here is also the Florentine chamber, of the same size, which contains over four hundred miniature portraits of the famous men of her time. Another little room has portraits of the Margravine and her family in all sorts of dresses, there being seventy-two different portraits of each. The building is full of this kind of display, too gaudy for the refined taste of the present day, and in most marked contrast to the austerity of the little chapel called the Hermitage near by, where the gay Margravine secluded herself in Lent, and by scourging, fasting, and prayer, made up for the sins of the rest of the year. Here she prepared her own meals and ate them at a table, on the other side of which sat waxen images of Jesus, Mary, and Joseph. Here she lived in seclusion and repentance all through Lent, and when it was over came out again, and was as gay and frivolous as ever. Neither the Palace nor the Hermitage are occupied now, but both are kept in the condition in which she left them, so as to show the method of one of the most remarkable lives ever passed in this part of Germany.

Baden-Baden and its surroundings are in every way prepared for the idler and the pleasure-seeker. Like all watering-places, it is a town of hotels and lodging-houses. It has its race-course, where some of the greatest racing contests of Europe take place; and its people so far recognize the fitness of things as to designate the place where the hot springs issue from the hill-side as "Hell." A church has, however, been erected near by, to remind the pleasure-seeker that there is something else to be thought of. These springs have been known and been visited by the invalid since the days of the

Romans, and their flow has been unceasing. Most of the
Baden-Baden hotels are very good; and it is of interest to the
American traveller to know that what he cannot get good in
most other places in Europe he can get to perfection here,—
and that is good ice-cream, which is equal to our home-made
article.

## LETTER XXXVII.

### TO STRASBURG AND BEYOND.

BASLE, September 17.

From Mayence, on the Rhine, all the way south to Basle,
past and near Carlsruhe, Baden-Baden, Strasburg, Offenburg,
and Freiburg, the Baden State Railway runs through the flat
plain that borders the Rhine. For hundreds of miles it is
a reproduction of the prairie of our West, the railway skirting along the edge of the hills and woods of the Odenwald
and Black Forest, and the flat plain being a perfect garden,
much of it irrigated, and all producing luxuriant crops. The
Germans who migrate from this region to our American
prairie States find exactly the same kind of land as they are
used to, but they do not find the myriads of statues and
crosses that are set up in the fields and along the roads, or the
strange-looking houses, with tremendous roofs, in which this
region abounds. I have seen plenty of one- and two-storied
houses here, with four- and five-storied roofs, each story of
the roof having its row of dormer-windows. Some of the
houses in the narrow streets of the villages project over the
pavements, and the roofs of the opposite houses almost touch
above. Other houses have on their enormous roofs ponderous
structures erected that look like bay-windows or hurricane
decks, and these are altogether the oddest-looking kind of
buildings. As the railway train rushes through the villages
the railway guards at the road-crossings stand erect with
helmets on their heads and their flag-staffs at shoulder arms.
The Government controls the railways, and everything is done
by military discipline. The engineer drills his train at the
sound of the bugle, and the train-men blow trumpets as well

as whistles. The stations are pretty, but they contain so many offices that are marked by so many curious signs, that the chief difficulty the American has is in ascertaining which is the name of the station. He is all the time selecting the imposing sign denoting in an unknown tongue the name of the baggage-room, or ticket-office, or toilet-room, as the name of the station, and causing shouts of merriment when the amusing mistake is discovered.

From this railway a branch leads by a short ride from the main line to Strasburg. It goes westward over the level plain, and all the way there can be seen standing up against the sky the tall Cathedral and its spire, which is the highest in the world,—four hundred and sixty-eight feet high. This railway goes through a region that has been riddled by shot and shell, and seems to be practically a succession of forts and other military works. Canals and ditches intersect in the flat land, being a part of the military net-work which has for many years been drawn around Strasburg, which is one of the strongest fortresses of the Rhine. Here, on the great river, the French and Germans for two centuries faced each other and each had a great fortress; the French at Strasburg and the Germans at Kehl. The railway first passes through the works behind Kehl, and then through those of Kehl and out on the bridge over the Rhine, with its draws at either end ready to be opened at a moment's notice, and each commanded by ponderous forts, for each nation formerly held one end of the bridge. Then going across canals and water-ways to Strasburg, the railway does not enter the city direct, for that would have interfered with the strong front the French presented towards the Rhine, but it goes completely around the city, outside the fortifications, and finally enters through them at the back. All the way there is multiplied evidence of the siege of Strasburg in the patched condition of the houses and the numerous places where the earthworks have been repaired. The whole of this is now German. The heroic defence and capitulation of the French are historical. The Germans, from their well-covered works at Kehl, bombarded Strasburg and did the city great damage. It was Louis XIV.'s great fortress, planned by his famous engineer, Vauban, who, by his system of sluices and overflows for miles around, added to the citadels and forts protecting the city, made it, for his day, impregnable. But the

American war taught the art of using long-range guns, and the Germans, as they shot their bolts over Vauban's ditches and overflows, laughed at them. But the Germans do not intend to be driven out of this fortress again if they can help it. The strongest side, as a French city, was towards the Rhine; they are now making its strongest side towards France. On the north, south, and west they have thousands of men engaged in building new fortifications on an enormous scale, and these works are of such a character as to throw the old ones, which they replace, entirely in the shade. Galleries, vaults, bomb-proofs, lateral railways, and every modern appliance are availed of to aid the defence that these stupendous works are expected to make against French attacks in the future. Strasburg is to be a German outpost, and the Kaiser, whatever people may think of his seizing it, intends to hold the city at all hazards as one of the most valuable military positions in his possession on the Rhine frontier.

## STRASBURG.

Strasburg is not a pretty town, nor a large one, but it is the easiest to get lost in of any of the towns on the Rhine. The Germans have re-named all the streets and squares in their language, so that the old maps are of little use, and whilst the Cathedral spire is a sort of landmark, the streets are so crooked and most of them so narrow that the spire is difficult to find. The Alsace women, with the broad black bows tied on the backs of their head-dresses, give a picturesque look to the promenades in the few places that there are any, but the discovery that the street cleaning is done by women sweepers, who go about in gangs of a half-dozen, and wield their birch brooms with much more vigor than many of the tired-looking old fellows who do such work in Philadelphia, rather takes the romance out of the Alsace female style of doing things. To go and see the Cathedral and the clock is the visitor's duty at Strasburg. The Cathedral was seriously injured, like almost every other building, by the bombardment, and the repairs are still going on. It is built of the dark-red stone usual along the Rhine, and stands up like a giant, its great height rendering the spire comparatively small. Its front is a wonderful piece of architecture, covered with images wherever they could be put to add to the adornment, and its inside effect is grand.

They show where shells went through, and where it was battered and broken by the bombardment, and the sextons tell in a language made up of words taken from a half-dozen tongues, and almost all mispronounced, of the Cathedral's danger and damages. But the Germans having almost knocked it down, are doing their duty in repairing it. The clock every one has heard of, and at noon every day it attracts a large audience to see it go through its motions. This clock was entirely reconstructed with new works forty years ago, and though still in its old case, it thus loses much of the flavor of antiquity. The Engle clock, which has been exhibited in Philadelphia, is not so large, and yet does all that this clock does, and much more, and does it better.

To my mind the chief achievement of the Strasburg clock is the crowing of the cock. It is an almost natural reproduction of chanticleer's clarion, which seems to be tuned to the same language in England, France, and Germany as in the United States. My little girl says the chickens in this country talk the same as at home, though the people don't; but she is sure the chickens here do not grow as large or lay as big eggs. The Strasburg clock, which is about forty feet high, is placed on the floor of the Cathedral, and, in a little gallery alongside, there is a carved image representing the first architect of the church, sitting as if looking over the railing out into the nave to admire his own handiwork.

The old church of St. Thomas in Strasburg is another edifice of interest, because it contains the magnificent monument erected by Louis XV. to Marshal Saxe, which is one of the finest monuments in the world. It represents the Marshal, baton in hand, as having raised the French standards and vanquished the animals emblematic of England, Holland, and Austria. He walks boldly down the steps that lead to the grave, whilst France, a beautiful female figure, with one hand tries to deter him and with the other endeavors to keep off Death, standing by the coffin ready to receive him. On the other side Hercules weeps over the coffin. The conception and execution of this monument, which exceeds anything in Westminster Abbey, are grand. The remains of the great Marshal lie beneath. This church has some other famous tombs, among them that of Oberlin. There is a tomb to a Strasburg man who starved himself to death that he might

ST. THOMAS'S CHURCH, STRASSBURG.

## STRASBURG. 217

leave his money to the church, and carved upon it is the startling form of his starved and emaciated body. But the strangest things of all are the glass cases containing the mummies of the Duke of Nassau and his daughter, aged thirteen, both being carefully preserved, and the Duke, who was killed in battle, wearing the same clothes and shoes as when he died. The preservation is almost perfect, but the bodies are repulsive to view, even though over two centuries old.

Strasburg is the centre of the trade in that epicurean luxury known as *pâtés de fois gras*, or goose-liver pie, which costly but not very toothsome dish is made by maltreating the poor goose until it gets the liver complaint, and the liver frequently swells until it weighs nearly as much as all the rest of the goose. By the cruel treatment to which they are subjected, the goose liver is sometimes grown until it weighs three pounds, and the overgrown article is then treated by the mysterious methods for which French *cuisine* is famous, and exported to all parts of the world. The gourmands of Europe were in trepidation during the siege, not because Strasburg was suffering, but because the geese were not suffering so much as usual and the trade in *pâtés* was, therefore, interfered with. All around Strasburg, besides the evidences of the siege, are also seen evidences of German intention to hold the place. Their troops are numerous, and they can be seen on their parade-grounds going through the manual of arms and other exercises.

The Baden State Railway, when it lands the passenger across the Rhine, at Basle, takes him out of German dominions and into Switzerland, and here the officials stand ready to make another Custom-House examination of baggage. It is, however, the merest formality. Nothing is opened. The traveller and the officer talk to each other in languages that neither understand, and the officer in disgust finally puts the traveller and his bags out of the station, forgetting even to chalk them. Neither knowing what to do, this probably was the best horn of the dilemma.

## LETTER XXXVIII.

#### ALPINE SCENERY.

LUCERNE, September 19.

The Swiss Alpine scenery has been praised by all men and in all ages, and it is worthy of all praise. Yet we have near home, at Philadelphia, scenes as lovely and views as fine as the northern approach to the spurs of the Alps by the railway between Basle and Olten. This railway, which runs for about thirty-five miles through Northern Switzerland, bears in many respects a strong resemblance to the Reading Railroad's Perkiomen route from Philadelphia to the Lehigh Valley. The resemblance is strengthened by the fact that this portion of Switzerland, like our Pennsylvania Hassensach, is German, and that the railway in each case twists in and out among the hills, running up the valley of a stream, the land being cultivated at the bottom, whilst the hill-sides are rugged and heavily timbered; and this railway also runs up grade to a tunnel at the summit, just as the Perkiomen Railway does, and then descends amid lovely scenery on the other side. This line is praised throughout Europe as one of the most famous in Switzerland for beautiful scenery; but it is no better than that seen on the railway I have referred to, which is almost within an hour's ride of Philadelphia. After passing Olten, however, the scenery exceeds anything that we can present, for whilst the immediate scenery becomes tamer, the distant appearance of the snow-capped Alps gives it a charm that has an almost electric effect upon the passengers. Thus, as the train runs along the famous little Lake Sempach all hands are agog jumping hither and thither to get a peep at the snow-topped peaks, which change their positions most provokingly as the very crooked railway turns about along the edges of the hills. The fact that here, five hundred years ago, Arnold Winkelreid " made way for liberty and died," and in doing it founded the freedom of the Swiss, is of much less importance than this, the first sight to many of the snow-covered mountains. Pretty little Swiss cottages, the perfect originals

## ALPINE SCENERY. 219

of the toy-houses that are sent to America, are quickly passed by the roadside; also any number of country wagons that look like Jersey charcoal-teams, and to some of which a horse and ox are yoked together. Everything is German in appearance and language, and finally the two grand peaks of Rigi and Pilatus rise up before us, and the train runs into the station at Lucerne, almost between them.

Here, at the bottom of the famous Lake Lucerne, which has the loveliest lake scenery in Switzerland, I look out of the room window as I write this, with forty-two Alpine peaks in full view before me. On the left hand Rigi mounts up against the sky, and on the right Pilatus with its serrated jagged top. They rise six thousand feet above the sea, and seen between them, but far off, over the calm waters of the lake, are the higher but more distant peaks of the Alps, many of them shining dazzlingly white as the sunlight falls upon their snowy caps. Clouds float over the water below these peaks, and fleece after fleece obscures the top of Rigi, the hotels on the summit being one minute hidden, and the next in full view. Little steamboats course over the lake, for the great numbers of tourists require several routes of travel. Tiny rowboats take out the fisherman, whose luck, however, is generally poor, and as the night approaches the shore lights up with hundreds of lamps in the houses of the town on either hand, which makes the scene a perfect fairy-land. It is no wonder, with this great attraction in full view in front, that Lucerne has so many hotels, or that their proprietors can afford to provide bands of music to help the guests eat dinner. Both continents pour out their tribute to the lucky landlords whose lot fell in this beautiful spot.

The light-house and the lion are the more immediate attractions of Lucerne. The meaning of the name of the town is the "light-house," and there it stands in the middle of the river Reuss, which runs out of the lake, an ancient tower, with a peaked top, a relic of the olden time. In the days when William Tell is alleged to have wandered about this lake and performed his feats of valor and roused the Swiss to resistance against the Austrians, the archives of the town were kept in this strange, old, mid-river tower, and they have been kept there ever since, so that it is looked upon now with much the same reverence as we regard Independence Hall. Thorwaldsen's lion is, however, probably the most noted attraction in Lucerne. In the rocky formations about the town there are not infrequently seen perpendicular walls of rock, that look as if they had been chiselled out, their faces are made so true. On one of these rocky faces is sculptured the famous lion of Lucerne, designed nearly sixty years ago by Thorwaldsen, to commemorate the valor of the Swiss Guards who were massacred in Paris in 1792, during the First Revolution. These troops were the guard of honor of the French King, and there were nearly eight hundred of them slain by the Commune. Their fate, with the names of the officers, is inscribed on the face of the rock, and above there has been cut out a massive lion twenty-eight feet long, dying from wounds, yet still protecting the shield of France, which he will not yield up. Thorwaldsen designed it, and a young Swiss sculptor carved it out of the solid rock, where it will probably stand to be admired for ages. A little fountain plays in front, and the carved images of wood and stone, reproducing the lion, are as numerous in the shops of Lucerne as the bears at Berne, or the cologne-bottles at Cologne. Lucerne bears every evidence of its ancient origin. Frescoes are painted on its bridges, and its church steeples are pointed, gradually tapering as they ascend until they seem to terminate in a point as sharp as a needle. Its ancient walls remain with their towers, and its great attractions enable it to thrive handsomely on the fortune Nature has cast at its feet.

LAKE LUCERNE.

The Lake of the Four Cantons is celebrated as not only being superior to all others in Switzerland in beautiful scenery, but also in historical attractions, its banks having been the early cradle of the Swiss Republic and the home of Tell. It is bounded by the four famous cantons of Uri, Schwyz, Unterwalden, and Lucerne, and the mountain peaks surrounding it give it the form of a St. Andrew's cross, from which comes that cross on the Swiss flag. Lucerne stands at the head of the cross, Uri at the foot, and Alpnach and Kussnach at the extremities of the arms. It may be imagined that such a lake formation when made by mountain peaks and ridges would give views of great magnificence, especially as through all the openings there is seen a broad expanse of water, and other peaks beyond. The giant guardians of the lake, Pilatus and

Rigi, stand, as it were, as the sentinels upon the outposts of the Alps, raising up their massive forms on the northern verge of the famous range, and looking out upon the comparatively level plain to the northward. As the lake proceeds southward peak after peak surrounds it, and the long L-shaped extension from the foot of the cross is gradually closed in by higher and higher mountains until it terminates at Fluelen, the beginning of the St. Gothard Pass over the Alps. Steamboat routes run in all directions over this famous lake, for it is the Mecca of most Alpine tourists. Little Swiss cottages are dotted all along its edges, the homes of lovers of the beautiful who can afford to live here. Hundreds of thousands of all nations come here every year and enjoy the fresh air, the fine views, the cloud and storm and sunshine that are all seen to perfection in this elevated region, for the lake is about fifteen hundred feet above the sea, and discuss the problem which the lake and its neighborhood always suggests,—did Tell shoot the apple from his son's head? One of the most magnificent scenes in nature is that selected by the Swiss for the building, near the water's edge, on the eastern border of the lake, of Tell's Chapel, erected in 1388, thirty-one years after his death, to commemorate his career. Here Tell leaped on shore from Gesler's boat, when being taken to prison, and escaped up the mountain, and during Easter-time this chapel is the scene of commemoration services by pilgrims from all parts of the country, who come in a picturesque procession of boats. Whether America believes in Tell or not, the Swiss do. He is their Washington, and reverence for him is a national characteristic. At Zurich they have the very cross-bow with which he shot the apple, and they would probably have the apple too, had it not succumbed to the laws of nature. The Swiss tolerate no doubters about Tell and his career. Sixty years ago it was boldly attempted by various skeptics at Berne to circulate a book which argued that the apple tradition was a myth, whereupon the people around this lake invoked the aid of the authorities, and the Four Cantons making formal complaint to the Government, all the copies of the book were collected and publicly burnt. The book perished forever, and no doubters have since dared raise their voices against Tell in Switzerland.

## THE RIGI KULM.

Every one has a desire to go up a mountain, but few like to walk up-hill. Therefore, when a mountain comes across the traveller's path up which a railway runs, he naturally desires to go up. So I went up the Rigi, over the famous Riggenbach cog-wheel railway, and, without unduly straining the muscles, was able to enjoy the charming view afforded. The Rigi and Pilatus, as I have already said, stand as sentinels on the northern verge of the Alps, looking out over the broad plain of Northern Europe. Both have been for years climbed by tourists, and both have hotels on top, but Rigi is the favorite, so much so, that eight hotels have been built on and near the summit, with accommodations for two thousand guests. Prior to 1870 over fifty thousand people climbed this mountain every summer to enjoy the view, for, although not a high summit, it has from its isolated position a magnificent prospect in every direction. It is the fashion to go up the Rigi in the afternoon, and crawl out of bed at daybreak to see the sun rise, the tourist being gratified by a reasonably good view of it about one day in the week, for the Rigi and the Alps, to the eastward, seem to be most prolific cloud manufacturers early in the morning. But, as I have said, the people, awakened by the tooting of the Alpine horn, crawl out of their warm beds, whether it be cloudy or clear, and stand shivering on the summit in the cold winds of the early morning to see the sun rise. They are a motley crowd, dressed in their old clothes and wraps, and whatever comes handiest, some with bedclothes wrapped around them, though the hotel-keepers put up signs worded in very doubtful English, forbidding " taking out of hotel bedclothing to see the rising sun ;" and with chattering teeth and shivering frames they express admiration, and then crawl back to bed again. But when, once in a while, it is done right, the sunrise is a magnificent sight from the top of this mountain,—too magnificent for me to find words to describe it. Therefore, I quote the guide-book language of an enthusiastic Swiss, whose zeal sometimes affects his English :

" The starlight night, far expanded and aromatic with the herbs of the Alps and the meadow-ground, now begins to assume a gray and hazy veil. A gentle breath of the morning air greets us from the rocky walls of the deep and brings confused noises from below. Then all at once a figure appears at first undefined and then with clearer outlines. Who can that be? 'Tra-da-tra-da-dui-da.' It is the signal for all who did not like to ascend so high without beholding the sunrise. Then a curious bustling crowd begins to rush up to the summit; a variety of strange costumes is displayed. The air is biting sharp; some are shivering, and, notwithstanding the charms of nature, cannot bring forth a single coherent word. Meanwhile the day breaks on bright and clear, a golden stripe getting broader and broader covers the mountains of St. Gall; the peaks of snow change their colors, indifferently white at first, then yellowish, and at last they turn to a lovely pink. The new-born day illuminates them. Now, a general suspense; one bright flash, and the first ray of the sun shoots forth. A loud and general 'ah!' bursts out. The public feels grateful,—it always feels grateful, be it a ray of the rising sun, or a rocket burnt off and dying away in the distance with an illuminating tail of fire,—and after the refulgent globe, giving life to our little planet, has fully risen, the crowd of people drop off one by one, some to crawl into their warm roosts again, some to write a long premeditated epistle, full of poetry, under the first impression of what they had seen, to send it to their friends at home from the summit of the Rigi, and some others to hasten to pack up and with a loud hurrah launch forth into the grand and splendid world of the Alps."

The summit of Rigi is elevated about one mile above the lake, and the view very much resembles that from a balloon. You can see all around. To the north you look over the broad plain of the northern country, which comes down to the waters at your feet. There are Zurich and Basle far away. It is all laid out like a map,—villages, lakes, fields, roads, houses,—and the outline gradually fades away into the clouds much like the view over the ocean. There are the little Swiss cottages far down below, looking as if they had been taken out of the toy-boxes and set alongside the little streaks that represent the roads. There are the little specks of trees on land, and the little specks of boats on the water, and an occasional steamboat, looking like a caterpillar crawling over the face of the lake. This is the sweep from the west around to the east on the northern side, a view over the land that is unexcelled anywhere. Here lies Lake Lucerne at your feet on the left, and Lake Zug on the right, with the little towns on the shore, and all set out like a chart. Facing to the south, the view is changed. It is a view far away over range after range of mountains, with no horizon limiting it, but a splendid amphitheatre of snowy peaks. There are at least two hundred peaks raising up their heads, many of them snow-covered, and all presenting the roughest and most rugged landscape that can be imagined. There is water on this side, too,—part of Lake Lucerne, and two or three little, isolated sheets of water among the mountains that seem to have no outlet. But it is essentially a view of mountain peaks high above you, proudly rearing their heads above the clouds. There are the Jungfrau and the Wetterhorn, and the Spielhorn, and the cluster of grand snow-covered peaks of the Bernese Alps. They lift up their heads twice as high as you, but are seen so far away over the intervening lower peaks that you seem almost as high. This view is unspeakably grand. With the telescope, glacier after glacier can be traced out, and on some of the lower peaks little houses are seen that venturesome beings have built there for habitations. The Rigi summit, like the seashore, is scant of verdure. There are no trees there, but the grass is luxuriant, and the small hairy Alpine cattle feed contentedly. Its view and its comforts far exceed those of Mount Washington, whilst the wind, though it blows hard, does not blow the great guns familiar on Mount Washington, for the buildings do not have to be anchored down. The clouds, too, whilst often unpropitious at sunrise on Rigi, generally break up and give clear views throughout the day, thus behaving much better than those on our bleak northern mountains. But we have not the genial climate of this region, and New England, therefore, cannot hope for all the glories of Switzerland.

## THE RIGI RAILWAY.

The Rigi Railway is constructed on inclined planes, running up both sides of the mountain. There are thus two railways running up to the summit, from Visnau on the west, and Arth on the east. Their greatest inclination is one in four. From Visnau, where the steamer takes visitors from Lucerne, the distance up the mountain is five miles, and this route is accomplished in about eighty minutes. The railway is of ordinary gauge, and along the centre runs a cogged track, into which a cog-wheel on the locomotive works, thus giving the power for the ascent. The train does not go faster than a brisk walk, and the engine, which looks like a vertical steam-engine, such as is put on a crane-derrick, pushes a single car before it. The engine-boiler is inclined forward, so that when on a level it looks as if tumbling over, but when on the inclined plane it stands vertically. The car will contain fifty people, and as they go up-hill the very curious optical illusion is presented of the trees, and houses, and telegraph-poles looking as if they were tumbling over. The passenger forgets he is on an incline, and his unpractised eye makes him believe everything else is. The houses actually seem to be toppling over, and not a tree grows straight. The sensation of rising is very much like the gradual upward motion of a balloon, excepting that the wheels grating along the cog-wheel track rather dispel the illusion of a separation from the ground. The railway line crosses several torrents, some of them at great heights. In one place it passes through a tunnel, about two hundred feet long, and then comes out on a curved bridge over a fissure five hundred feet deep, through the bottom of which a little stream runs. In another place it crosses over a waterfall. It goes up on the Lake Lucerne side, so that the lake is always seen, and to give the better view the seats are all arranged so that the passengers ride backward with the lake spreading out down below before them. As the car rises, one snowy peak after another comes up to view over the distant rocky ridges, and the beautiful cross formed by the lake gradually unfolds. Here and there a solitary goat browses on the summit of a hill and raises his head to watch the slowly-passing car. The railway twists around corners of rock and runs through deep cuttings, but though it rises so high it nowhere gives the frightful sensation that is made by running along the edge of a precipice. In fact, the engineers, in laying it out, seem to have avoided this whenever they could. At the five or six stations on the way up, the line is made comparatively level, so that the car can be brought to a stop, and at the kulm or summit there are engine- and car-houses and a neat little station. There are ten engines used on the line, and several trains run each way daily. Whilst steam-power

K*

is used in going up, the brakes in going down are worked by atmospheric pressure, and the engine goes before the car, there being no greater rate of speed attempted in going down than up. The construction of this five miles of line, which in its ascent overcomes about one mile of altitude, cost about three hundred thousand dollars, and it pays a very good interest on the investment.

The ascent of the Rigi is about the easiest way of getting a mountain view, and the isolated situation of the peak rewards the observer with a better view than if he had toiled up higher ones. The higher Alps are so surrounded by mountains, that distant views seem almost impossible, whilst Rigi has the great advantage of land and water scenery all around it far below, of mountain views beyond, and a summit so situated that the observer can see all around. The hotels on top are some of them very large establishments, and they can be seen from afar off. There are little booths on the summit where souvenirs and photographs are sold, whilst intelligent Swiss have very good mountain-telescopes mounted there, through which the views are excellent. The peak is far above the lower strata of the clouds, and one of the most interesting studies is to watch their formation and dissolution. The feathery cirrus clouds, however, those light and airy formations that scarcely make a shadow, were still far above us, and seemed to rise above all the peaks in the neighborhood, though below the snow-clad Alps beyond. The sight and its sensations taken altogether will be long remembered.

The season on these Swiss lakes is much like our own watering-place season, beginning in July and ending in September. It will soon taper off to a close, and the Alpine tourist will leave for more congenial climes. But it is still in the full tide of prosperity, and as I sit at my window on the border of the lake, with mountains dimly traceable in the darkness far away, the lights of the town dancing over the water, the music from the hotel bands floating in on the evening air, the scene is one that is most charming. Yet, with all its charms, I am reminded of home, for our September friend in Philadelphia—the mosquito—is wafted in at the window and mingles his music with that of the concert below, to remind poor humanity that, even on the delicious Lake of the Four Cantons, we are still subject to mortal ills.

# LETTER XXXIX.

## AN ALPINE PASS.

GIESSBACH, September 21.

To cross an Alpine pass is the best way of getting an idea of Alpine scenery. Therefore I determined to cross the Brunig Pass, between Lake Lucerne and Lake Brienz, and chartering one of the curious carriages of this country that are built with two or three gig-tops, so that everybody can have a seat giving a front view, and having a driver with an immense Panama hat, and a long whip which he cracked every minute, we set out early in the morning. The route was along the bank of Lake Lucerne and around the foot of Mount Pilatus to Alpnach. This part of the road was a dead level, along which the horses trotted briskly. We passed through the beautiful valleys bordering Lake Lucerne on this side, and finally entered the forests of magnificent timber that clothe the mountain-side. There were numerous timber slides passed which are used to shoot logs down the mountain to the edge of the water. The slide at Alpnach is famous for being eight miles long, and the logs shooting down attain a speed of a mile in a minute, and if they jump the track they break off the trunks of trees like pipe-stems. The road, which is as fine as the best in Fairmount Park, and continues to be as fine throughout the entire pass, goes through frequent Swiss villages, where the steeple-clocks have but one hand, that pointing to the hour, and the houses are all shingled on the sides with miniature shingles, about four inches long and an inch and a half broad, rounded at the projecting ends, so that the walls look as if covered with scales like a fish. The saw-mills are numerous, but they are very old-fashioned, and the little mountain streams on which they stand all give evidence of being torrents that rage fiercely when the snows melt in the spring, though now they seemed only little rivulets in their broad stony beds. The crops in the fields were frequently varied by small patches of corn and tobacco, and all the inhabitants went about with baskets on their backs, slung fast to their shoulders. The juvenile population also seemed to drive a brisk trade at selling fruit, cakes, and milk to the passers-by, for this route is much travelled and the coaches are frequent.

Having gone the entire length of Lake Lucerne the route passed up the valley beyond Alpnach, towards Lake Sarnen and along the bank of that lake. It still kept its level character, though huge mountains enclosed it, and the road did not begin to rise until Lake Sarnen was left behind, when there was quite an ascent to the pretty little Lake Lungren. This lake nestles among high mountains and seems to have no visible outlet, though a tunnel can finally be detected through which the surplus waters flow out. Its level formerly was much higher than now, but the inhabitants wanting land much more than water, opened this tunnel, by which they lowered the depth and thus reclaimed a large surface. At Lungren, where the mid-day halt was made, we were introduced at the inn to the Swiss National costumes, for all the servant-girls wore them. These costumes, which look so pretty in pictures, are seldom seen now in real life, but they are an additional attraction to an inn, and are, therefore, adopted. At this place the ascent of the Brunig Pass begins, and the road toils zigzag in and out, up the face of the mountain, around rocks and among the trees, making all sorts of circuits, and still going higher and higher, though apparently not making much progress, until it raises the traveller far above the valley and the lake, and gives a fine view of the mountains behind us. The day, which opened well, proved to be lowering, for the Alpine cloud-factory was briskly at work, and as we toiled up the hill, the clouds were seen rolling along the mountain-side above us. We finally went high enough to get into them, and enveloped in the thick fog, with everything saturated and dripping, and the clouds so surrounding us that scarcely anything could be seen, we crossed the summit. Here at Brunig were several hotels, for it appears impossible to do anything without drinking in this country, but the cloud and fog made them look rather inhospitable, and after spending about twenty minutes crossing the flat summit, the driver fastened a drag on his wheels and the descent began on the other side of the mountain. The road continued of excellent character and showed skilful engineering. In many places it was hewn out of the solid rock, and sometimes

THE FALLS OF THE GIESBACH.

galleries had to be cut to provide a passage. Vast overhanging masses of rock threatened to fall upon the road, whilst the precipice descended abruptly below to an abyss that could not be fathomed, the clouds were so thick beneath us. We had not gone far down the slope, however, before we got below the cloud line, and then, at a turn in the road, there burst upon the vision one of the finest views in Switzerland. The green valley of the Aar was stretched out at our feet, that stream flowing between the dykes that make its banks, like a canal, for the Swiss have embanked it throughout, so as to cultivate the valley, over which much of it formerly spread. For many miles each way this beautiful valley could be seen spread out far below, whilst away off on the right was the Lake of Brienz, and opposite the massive wall of rock that seemed to rise up perpendicularly many thousand feet. On its surface three pretty waterfalls could be seen, one of them with its attendant cascades being at least two thousand feet long. The road wound down the mountain-side, and for an hour kept this magnificent panorama in full view, until we had got completely down to the bottom of the valley. Here the natives were found to be chiefly wood-carvers, and they swarmed along the road, offering carvings for sale, whilst nearly every house was a wood-carving warehouse. Brienz, which is an ancient town, though so well situated, is the centre of this trade, and from its quaint old houses, which seem to be stuffed full of wood-carvings of all kinds, they are exported to all parts of the world. Solemn goats also became numerous on this side of the mountain, there being large herds of them. In crossing the Pass the whole day had been consumed, and before the little steamboat had set us across Lake Brienz to Giessbach it was dark.

## AN ALPINE WATERFALL.

A waterfall in a country like Switzerland is a great thing, for the mountains give it an excellent chance to make an exhibition. If Niagara's lot had been cast here, it would probably have fallen several thousand feet and had cascades above and below, and generally improved its splendors. The Falls of Giessbach are a series of seven cascades descending thirteen hundred feet, and though they come out of the mountain where it rises up apparently almost perpendicularly from Lake

Brienz, nature has been kind enough to put a small spot in front of them sufficiently level to build a hotel. This spot is about seven hundred feet above the lake on a mountain eight thousand feet high, which looks almost too abrupt and perpendicular for any one to attempt to climb it. But Swiss ingenuity has carved a zigzag road out of the rock, and up this strange course the passengers go to the hotel. When the steamboat lands at a little ledge on the water's edge, instead of finding boisterous hackmen, you are pestered by a noisy crew of chair-carriers, and the traveller whose pedestrianism is not well developed, goes up the seven hundred foot hill to the hotel door in a sedan-chair carried by two men. This is an unique hotel coach, but it is comfortable. The attraction at Giessbach is the Falls, and the chief attraction of the Falls is at night, when they are illuminated. At half-past nine o'clock the ringing of a bell and the firing of rockets warn the visitors to be on the alert, and then the entire series of cascades is illuminated by Bengola lights, some behind the water in grottos, and the Falls are thus illuminated from top to bottom, making one of the grandest exhibitions it is possible to produce. Foaming water, when illuminated, is always beautiful, and here we have a series of cascades, down which falls a large mass of foaming, bubbling, rushing water, lighted up with intense brilliancy in changing colors, and the effect is as novel as it is grand. It is worth trudging seven hundred feet up-hill to see, and its fame makes a profitable trade for a large hotel, where the waiters are all girls, clad in the picturesque costumes of the Canton Berne. The Falls do not at this season have a very large amount of water, but they are so broken into cascades, and so well surrounded by shubbery, that the broken line of foam, bordered by dark-green foliage, is by daylight very beautiful. This fine exhibition is in full view from the hotel windows. The Niagara-like roar lulls you to sleep at night, and in the morning the free exhibition of Nature's handiwork is a solace whilst dressing.

This region, a hotel perched on the mountain-side, the top of the mountain obscured by clouds and the foot washed by the pretty waters of a narrow lake far below, whilst fine to look at, is a dangerous one in which to venture out. There is every opportunity provided for making a first-class newspaper item by falling over the edge, and, whilst tempted to do it in the interest of our profession, I hesitated, because no brother journalist was at hand to properly record the event. To outward appearance this is an almost inaccessible region, yet, when once in it, the Swiss are found to develop an amazing ability with their spiked staffs to scale the mountain-side, and during the night they clambered up the edges of the great cascade to fix their Bengola lights for the illumination, with a skill and daring that belongs only to mountain races. These people think nothing of walking an entire day over these mountains and carrying heavy burdens upon their backs, and the farther you penetrate into this rock-ribbed country the greater is the veneration for William Tell and the admiration for bears. The hotels are all named for one or the other. Finely-carved images of Tell shooting the apple off his son's head are set up in front of some of the inns, whilst the carvings, large and small, of bears, doing all sorts of things, and in all sorts of positions, and the fact that every inn that is not a " Gasthaus Tell" is a " Hotel of the Bears," is a strong reminder that we have got into Canton Berne, where hero- and bear-worship go hand-in-hand. In clambering about the rocky precipices that surround these pretty Giessbach cascades, we pass over the paths that are haunted by the chamois goat, and his delicate horns and hoofs are worked into many a keepsake by aged goat-hunters who are too old to follow the chase, but not too old to turn an honest penny by keeping booths. These venerable natives, with flowing beards and goat-skin clothes, come out of the woods looking like veritable Rip Van Winkles, and sell their knick-knacks to the traveller. They tell grand tales of the chase as it was in days gone by, and they look out at the distant mountain-sides over the lake and point to places where once the goat-herds were numerous, but now there are none. We descend the precipitous mountain-side, and, with a farewell look at the tumbling waters of the succession of cascades, bid good-by to Giessbach, of which will be recalled many pleasant memories.

## LETTER XL.

### AN ALPINE VALLEY.

INTERLACKEN, September 22.

The last letter left me at the foot of the mountain at Giessbach, after a visit to its pretty waterfall. Clambering down to the landing I embarked in a rowboat on Lake Brienz, and the "ash breeze" proving propitious was soon set over on the opposite shore to resume the journey in the gig-top carriage. The road ran along at the foot of the mountain, with a glorious view across the lake at the almost precipitous side of the opposite mountain beyond. We drove for nearly three hours along the bank, across the beds of torrents that had been dyked in, but which evidently in the spring frequently overflowed their banks and brought avalanches of stones and débris down the mountain-side. The road went through the most primitive Swiss villages, thoroughly illustrating the race. Stones were piled on the house-tops to keep the shingles from blowing off, whilst the fronts of the houses were frequently remarkable for their wood-carvings. This being the country of the wood-sculptors, they plied their art not only in making little images and keepsakes, but also in beautifying the housefronts, some of which showed great labor and skill. Through the windows the men could be seen, pipe in mouth, busily carving wooden images; and fence-posts, signs, and pretty much everything bore evidence of their trade. The country, however, gave some indications of poverty. The buildings were poor, and the people could get very little from the sparse vegetation, whilst wood-carving must be but a slight reliance for a fixed income. Every house had its little pile of hard wood, seasoning under the eaves, so as to be prepared for the knife. Saw-mills were frequent, but they had most primitive wheels, driven by the torrent streams. The goat looked down upon us from his perch, as we passed, but he seemed thin, and not to thrive well, probably because there was no waste paper to eat, and the flaxen-haired children paused in their work— for all, young as well as old, seem to work in this country—

to see us go by. As we approached Interlacken, the road contained frequent squads of people coming from that town. Families trudged along with the ever-present baskets on their backs, or else the men were drawing little hand-carts, in which pigs and children nestled, a happy family. Men would come leading cows and goats, their families following, the cows and goats showing the usual desire, bovine as well as human, to go the wrong way. After seeing much of this, especially the dragging of pigs in hand-carts along with the children, curiosity prompted inquiry, and it was discovered that a great fair was going on at Interlacken, and these people had gone there for a frolic and to buy animals and were returning home. The road finally came out over the pretty valley between Lakes Brienz and Thun, through which runs the Aar connecting them, and after descending the hill we were soon in the famous town.

Interlacken, as its name signifies, lies between the lakes. Imagine two ridges of precipitous mountains curving gradually around, running almost parallel for fifty miles, and rising six thousand feet high, with a depression about three miles wide between them, and an idea can be formed of this extraordinary region. To the east the depression contains the valley of the Aar; then proceeding westward Lake Brienz, then the valley between the lakes, then Lake Thun, and far away to the westward the sunset can be seen in fine weather through the opening apparently at the end of the mountain ridges. It is a most massively grand exhibition of the upheaval that has made the Alps. At the centre is this town of hotels and boarding-houses, with a portion of very crooked streets and old buildings, some of them seven hundred years old. The great attraction of Interlacken, however, is not the view either way along the valley, but the view through a depression in the mountains on the southern side. It is known as the "City of one View," but through this one view, when clouds permit, is plainly seen the Jungfrau and her attendant galaxy of noble Alpine peaks, covered with snow and rearing their heads far above the horizon. The fair was about ending when we reached Interlacken, but we saw enough of it to show that all the neighborhood had been in town in their Sunday clothes. Some of the women were dressed in the peasant's waists, velvet collars, and silver ornaments of the Canton Berne costume, whilst the men came out in their butternut homespun, and looked very much like an ex-rebel regiment scattered through the streets. The wonderful part of their garb was the short-tailed coat, the counterpart of that frequently worn by the negro minstrel, in which the back buttons are between the shoulders, and the continuation below stops much too soon to satisfy the pantaloons, which latter were also as short proportionately as the coat. In this strange garb the Switzers lounged about the streets, bargaining for goats and cows and pigs, and smoking very bad cigars. But it gave an idea of human nature among the Alps, and was so accepted, for it was a curious exhibition, and one that few travellers see.

#### ALPINE HOTELS.

That we have got into a wood carving and fashioning country is plainly shown in the hotels that have accommodated us during the past few days. Journeying southward through Germany we gradually came into the region of waxed and fancy wood floorings, the artistic character of the floors increasing as we have progressed into Switzerland, whilst the carpets have grown smaller and smaller so as to show the ornamental borders. I am now writing in a bedroom the floor of which is a wood mosaic of great beauty, waxed until it is as slippery as glass. A small floor-cloth in the centre of the room, and a rug at the bedside, are the only covering. The joiner-work of the floor is as artistic as its design, and both testify the wonderful ability of the Swiss as wood-workers, though cold floors, as the mercury declines in these Alpine regions in the autumn, are anything but pleasant. Still sleeping under the feather bed instead of on it, the Swiss have the same rule as the Germans, but all the beds are single, and throughout the entire country most of the bedsteads are too short. How a six-foot Swiss stretches out in these short beds I cannot understand, for their meagre length sometimes compels me, who always march with the ponies, to sleep "bias." But otherwise the beds are all good, even though the bolsters are wonderful constructions of springs and coverings, made on the inclined-plane principle, while some of the bedsteads are so high that you have to use a chair to get into them. Travel is a wonderful seasoner of sleep, and after a day's duty at sight-seeing one is ready to sleep in any bed.

This is a great country for good hotels, the service, the food, and all the adjuncts being excellent, whilst the charges are not exorbitant. Instead of having the American rule of *per diem* charge, they have the universal European custom of charging each thing as a separate item, so that a couple of days' sojourn produces a bill of great length, if not of large amount. These hotels in Switzerland gratify the Americans by putting fresh drinking-water on the table at meal-time, instead of requiring, as in England and France, a special order for a drink of water, which is, after much trouble, grudgingly doled out in small quantities. Switzerland has so much water in the shape of ice and snow, clouds and rain, lakes and mountain streams, that it is cheaply furnished and very good. Even now the great cloud-factory in the Jungfrau is hard at work, and is pouring down free libations all around us. We, therefore, cannot see the great sight of Interlacken, the Virgin Mountain, leaning over, a white-hooded maiden, ever confessing to the attendant Monk standing by her side. Both of them, with the Wetterhorn and the hundred snow-clad peaks attending them, and covering about three hundred square miles just south of Interlacken with ice and snow, are hard at work to-day manufacturing the materials for a cold equinoctial storm, which is spreading all over Southwestern Europe. But to return to the hotels. They are usually very economical in the use of gas. They have it in the lower stories and in the public rooms, but the supply is generally very weak; whilst in the chambers candles only are furnished; and the ever-present charge for "bougies" is found in every bill. They give you towels, but no soap; this must be carried with you. It is easy to get into these hotels, but hard to get away without passing through the gauntlet of "tips," and "pour boires"; but in two places, Lucerne and at Giessbach, the hotel proprietors have boldly braved the universal custom, and forbid the servants receiving "tips." They pay them wages, so that they do not have to depend on the dole from the traveller. Elsewhere, however, the system reigns in all its comprehensive splendor; the waiter, porter, luggage-carrier, boots, and omnibus-driver must always be "tipped" on leaving, and they do not forget to ask for it if the traveller overlooks them. These men are the best linguists in the country; they can ask for money in every known tongue, whilst throughout these beautiful regions small change is always at a premium. In the matter of decoration these hotels exceed those of America. They have magnificent halls, skylights, mirrors, and ornamental marble and wood-work, the same as we have; whilst to it they add the most elaborate floral displays both inside and outside the house, extensive gardens, fountains, statuary, paintings, armorial ornaments, and everything that can please the eye. This appears to be the rule both in Germany and Switzerland. Whatever profit the landlords make seems to be largely devoted to beautifying the hotels, and some of these are themselves as great curiosities as the towns containing them can present. But by the time you have been a week going in and out of these grand caravanseries, every tendon in the limbs is sore from the extra effort necessary to keep upright on the slippery waxed and polished floors.

## LETTER XLI.

#### THE BEARS OF BERNE.

LAUSANNE, September 23.

A great many years ago Berthold de Zahringen, of whose history you probably know as little as I do, travelled much in Switzerland, and coming to a certain point on the river Aar, where that very crooked stream makes a double turn around a flat-topped hill a hundred feet high, he killed a bear. Bears were plenty in that part of Switzerland, and Berthold founded a town there to commemorate the bear-killing, and he enjoined upon all the inhabitants to make friends with their ursine neighbors. As Berthold was a great duke the people obeyed his instructions, named their town and the surrounding country after the bears; kept pet bears in the town ; set up images of bears on all sides, and for seven centuries have continued to thrive and to show their devotion to the Ursa Major. Baren is German for bears; hence comes the name of the Canton Berne and the city of Berne. As we travel through the famous canton up to the city, the indications of popular bear-worship become more and more general, and when we get into

## THE BEARS OF BERNE. 237

the town and stop at the "Hotel of the Bears," the earliest glance around shows plainly the genius ruling the place. It is bears in French, and bears in German, bears on coats of arms, bears as card-receivers and hitching-posts, bears as signs, bears on top of fountains and flag-staffs, bears on clock towers to strike the hours, and in one case, whenever the hour is struck, a solemn bear nods his head at every stroke, whilst the great Berthold sits by and opens his mouth and swings his sceptre, and a procession of other bears march around. In the baker-shops the youth's favorite gingerbread is made as a bear, with Bruin's presentiment stamped upon it. All the children's toys are bears of various sizes doing all sorts of things,—sitting on their haunches, walking on their hind legs, smoking pipes, playing billiards, nursing their cubs, wearing spectacles, and in all manner of grotesque positions. And, to complete the bear-worship for which Berne is so famous, there are a half-dozen bears kept at the public expense in two magnificent bear-pits, where the population go to pay obeisance and feed them. The old grandfather bear, whose venerable looks betoken his great age, still sits on his haunches and begs for bread, whilst a woman keeps a stand near by to kindly sell it to the inhabitants. As I looked upon this ancient idol of the town,—this veritable Ursa Major,—the Philadelphia Zoological Garden was recalled to mind, and I marvelled how the old bear could be content to live so long and yet in all these years not have tasted peanuts! For many centuries these bears and their ancestors have been Berne idols. In 1798, when Napoleon despoiled almost all Europe of its most famous treasures to take to Paris, he carried thither the bears of Berne. They lived for several years in the Jardin des Plantes, but Berne was inconsolable, and when Napoleon was finally laid low the Swiss stipulated for the return of the bears, and they were brought back to happy Berne with great rejoicings. They look placid in the pits begging for bread, but it does not do for the visitor to throw himself as well as the bread over the balustrade. An English officer, by some mischance, fell in not long ago, and after a desperate struggle was torn to pieces. The people are proud of their idols, and prohibit, under severe penalties, throwing anything at them but fruit and bread.

## OTHER THINGS IN BERNE.

Whilst the bears are the chief curiosity of Berne, it is also noted for some other things. It, like most Swiss towns, is especially devoted to those useful people, the washerwomen. The chief street, and in fact almost all the streets, have fountains set up at frequent intervals, from which spouts run a perpetual supply of water for their especial use, whilst near by permanent tubs and washboards are established, at which, during almost all hours, both day and night, the women can be seen washing clothes and vigorously pounding them with paddles. Berne thus publicly recognizes the virtue of cleanliness, and also runs down the centre of its chief street a great sunken gutter for the especial drainage of these fountains and tubs, over which sundry bears, knights, and curious statues are set as guardian angels. This is called in one portion Market Street, and it would be a novel sight in Philadelphia to see on our Market Street all the city's washerwomen (including the Chinese) distributed at their tubs along the middle of the street, talking scandal and beating a tattoo on their washclothes. This is one of the sights of Berne.

The streets have no sidewalks in the older portion of Berne, but the ground-floors of the houses are made into arcades, along which people walk, whilst massive arches hold up the houses above. This makes a very strange-looking system of pillars and arches extending along the sides of the streets, while the old gateways and clock towers remain in the centres of the streets. The finest building of modern construction in Berne is the Federal Palace, where the Swiss National Council, or Congress, meets, Berne being the capital of the country. Unlike our Congress, however, which generally wants to be in session almost the whole year, the Swiss Congress is usually content with a single month's session in July, a moderation which is probably due to the fact that the debates are carried on in French, German, and Italian, and after three or four weeks the members get so mixed up that they find an early adjournment the best solution of the linguistic riddle. Berne was full of Swiss soldiers when I was there, as were also the trains coming into and going out of the city. They trudged about in immense top-boots, with rattling swords and a ferocious look, and appeared and acted decidedly more warlike than any of the troops I have seen either in England, France, or Germany. This was probably due to the peculiarity of the Swiss situation. Its neutral necessities forbid fighting with anybody, but there is nothing like keeping up good business appearances. Berne's position, perched up on a bold hill, with the swift-flowing Aar washing it almost all around, is most beautiful, the window-gardens in the city also adding to the pretty appearance which smiling gardens and green vineyards enhance on all sides beyond the town.

To get from Interlacken to Berne the journey is made along the Lake of Thun by steamer, and then by railway down the valley of the Aar. The lake, beginning among high mountains and the most rugged scenery, as the valley in which it lies gradually passes out of the Alps, becomes a quieter scene of smiling, highly-cultivated shores and pretty cottages. The broad valley of the Aar, after it flows out of the lake, is cultivated to the highest degree, the people having embanked the stream, so as to save as much land as possible. The little town of Thun is embosomed in the richest verdure, and the ride to Berne is through a rolling, highly-cultivated country, much like the farming land in the neighborhood of Philadelphia. The Swiss have not much ground to cultivate, but what arable land they have is made the most of. In all the lowlands peat was being gathered and dried for fuel, being extensively used in this part of Switzerland.

## FROM THE RHINE WATERS TO THE RHONE.

The Swiss railways charge low prices, but they manage to run the trains slower and waste more time at stations than any other railways in the world. They are among the crookedest, too, and the hilly region through which they run compels steep grades, high viaducts, and frequent tunnels. The cars, they tell us, are American cars, and so they appear outside; but when you get inside, and see how they are fitted up, you repudiate any idea of their being American. They have the aisle down the middle, but that is all. They are divided into compartments, with partitions between and doors, and the seats are straight-backed and uncomfortable, and, being fixed, half the passengers always have to ride backwards. The Swiss have built a car in which they attempt to combine both the American and English systems, and spoil both. The passenger, who is naturally disgusted at his discomfort, is told that it is an "American car"; but if he be an American, he makes haste to repudiate it on behalf of his countrymen. They have probably attempted to thus most incompletely imitate the American car out of compliment to the race who are the chief travellers in Switzerland. I am told by the hotel-keepers and railway people here that there are more American travellers in Switzerland than all other foreigners put together, and that were it not for the money left here by the Americans, the hotels, railways, storekeepers, livery-stable owners, and possibly the whole country, would be in danger of bankruptcy. As our nation, which contains the greatest travellers in the world and the most of them, is thus generous to Switzerland, the people here, in return, show us great friendliness. They overlook all mistakes in language so long as the cash is freely paid out, and in one way or another a very large part of the Swiss population subsists upon the constant stream of gold and silver, amounting to many millions in a year, which is generously poured out by the American sight-seer. If the Swiss railways are crooked and the trains slow, the railway managers are careful. The passengers are penned up in the stations until almost the moment for starting the train, for fear they may get in the wrong cars, and then there is a rush for seats that equals anything in that line elsewhere. Then about every ten minutes, on an average, the conductor comes around to examine and punch tickets. With stentorian lungs at all stations they call out the names and instructions what to do; but as it is always done either by a German speaking French, or by a Frenchman speaking German, the American is about as wise as before the oration began. I have often listened at home to railway hands who call out the names of stations with a musical twang and a foreign pronunciation that no one can comprehend—and they do the same thing in Switzerland. Thus are new countries always reproducing the customs of the old.

On one of these Swiss railways—after the rush for seats and the struggle with baggage and umbrellas that always persist in getting mixed up in car-seats when you are in a hurry and some one else similarly obstinate blocks the way—I went from Berne to Lausanne. The line ran through a rich and rolling country, very much like what we see at home, from

INTERIOR OF FREIBURG CATHEDRAL.

Berne to Freyburg, where it crossed the Sarine River on a viaduct two hundred and fifty feet high, and proceeded up the valley of that beautiful stream. It was near here, at Lake Morat, four hundred years ago, that the Swiss defeated the unfortunate Charles the Bold, of Burgundy, and slew fifteen thousand of his troops, whose bones were gathered into one sepulchre, where they remained for centuries, until the Burgundians, desiring to efface the memory of the defeat, scattered them. Then, according to tradition, began a race at carrying off the bones. Every Burgundian passing the field patriotically took a bone home to bury in his own country, whilst every Swiss carried them off to carve into knife-handles or bears, the bleaching of years having given them a remarkable whiteness, causing them to be in great request. These Morat knife-handles are still sold, and are in good supply at high prices,—but several millions of these bones having heretofore been disposed of, I did not invest. A lime-tree stands near the field, thirty-six feet in circumference, under which the Swiss are said to have held their council of war before the battle. It is on a hill that overlooks the field. Another lime-tree at Freyburg bears even date with the battle, and is almost as large as this. A young soldier was sent to Freyburg to carry news of the victory. He ran so fast that he sank down exhausted on arrival, was only able to say the one word, "Victory!" and died. In his hand was a branch of the great lime-tree at Morat, and they planted it and it has grown to enormous size. Freyburg, which was also founded by Berthold de Zahringen, has, over the Sarine, the greatest suspension bridge in Europe,—one hundred and eighty feet high and nine hundred feet long. Until the great suspension bridge at Cincinnati was built, it was the longest in the world. Freyburg also has an ancient cathedral, in which there is a great organ, considered the finest in Europe, with sixty-seven stops and eighteen hundred pipes, some of them thirty-two feet long. The most curious feature of the town, however, is the line of demarcation between German and French Switzerland passing through it. The German is spoken on the northeast, and the French on the southwest side of this line, and all the way on as the railway runs towards the Lake of Geneva, the language spoken is French. The railway continues some distance along the Sarine, and then, leaving that river, abandons the water-courses flowing north to cross the watershed to those flowing south. Heavy grades, deep cuttings, and tunnels carry the line over the summit, and we leave the affluents of the Rhine, whose waters go to the North Sea, to pass over to those of the Rhone, flowing into the Mediterranean. A few minutes accomplishes the change; the train passes into a tunnel, and on coming out we find ourselves almost on the edge of the Lake of Geneva, but elevated far above it, whilst away across on the other side rises the snow-capped peak of the Dent du Midi, nearly eleven thousand feet high. Then the railway runs along the tops of the hills, through vineyards and gardens, which gradually slope down to the lake, and as it passes on steadily comes down towards the shore, when it runs into the station at Lausanne, which famous watering-place has a situation of surpassing beauty. Here I sit in the garden where Voltaire often wrote, and where Gibbon composed much of his great history. For, whilst formerly their home, it has since been made the garden of a hotel, and it gives a view of grand attractions across the placid lake to the mountains beyond. But here too I found, as so often on this journey, that the lessons of school had to be unlearned. No one knows the Lake of Geneva here, for they all call it Lake Leman, the name the Romans originally gave it.

## LETTER XLII.

### THE GRAND ALPINE FILTER.

GENEVA, September 25.

The river Rhone collects the water that falls on the south side of the Jungfrau and her attendant peaks in the Bernese Oberland as the river Rhine collects the drainage of the northern slopes. Glaciers come down the deep furrows of the mountains on both sides. At the top they are accumulations of snow, at first soft and ductile, then, as it gradually slides down the fissure and is jostled and constrained by the impassable barriers of rocks that hedge it in, the glacier becomes more compact, compressed, and icy, and with slow progress, with many a crack and groan and upheaval, it changes from a river of snow, fed by avalanches, to a river of ice. All the time it wastes by melting, the water going to the bottom, but equally all the while it is renewed by supplies of snow at the upper end. It bears all sorts of spoils on its surface,—rocks, stones, timber, mud, and débris of every description, and finally, at the point where it attains its greatest dimensions, the waste of the glacier begins to predominate over the supply, the spoils sink to the bottom, and it gradually resolves itself into water. Out of the dirty, shrivelled, and wrinkled remains of the glacier there springs a torrent stream, which bounds merrily down the mountain-side, through gorges and over waterfalls, carrying with it mud and stones and all kinds of débris. This is the nature of the source of all the Alpine streams that flow from this famous chain towards all points of the compass, to feed all the seas that environ Europe. Scores of such torrents unite to form the river Rhone, which flows, a rapid stream, past Leuk, and Sion, and Martigny, and Bex, until it enters the Lake of Geneva. Above that entrance the Rhone is chiefly conspicuous for its dirty character, and for the spoils it bears in its turbid current. The falls at Fairmount in their time of greatest freshet do not carry down a worse coffee-colored liquid, full of all sorts of rubbish, than the Rhone, when swollen by floods, bears into the lake, which is practically a crescent-shaped widening of the river to a breadth of five to ten miles, for a distance of about fifty miles. The Rhone pours its muddy current into the lake to be purified as it passes through. The discolored liquid of the eastern end issues from the lake a delicious blue at Geneva, the water being the clearest I ever saw, so that the fish can be seen disporting far below, and the aquatic plants growing on the bottom can be distinctly traced. Thus is the famous Lake Leman, as they call it here, acting the part of an Alpine filter, and filling up its eastern end slowly, by the accumulation of mud and stones poured into it. The lake is about twelve hundred feet above the sea-level, and that is also its average depth; but the drainage of its banks sends the Rhone out of the lake with three times as much water as it brings in.

This famous lake begins among enormous snow-covered mountains at its eastern end, and gradually subsides to tamer scenery at the western end. The snow-capped Alps border the entire southern bank; but, as Geneva is approached, the range retires southward from the bank of the lake, and leaves only hills of twenty-five hundred to three thousand feet high near the shore, which little fellows are of no account in this region, being merely regarded as moderately rising ground, when Mont Blanc, looking like a long-backed, recumbent elephant covered with snow, rises behind them to the height of fifteen thousand seven hundred and thirty feet, the highest mountain in Europe. Mont Blanc is, from one end of the lake to the other, its southern sentinel, for, as the crescent curves, it leaves the mountain almost equi-distant from all points,— when the great Alpine cloud-factory permits you to see it, which has been seldom this autumn, much to the disgust of the hotel-keepers hereabout, who complain that their season is spoiled. But when it is seen its great long side stands up a snow-covered wall, its length preventing a proper appreciation of its height. Amid these mountains on one shore, and in full view of them on the opposite bank, stand many famous places, for the lake is a popular resort, and its vine-covered banks are dotted with cottages, boarding-houses, hotels, and many a building of renown. It is Savoy, in France, on the south side, and the Swiss cantons of Vaud and Valois on the north side. To recapitulate a few of the famous places on the lake, here is Coppet, where Madame De Staël lived and held her intellectual court, dying there in 1817; Nyon, founded by Julius Cæsar; Prangins, where Voltaire lived for two years; Rolle, where General La Harpe, the tutor of the Emperor Alexander of Russia, is buried, on a small island in the lake; Aubonne, where the great traveller Tavernier built his home, declaring it the place having the most enchanting view he had seen in all his voyages; Morges, with its castle nine hundred years old, from which the Swiss quickly banished the First Napoleon when he landed there on a visit when a young lieutenant, thus early having an instinctive dread of the race; Ouchy and Lausanne, famous, the former as the place where Byron wrote the " Prisoner of Chillon," and the latter as the home of Gibbon and Voltaire; Vevay, the resort of invalids, the hotel landlords proving by any amount of statistics that people are longer-lived here than anywhere else on the globe; Charens, of which both Rousseau and Byron have sung; Montreux, another favorite resort for invalids; the forbidding

Castle of Chillon, standing on a rock one hundred feet from the shore, where the prisoner Bonnivard was immured six years; Evain, with its mineral springs, where the gamblers, driven from the German watering-places, are endeavoring to revive the public gaming, but with doubtful success; and finally Geneva. These places are all located on the shore, which extends not much over one hundred miles in length around the lake.

Lausanne (which, like most of these Lake Geneva watering-places, is a city of hotels and boarding houses) was almost completing its season when we left it, for the Swiss resorts are chiefly closed by October. The view of Mont Blanc and the other snow-capped mountains across the lake had been superb the previous day, but clouds and rain obscured them as we left the hotel on the hill and went down on an inclined-plane railway to Ouchy, to embark on the steamer. Here one of those kind individuals who is always dying in these countries and leaving his accumulated millions to the cities and towns for the public benefit, had established a beautiful garden, with an ample endowment for its maintenance, and in it we awaited the steamer. The storm and wind steadily increased, until the lake was lashed into an angry ocean, and the waves dashed high over the breakwater that protected the little port. We embarked, got treated worse by the fresh-water Neptune than we ever were by his salt-water brother, and the steamer took a lot of woe-begone sea-sick passengers into the breakwater that guards Geneva. But we had the satisfaction of knowing that all this row was kicked up by the beautiful Lake Leman, and feeling that it must be all right, were content.

## MUSIC AND THE LAUNDRY.

There are only required a few hours in Geneva to convince one that the city is devoted to washerwomen, musical boxes, and watches. Mont Blanc and the Alps step down from the high pedestal, whilst the first duty of Lake Leman's beautiful blue water is to furnish a copious supply for the public washhouses along its shores. At Geneva the lake narrows with swift current into the river Rhone, and is crossed by several bridges. Jean Jacques Rousseau's Island stands in midstream, and around and below it the swans and pretty ducks are kept, whilst on both shores the city stands, fronted by the sheds floating on the water, where those useful people, the washerwomen, do their work. Whilst all Swiss towns provide for them, Geneva does it on probably the most extensive scale. You look out of the hotel window at Mont Blanc far away, the snow and clouds around its top, or the vine-clad hills nearer, and the city, with the beautiful blue water of the lake in front, or the island and the bridges and the swans, the little steamboats and fishing-craft that sail ; along and as a foil to the poetry the enchanting scene inspires, there are a hundred washerwomen right in the foreground, beating a tattoo on about the dirtiest lot of clothes that ever sought the laundry. And they are no slouches either, these nymphs who thus lave on the edges of the beautiful lake. They are up with the lark, and keep at it till dark. They use paddles and clubs to beat the dirt out, and put huge hand-scrubs on refractory cases, and slap the clouts around, and rinse out the water with heavy rolling-pins, till you sigh to think of the crop of buttons that must go floating down the Rhone, to be gathered up by the future geologist in the Mediterranean. Thus they keep at it winter and summer. making a racket almost like a kettle-drum corps, in beating the clothes, and teaching all the hotel guests how the thing is done. Geneva has from time immemorial thus honored its most useful citizens, who untaxed and untrammelled publicly teach and execute cleanliness on beautiful Lake Leman. It thinks far more of this than Alpine scenery, whether its visitors do or don't.

The Genevans who do not engage in the laundry business, chiefly manufacture watches and musical boxes. There are clocks and watches of all kinds and styles exhibited by the acre, but the Swiss watch-maker is in sore dread of his American competitor, and is sorrowing because one of the chief markets is thus gradually closing against Swiss wares. But in musical boxes Geneva takes the front rank. When the hotel is entered you hear them playing on all sides, even in the elevator, and the automatic singing birds chirp out their pretty songs among the flowers that decorate the dinner-table. The city is full of large manufactories of these boxes, and the reader will miss nothing by coming with me a few moments into one of them. You enter and shut the door behind you, and it strikes up a tune; you sit down in a chair and it plays the " Marseillaise"; a footstool is pushed to you, and the moment the foot is upon it, it starts up "Coming Thro' the Rye." If thirsty, the water-pitcher that you lift and the glass you drink from both play tunes. You look at pretty work-boxes and jewel-caskets, and, on opening the lids, some will start music, whilst out of others jump little birds to carol their lays. A complete orchestra of monkeys, with most amusing gyrations, play the Swiss favorite airs, whilst if you take a cigar, the cigar-case opens to music; and the clock cannot strike without giving an opera overture. Music is concealed in everything around, and a hundred pretty miniature Swiss cottages stand on the shelves, to discourse music if started. The ingenuity of the Swiss in thus putting music into everything is remarkable, and they are also wonderfully proficient in the manufacture of the more elaborate boxes, with harp, drum, bells, flutes, and sometimes full orchestra accompaniments.

The Duke of Brunswick, another of those kind people to whom I have referred, has recently died and bequeathed Geneva a fortune of five millions of dollars, and the happy people are putting up a monument in his memory alongside my hotel. It is to be two hundred feet high, and will take a long time to complete. It will be visible many miles along the lake, and be another of the many attractions of this beautiful city. It was in Geneva that John Calvin lived many years, and John Knox came here when exiled from Britain. Relics of both are frequently shown. Geneva also has memories of Voltaire, but seems most to cherish those of Rousseau. Whilst famous for her history, ancient and modern, for it was here the Alabama Claims Commission made the fifteen million five hundred thousand dollars award against England, I must not forget to mention, among other Genevan characteristics, her chimney-pots. In other parts of the world the builder of the chimney-pot, no matter how numerous or how strange looking they may be, is content to have them stand upright, but Geneva, whilst imitating every other chimney-pot absurdity elsewhere invented, adds the additional grotesqueness of having them all bent and twisted at angles. Millions of them seem to be thrust out on top of the houses, and they are all intoxicated,—all apparently falling over in different directions, making the most ridiculously absurd chimney-pot exhibition that can be conceived of. But the town has redeeming qualities, and one of its most charming spots is Jean Jacques Rousseau's Island, a most lovely little place in the mid-river just where the lake pours out its torrent into the Rhone. Here, watching the swans, and the clouds, and Mont Blanc, the people love to sit and sip their wine and beer, dispensed at a conveniently-located restaurant, whereto the proprietor thinks he is alluring the American visitor by displaying a sign announcing that he can successfully concoct that well-known American drink, which his sign describes as a "sherry-gobler."

## LETTER XLIII.

#### GOING INTO THE ALPS.

CHAMOUNIX, September 27.

Amid clouds and rain, and with the mercury almost down to the freezing-point, we started early in the morning from Geneva to pay a visit to that exalted curiosity, the King of the Alps, Mont Blanc,—or, in English, the "White Mountain." It has heretofore been noticed that the highest mountains of the world are always called the "White Mountains" or the "Snow Mountains." As the highest mountains are always snow-covered, they therefore appear white, and the earliest lookers at them naturally named them according to their color, so that, if we trace out their names in the various languages, they are always found to be, when translated into English, the synonyme for "white" or for "snow," whether those names be given in Savoy, or India, or Thibet, or Africa, or America; whether it be the White Mountains of New England, or Cotapaxi in the Andes, or the Sierra Nevada, or the Himalayas, or Mont Blanc, or other distinct mountains or ranges. Having thus properly introduced the white-topped monster of Savoy, who has probably been studied and visited the most of all the famous mountains of the world, I will go on to describe the journey we made to see him, in another of those gig-topped carriages, with three horses driven abreast, with which this celebrated but very hilly region abounds. We huddled together closely, for the air was keen and the north wind came sweeping down Lake Leman, but we were told the rain would soon cease for better weather was indicated by the unfailing barometer the lake afforded. As a lighter atmospheric pressure indicates a storm, so a heavier pressure presages its cessation, and the lake acts just like a barometer. Its surface will rise and fall sometimes as much as five feet in a brief period, this being caused entirely by changes in atmospheric pressure. So the Genevans, in a rain-storm, by looking out of their windows at the current in the Rhone running out of the lake, can immediately tell a heavier pressure by the swifter running of the water; and so it was when we started, they foretold a cessation of rain, and the rain ceased within two hours, though the clouds hung about all day.

We started, drove over the bridge across the Rhone, and passed through the portion of Geneva which rejoices in possessing the three streets—Hell, Purgatory, and Paradise. If you are in Purgatory, you turn round the corner at one end into Hell, and at the other into Paradise. We did not stop in either, and only had time to notice that a woe-begone lot of draggled people were in all three places. Our driver cracked his whip and chirruped the horses, and each merrily jingling a long string of sleigh-bells they briskly trotted along, showering mud on all behind them. Every animal carries a bell in this country. The horses all have bells; also the goats, and also the cows, and no properly-regulated Alpine cow is satisfied with the very modest bell that suffices in our country. They carry bells of the largest size,—some big enough for church-bells, and most of them large enough for a steamboat. Thus we went briskly and noisily along the road towards Chamounix, the driver cracking his whip and making a great row whenever we passed through a village, in order to duly impress the gaping inhabitants, and get all the idle dogs to bark after us, and in a short time we were out of Switzerland and crossed the frontier of France into Savoy. There was no Custom-House examination, this region of the High Alps being exempted, and we had not left Geneva long before we crossed the Menage River on a high bridge, and were at once introduced to picturesque scenery. The road then sought the valley of the swift-flowing Arve, and followed this stream all the way up to the foot of Mont Blanc. It was one of the greatest rides that any one could take, for it passed through scenery that gradually changed from a broad

L*

and fertile valley to a mountain gorge, or cañon, where tremendous precipices were far above, and abysses far below, and the rugged mountain-sides poured out their torrents of water, mud, and stones, until they divested the valley of almost all chance of fertility. Yet through all this inhospitable region there was constructed one of the best roads in Europe, a wagon way everywhere at least twenty feet wide, solidly built, with a smooth surface as good as any in Fairmount Park, curbed and thoroughly drained, and with gradients easy enough for a railroad. It was a triumph of engineering, the most of it having been made by Napoleon III., and it was of the costliest description, for miles of it have had to be blasted out of the solid rock or supported on walls sometimes fifty feet high. Its bridges were all solid stone structures, and it followed the river up, sometimes on one side and sometimes on the other, as the best opportunity for construction was afforded, until it brought us to the Valley of Chamounix. As we progressed the mountains became higher, and their sides more precipitous. Sometimes we passed around bends in the gorge that were like tremendous amphitheatres; sometimes through fissures that looked as if an earthquake had rent them solely to let the torrent stream and the road pass through. Waterfalls frequently shot over the mountain-side, and sent rushing torrents under us and into the Arve. One of these, the cascade of Arpenaz, said to be the highest waterfall in Savoy, comes down a fissure in a mountain nine thousand feet high, shoots over a projecting precipice, and falls so far that it is entirely dissipated into spray; then collects again on rocks a thousand feet below, becomes a tumbling series of little cascades, and finally hurls itself into the Arve. Other falls jump over the rocks, bury themselves in subterranean passages, and finally come out again as bubbling fountains far below. Every torrent is bordered by the vast accumulations of stones and débris which it brings down in spring-time freshets and scatters far and wide. They all have to be given broad beds, for when the snow melts fast in the spring they carry all before them. The Arve was filled with huge boulders, and had along it many snagged trees, the relics of the last freshet, and it, even now in its gentler mood, swept down the valley with a roar like a young Niagara. All the way the road went it gradually mounted an ascent till it passed around a sharp point of rocks, went through a tunnel, and in the midst of snow-covered mountains and glaciers gradually resolving themselves into torrents, it passed through a tremendous gorge, and brought us into the Valley of Chamounix, which is elevated eighteen hundred feet above Geneva, and three thousand feet above the sea. Here, with snow-capped mountains all around, and in a place which, before the great road was made, few travellers visited, we alighted after ten hours' brisk riding, with fresh relays of horses, and passed the night.

## CHAMOUNIX AND MONT BLANC.

Chamounix is the goal of the Alpine traveller. It brings him face to face with Mont Blanc, surrounds him with snow and ice, reduces his temperature, gives him plenty of clouds and dampness, and depletes his purse in fees for guides and mules. The whole world around Chamounix is set on edge, and every visitor is expected to climb over the top of it. The more fatiguing the expedition taken the more he has to pay for it. For sixty to one hundred dollars you can have the privilege of climbing up Mont Blanc at the risk of your life, and after getting tired enough to require a month to rest, have your name spelt wrong in the official list of the "*Ascensionistes en Mont Blanc,*" one of the most sadly-printed books I ever saw, and the English names in which, judging by the way they are misspelled, seem to have been set up by an Italian in the French language. For a less sum you can take a less risk, and may be less tired. The people at the hotels here talk only of Alpine ascensions; of going up Mont Blanc to get an appetite for breakfast; of tramping over glaciers and scaling rocks; of skipping with light hearts (by the aid of the omnipresent Alpine stick) over little hillocks eight thousand feet high; of riding forty miles a day on a mule; and similar feats. To walk on level ground is undignified, they all prefer going up-hill. And so they jabber away in Anglicized French in the sitting-room as they gather around the fire these cold nights, and tell of what somebody else said he did yesterday, and what they expect themselves to do to-morrow. Chamounix is a town of hotels and boarding-houses, all with grand views, for look where you will, there are snow-capped mountains and glaciers,—but it has not yet been reached by the railway, though one could be easily constructed along the magnificent road with the easy gradients that brought us from Geneva, and perhaps will some day, for nowhere else than in this secluded vale, away up in the Alps, can a better idea be got of snow-covered mountains. Chamounix gets its name from the Latin words "*champs munis*," or "fortified grounds," alluding to its strong mountain defences; but the residents prefer to derive the name from the chamois goat which flourishes on its mountain-sides, and it gets its fame from Mont Blanc, which rises fifteen thousand seven hundred and thirty feet high on its southern edge. One hundred and forty years ago adventurous scientists began to visit and study its glaciers, but it was not until 1786 that Balmat and Dr. Paccard made the first ascension, and 1787 that De Saussure made his ascension with Colonel Baufroy. The first lady— Mlle. Paradis—ascended the mountain in 1809, whilst the first Americans—Messrs. Howard and Rensselaer—ascended in 1819. On the 6th of September, 1870, three persons, two of them Americans, attempted the ascension, with three guides, and all perished. Now the ascensions average fifty a year, and are considered safe to make, though very fatiguing and occupying two or three days. The first day the visitor goes to the huts of the Grand Mulets; the second, he starts at midnight and goes to the summit in time to see the sun rise, and then he descends on the second and third days, unless he is robust enough to compress the fatigue into one day. The view from the Valley of Chamounix is of most extraordinary description. It is a deep, narrow valley, with a slight curve, bordered by tremendous precipices, snow-covered at the tops, and rising to the height of nine thousand to ten thousand feet on the north side, and much higher on the south. Out of the snowy tops are thrust the bare, jagged, pointed rocks, that are the higher Alpine peaks, generally bare of snow, because they are too steep for it to stay on them, and looking like blunt-pointed needles, which leads the people here to call almost all of them by that name. Great fissures are rent in their sides, down which come glaciers, or the dry beds of spring-time torrents. Below the snow verdure covers them, gradually changing from grass to bushes and trees as the mountain is descended. At the bottom of the valley is a flat fertile surface, which is carefully cultivated, but it forms but a small portion, and is frequently crossed by great stony morains, whose torrent beds run into the Arve. There are a few villages here, of which Chamounix is the chief, but it would be of very little size were it not for the hotels and boarding-houses. In fact, almost the entire subsistence of the people in this nearly-desolate valley is upon the stranger. Visitors come to see the sights, and the people earn a subsistence by serving them as guides, chair-carriers, muleteers, coach-drivers, and hotel-servants. Mont Blanc and the glaciers, and the snow-capped hundreds of mountain-tops around, bring Chamounix its wealth; yet the people, like many elsewhere, are unsatisfied with this, and are endeavoring to get for their valley a reputation because it contains mineral springs. How strange some people are! This valley is unknown abroad excepting as a mountain vale, yet its people want to make it a bathing-place for invalids, and cover the hotel rooms with placards that describe it, in very queerly-worded English, as a prospective Baden or Saratoga. A great bath it can never be, but the chief resort for getting glorious mountain views it will probably remain as long as human beings love sight-seeing.

## GOING UP THE ALPS.

On the morning of Thursday, September 26, 1878, there was seen solemnly marching out of Chamounix, with the undersigned bringing up the rear, a procession of seven donkeys, in single file. It might have been doubted which were the donkeys, the quadrupeds who did the marching, or the bipeds who rode them, but, judging from the remarks of some of the bipeds, *they* had no doubt on the subject. There were three ladies, two little children, and two men, with four guides leading the animals, a necessary precaution because the latter understood only French, and all the American "get-ups" and "whoas" that were uttered, no matter how vigorously pronounced, were entirely lost upon these long-eared beasts, that had only been educated in the polite and diplomatic language of the Court of Versailles. It was a picturesque party, with heads muffled in shawls, stockings drawn over shoes, and wearing ancient clothing, and those who had never been on mule-back before carried it by a large majority. The procession started amid clouds and unpromising weather, and slowly wound around among the little fields and stunted bushes of the valley, until it reached a zigzag path up the mountain-side. Then up the narrow, stony, crooked bridle-path it mounted to scale the Alps. Gradually, as each angle in the road was turned, the procession was raised above the valley towards the clouds that obscured the mountain-tops, and before very long it entered the clouds whilst still toiling up the ascent. Then nothing could be seen, though far below the roar of the rushing Arve could be heard, and also the twanging of at least one thousand cow-bells, for those useful animals were feeding all down the mountain-side and in the valley, each with a boy or girl watching it, as no cow pastures in this mountain region uncared for. Everything was dripping with moisture, and everybody was very cold, but they nobly toiled up the ascent in search of the unseen heights above. Yawning precipices opened alongside the narrow path down which a misstep would have thrown us to destruction, but the beasts, whilst not pretty to look at, were sure-footed, and if they did try once in a while to rub off their awkward riders against a stone, or stopped short, whenever they felt like it, regardless of the torrent of orders given them in the strongest American language, the offence was pardoned for the safety they insured. The guides would beat them, and cry "Vit!" and "Allée!" which is horse-talk in French, but the beasts knew they were masters of the situation and went along as it suited them, finally bringing the procession up to the region of snow. Then the clouds thinned above us, and we knew we were getting above them, and, finally, the sun burst out in all his radiance, for two hours' zigzag ascent of the mountain had raised us above the clouds, and there thrusting out their jagged heads in all directions around us were the peaks of the Alps, snow covered where the rocks were not too steep to hold it, whilst all below was encompassed in clouds. Still we toiled up the ascent, and the view became grander and grander, until having reached the top with the sun pouring his hottest rays upon us, we saw a sight which it was worth travelling four thousand miles from America to see. In every direction were thrust up the rocky peaks, pointed and needle-like, which mark the highest Alps. Snow lay in every fissure. There was no sign of vegetation. In scores of places glaciers flowed down, making those amazing rivers of ice, which look like a sea in a storm suddenly stilled and frozen, and snow then powdered over it to smooth the rougher edges. There was nothing in view but peaks and snow above and around us, and clouds below. But the sun's rays finally prevailed over the clouds, and, dissipating them, gave a view of all that was below; of the mountain-side that we had ascended, rocky and snowy at the top, gradually changing to trees and verdure below; of the great glaciers coming down enormous fissures in the mountain, and then uniting into the grand Sea of Ice, which flows slowly down the inclined plane between two mountains, cracking, groaning, and melting, until it resolves itself into the seething torrent that courses down to the valley far below to swell the Arve. The valley could be traced, its stream like a silver streak, its villages like spots amid the green, its course curving grandly around far away on either hand, amid two magnificent rows of snow-capped mountains, with Mont Blanc guarding it on the south and sending many a silvery glacier into it. The snow, which had fallen copiously during the early morning, was melting, so that it was damp underfoot and everything seemed to be resolving itself into running water. But we cared little for that. We had mounted many thousand feet until we had gone far above the clouds and the snow line, and there amid peaks twelve thousand to over fifteen thousand feet high, we were enjoying what all travellers agree is the greatest mountain view the world affords.

But we could not stay there forever, and, as the day waned, we must come down again, and here we learned additional experience. Going up-hill on a strange mule is one thing, going down is another. The beast is probably as sure-footed one way as the other, but the rider, as he thinks he is about pitching over the animal's head, don't always think so. Two minutes' mule-riding down the Alps made us forget all about grand views, glaciers, and glory. The beast has a fashion of raising his stern when going down-hill,—that is, to say the least, exciting, and the deeper the yawning abyss before you, the more sudden seems the rise. Then he has no regard whatever for the rider's legs, but goeth where he listeth, heedless of the jagged rocks protruding almost across the path that threaten to sweep the rider off. It was useless to talk to him, for he knew not the strange tongue, and whether threat or caress, the effect was the same. The guides understood no better than the beasts. When the animal threatened to throw you about seven thousand feet down the mountain-side, your eloquent remarks on the subject were entirely lost on both. The mule ahead never seemed to go fast enough to keep out of the way, and the mule in the rear was always running against you. It is hardly necessary to say these electrifying experiences of the devious, narrow, and very dangerous mountain-path soon drove all the cold out of the entire party and put every one in a profuse perspiration. But all things come to an end in this world, and the hours of zigzag winding down the mountain-side, all the time in full view of and almost over the town, ultimately brought us to it. There was a thankful party arrived from the journey, and when we looked back up the steep, the top was again obscured in clouds. But we had scaled the Alps, seen their greatest view, triumphed over the mules, and were happy.

## LETTER XLIV.

### AN ALPINE NEGOTIATION.

GENEVA, September 30.

Although Chamounix is a magnificent place, and displays the glory of the Alps in the highest degree, it is not a very comfortable region in which to spend the winter, and as the mercury persisted in going below the freezing-point, we were admonished after some days that it was time to leave. But leaving this remote place is involved in some difficulty, for it is far away from any railway, and carriages have to be taken for the purpose. We could have retraced the route to Geneva, but preferred if possible to go another way, yet the only other ways offered were routes over the mountains to Martigny, which stands on the Rhone away up the valley beyond the head of Lake Geneva. There are two such routes, one available only for mules, and the other for a peculiar style of open wagon they have at Chamounix, built very narrow and light. We had had enough, however, of donkey exhibitions, for all hands were sore from their experiences in that line, so we selected the wagon-route, known as the "Pass of the Tête Noire," and began to negotiate for wagons. The people of the

United States always have a profound sense of their own superior business abilities, and they will be glad to hear that in this negotiation it was demonstrated to the fullest extent. The tariff of prices set up in the hotel, which it was declared was never deviated from, required the payment of one hundred and fifty francs for two wagons, which were necessary for carrying the party, and it was signed in bold characters by the chief of the Association of Wagoners of Chamounix. This tariff was duly conned over and inquired about, and we were assured that it could not be broken or the price cheapened. But we had come from America, where in some localities there is a fashion of making laws that are not always enforced, and, having an idea that Savoy might have learned the same thing, inquiries were begun outside. A day's negotiation led to the most wonderful results. The Trade Society of Wagoners could not lower their prices, but there appeared a man who thought, if Monsieur made it an object, that he could find some one who would. So he soon discovered a Swiss who proposed to do the work for less money. There appears to be an enmity between the Swiss and the Chamounix Savoyard, and this cheapening being announced, the Chamounix society, having got a new light on the subject, thought they might do better. Each side abused the other's wagons and drivers, as they gradually came down in prices. The bidding was spirited, and the one hundred and fifty francs were lowered to eighty francs, and the Swiss still held the field. This had gone on the best part of the day, and seemed to be the chief subject of discussion among the townsfolk, when just at dusk new negotiators appeared offering even lower prices, and finally a committee waited upon us, consisting of the leading men of the Association, with the chief at their head, whose authorization was affixed to the tariff. They appeared, hats in hand, and said the Chamounix people were poor; that the Swiss came up there from Geneva and tried to take away their occupation from them; that they loved America; and finally, what was more essential, that they were very anxious to serve us, to vindicate their society, and would gladly do the work for sixty francs, promising their best wagons and best drivers. We closed the bargain, and Savoy triumphed. They gave us good wagons and good drivers, and after we went over the horrible road, with its fearful hills, we were sure the job would have been cheap at thrice the money, and that the horse makes a mistake when he is born in Switzerland or in Savoy.

### THE "MAUVAIS PAS."

We started soon after daylight on a cold, clear, frosty morning. Mont Blanc and all of the two grand ranks of snow-covered mountains that enclose the famous valley were clearly visible. The glaciers glistened and the hoar-frost whitened everything. The town was all astir, for the negotiation had excited the people, and they gave us a royal send-off in honor of the victory over the Swiss. The chief assisted us into the wagons, and the men and women all along the road, as we quickly trotted out of the town, bade us God-speed. It was the first time ever I knew hackmen to be so much more delighted at taking less. We were pleased too, as they were, though it was very cold, and Jack Frost made the ears and toes tingle. Yet cold as we were, there were women and children out in the little cultivated patches of ground, some of them barefooted, digging potatoes, and the entire valley was resonant with cow-bells, as all the animals were being driven to pasture, each with its tremendous bell and its guardian, the latter often being women who carried babies, or knitted as they trudged along. The road passed eastward up the valley, with the swift-rushing Arve coursing along, first on one side and then on the other. It was a narrow, winding way, originally intended only for a mule-path, and all along huge stone-piles were placed on one side, intended as buoys to mark the route when the valley is covered with snow. We passed the Mer de Glace (Sea of Ice) with a magnificent view, and the little stream into which this great glacier resolves itself, came rushing, through a vast morain of débris, down to our feet. Then we toiled up a tremendous hill, and came in full view of the mountain known as the Silver Needle, which sends down another great glacier, and getting gradually into a ravine which led away from the Arve, we mounted up a height of five thousand feet, and crossed the summit of the mountain pass known as the Montets. This was one of the wildest and most desolate regions I ever saw. Nobody lived there; nothing grew but stunted grass and moss; there was scarcely a tree or bush to be seen, but the whole place was covered with huge boulders dropped about indiscriminately, and some of them as large as a three-story house. Even the cows and goats which we saw almost everywhere else avoided this inhospitable region, around which barren rocks kept guard, running up to the snow-covered mountains, whose rocky, bare peaks stood out against the sky. It was a tremendous hill to climb, but the Chamounix horses were used to the work. The men all walked, thus lightening the load. Having crossed the summit, the head of the Eau Noire, or Blackwater, appeared, and we began descending on that side, to go around the dark and repulsive mountain that gives its name to the pass, the Tête Noire, or the Black Head. Rocks and desolation reigned on this side, but the road was down-hill, and that was a satisfaction, though it brought us deeper and deeper into the dark and narrow valley. Here to comfort us was a monument erected to a French nobleman, some time ago overwhelmed in this pass by an avalanche. Down through the savage and barren region we jolted at a brisk pace, because the Swiss and Savoyard horses always trot down-hill, as it is the only chance they have to trot at all, but the road was frequently a breakneck one, narrow, filled with stones, and as uncomfortable to ride on as some of our Philadelphia cobble-stone streets. Directly an occasional hut appeared, and then a cow or two was seen hunting for herbage, and afterwards we passed some little sad-looking villages, with miserable houses, and a most poverty-stricken appearance. Getting finally to the bottom, we passed the pretty cascade of Barberine, and just beyond it crossed the boundary between France and Switzerland, marked by a square stone at the roadside. There was no custom-house, for there did not appear enough vegetation in the whole valley to support a revenue officer. Then we left the Blackwater, and gradually toiling up the side of the Black Head Mountain, mounted towards the terrible-looking gorge which gives this route the name of the "Mauvais Pas," or the Bad Pass. Here, at a small inn by the roadside, we stopped to refresh the horses. From the front door you looked up thousands of feet to the mountain-top, whilst from the back door a stone would drop a thousand feet into the torrent below. At this inn were a half-dozen of those famous St. Bernard dogs that do such good service in these Swiss passes in times of snow. They were large, good-looking, and hungry, and, very much like dogs at home, gathered around the table to pick up scraps. For a hundred francs I could have bought a little fellow four weeks old, that the landlady was anxious to sell, as she had enough St. Bernard boarders already.

After the rest we started again, and found that the route diverged into two gorges, one going off through the Trient, and the other, which we took, turning suddenly to the right between two mountains. This was the worst portion of this very bad pass. The narrow, devious road, more fit for mules than wagons, and on which there was only occasional room for two wagons to pass, toiled up-hill again, being hewn out of the rocky side of an abyss, the bottom of which, far down below, was filled with boulders, snagged trees, and all sorts of rubbish brought down by the torrent. Up we toiled through the narrow defile, occasionally peeping over the edge, or dropping a stone, whose fall was so far off we could not hear it, and this was unanimously voted about the worst-looking region that Nature could possibly invent. There was not a redeeming feature, and scarcely a foothold for the road, excepting what was artificial. But we got through it safely, though sometimes with bated breath, and, coming out, saw in full view in front of us the glacier of Trient, flowing down the mountain-side, which forms the torrent that runs through the bottom of the defile. The mountain stood up in front of us like a wall, but away up in a little indentation was a hut. We asked if men could possibly live in such a place. The answer, laughingly given, was that they could, and that we would see how they lived there, for that hut stood on the summit of the Forclaz, the mountain that we must go over, and that the road led to the hut. We were astonished, but submissive; in fact, were willing to go anywhere to get away from the miserable region we had just passed through. Then the road began to ascend, zigzag, roundabout, turning and twisting, up the almost perpendicular side of the hill. It was a hill of hills; a most exhausting drag up, but we did it; got to the hut on the summit; found it a little inn, and then were rewarded with a magnificent view. On one side of the narrow ridge on which we stood was the deep valley and the terrible defile through which we had passed, with all the Mont Blanc range of Alps behind it. Walking a few feet to the other side was seen the Valley of the Rhone, the two great mountains guarding the head of Lake Leman, and the Jungfrau and the Bernese Alps far away behind them. The horses rested a few minutes and then started down-hill again, for the road zigzagged down that side in the same fashion as it zigzagged up on the other. There was Martigny, almost beneath us, looking so near, though far below, that you could almost throw a stone and hit the little church spire. We trotted briskly down-hill, sometimes in imminent danger of rolling over a precipice; sometimes through woods and bushes; sometimes on so narrow a ledge that there was scarcely room for the wagon; and the farther we went, though still down, down, the more distant seemed the town. Occasionally a cow disputed the road with us, and there was as much trouble getting her out of the way as there usually is with a cow on a railroad. We jolted over stones and went around sharp angles, all holding on tight, and the wagon-brake fixed firmly. It was one of the worst rides that any one could take, and after two hours of it down-hill, with every bone bruised sore, we at length got to Martigny, which had seemed from the summit to be so near; and near it was, so far as horizontal measurement went, but perpendicularly it was a great way off. After a nine hours' ride we turned into the great St. Bernard road, and the horses trotted merrily into the town. They had accomplished the worst day's work they could be put to, and we had ridden through the worst pass in Europe.

## MARTIGNY.

Martigny is not a very attractive town in itself, but it stands in a magnificent position. Snow is all around, also high mountains and the most terrific-looking rocks and gorges, yet the valley in which it stands, like most of the Swiss valleys, has a level, fertile surface, bordering the swift-flowing, muddy Rhone, and is highly cultivated. Up on the hill side, several hundred feet above the town, stands the ancient castle of La Batiaz, built six hundred years ago by Peter of Savoy, and its dark-gray, round tower, over which floats the red cross of Switzerland, commands a view of the three deep, narrow valleys that diverge from Martigny, that from La Forclaz, down which we had come over the mountain from Chamounix; that along which the Rhone flows from the Simplon; and, turning a right angle, that by which the Rhone flows on to Lake Leman. In the centre of the town there is a little grove of trees, in which is set up a modest graystone monument where two roads diverge. This little monument marks the point where two roads of world-wide fame start to cross the Alps. On one side it bears the word "Simplon," and on the other "St. Bernard." The famous Pass of the Simplon, constructed by Napoleon as a military road, begins at this little monument, and starting at right angles from it is the road over the other famous pass, the Great St. Bernard. Both are fine roads, toiling up the Alps by devious ways, and across their top in the lowest available places, and down again on the other side into Italy. Martigny's chief business seemed to be to furnish guides and carriages for these passes, and for that to Chamounix. It is a sad-looking, sprawling village, scattered in bits about the valley, with generally poor houses, and with a great number of cases of goitre visible among the inhabitants, this disease being prevalent in Switzerland, and particularly so at Martigny, owing to the swampy land near there. The Rhone tumbles through the town in a bed about eighty feet wide, and comes from the great glacier away up near the Pass of the Simplon, for it drains all the Alps in that direction, and receives many a little torrent on its way down, and then it courses on through the valley to the lake. Martigny's only events are the occasional arrival and departure of railway trains and wagons; it subsists on the passing traveller; its mornings are sonorous with out-going and its evenings with in-coming cow-bells; and so it will probably continue till the Alps engulf it, or till the end of time.

### TURNING HOMEWARD.

Martigny was the farthest point from home of our tour, and from here begins the backward journey, for the American Line steamer is to take us home on October 16, and there is not time for any farther wanderings across the Alps into Italy. So, after several days of Alpine jolting, we again took the comfortable railway to get out of the cold and cheerless region into a more favorable climate. We went down the Valley of the Rhone, which flows through gorges that seem to be rent for its special passages, among enormous snow-covered mountains, and we passed a dozen waterfalls, the chief being the celebrated Pissevache, which is a magnificent cascade of the height of Niagara, though not so wide. A copious stream pours out of the mountain, and tumbles, a perfect waterfall, into the valley below, and then rushes a torrent into the Rhone. Some of the formations along the sides of this remarkable valley are like those of the Havana and Watkins Glens, well known to your readers, where the water has been boiling around like a pot for ages, has made both circular and square formations, and has then been let down and has all run away, so as to disclose these strange, but massive, workings in the rocks. As we pass down the valley two enormous snow-covered mountains guard it on either hand, and appear to come together in front and bar the passage. On the left is the Dent du Midi, and on the right the Dent de Morcles, each over ten thousand feet high. In the German Alps all the peaks were called "horns"; at Chamounix, in France, they were all "needles"; and here among the Italian Swiss they are all "teeth." These mountain peaks have resemblances to all three. The two "teeth" of which I have spoken, however, do not entirely close the valley. There is in one place just room for the river torrent to rush through; whilst over it the high road passes on a bridge, having a buttress resting on each mountain; and there not being room for the railway, it takes to a tunnel. Above this comes out the romantic Gorge du Trient, the other end of which was passed on the road from Chamounix to Martigny. It looks so tall, so narrow, and so deep, that it seems as if some Titan had chopped it out of the rock by a single blow of a massive axe. Away up on the mountain-sides were houses clinging to the rocks, making one wonder how people ever get up to them, and even there, at the risk of their lives, men and women were cultivating little patches of soil. All along these places there is in the spring and early summer constant risk of avalanches, and they tell of terrible disasters that have in this way occurred.

The Rhone flows into Lake Leman, and the railway passes out of the valley to run along the edge of the narrow lake. The train stops at the stations and the passengers get in and out, and as the new-comer lifts his hat, you think, returning the salutation, how very polite these Italian-Swiss are. But the new-comer sits down and, after the requisite preparation, lights up probably the most villainous pipe in all Switzerland, and your opinion is changed. The rule on these railways is to smoke everywhere excepting where it is expressly forbidden, thus reversing the American system. The railway runs all the way from one end of the lake to the other, and on its route passes the famous Castle of Chillon, where Byron's "prisoner" was immured. It is not far from the head of the lake, and Bonnivard's imprisonment does not seem to have much shortened his life, for he lived after his release until he was seventy-five. The Castle is a thousand years old, but its present form dates back six hundred years. It is a light-gray aggregation of a half-dozen square and round towers, coming up apparently out of the water, for it is built on a low rock near the shore. It does not look very inviting, and must have been a vile prison. It is now used as an arsenal, and over the entrance the Swiss have written "God bless all who come in and go out." The railway runs through an almost constant succession of vineyards as the lake gradually widens, and away across the water can be seen the snow-covered mountains with Mont Blanc's flattened top crowning the range. Thus through the vines, on a genial September day, the lake, as we passed, gradually changing its color to a delicious blue, we rode back to Geneva. The windows were open, the sunshine warm and the air balmy,—a most remarkable change from the Arctic experiences we had had such a short time before.

## LETTER XLV.

### JOURNEYING DOWN THE RHONE.

Lyons, October 1.

The city of Geneva is so surrounded by mountains that railways have some difficulty in getting out. There are only two available routes, and these require much costly construction. The road from Geneva to Paris, therefore, is by either a roundabout one, for the railway in one case has to go southwest down the Valley of the Rhone, and in the other northeast along the edge of the lake until an opportunity is offered near Lausanne to climb the hills. Both routes at first lead away from Paris, yet one or other must be taken to get to that city. We started down the Rhone so as to go to Paris by the way of Lyons. The railway kept closely to the riverbank, for it was the only means of getting through the enormous hills of which the whole country in that neighborhood seems to be made. On one side of the river were the spurs of the Alps, and on the other the mountains of Jura. The river ran in foaming torrents deep down in the narrow valley, whilst the railway was constructed on ledges in the rocks away up on the mountain-side, winding about among the hills, which projected in great knobs, making the course of the Rhone very crooked, running through frequent tunnels, and out over high viaducts that led the line far up above little boiling cascades that came down from the hills. The whole formation of this strange region was a series of vast rocky amphitheatres, each opening by narrow gateways into the other, with evidences, such as are seen at Watkins Glen, that at some time the water had been penned up in them and had been boiling around, fashioning out a succession of huge cauldrons. Thus the line coursed down the Rhone, giving magnificent scenery to look at, and quickly taking us out of Switzerland and into France. The frontier is about as plainly marked as a national boundary can be. Chancy, the frontier town of Switzerland, is passed, and beyond it two mountains rise up almost closing the way, the river having evidently burst a passage between them, as it had done in a dozen other places above and below. These mountains guard the entrance to France, Mont Vouache standing on the Savoy side and Mont Credo on the other, the outermost peak of the Juras. The river runs through a wild and narrow gorge; the almost perpendicular sides of the mountains bar out the sunlight; and on the frowning sides of Mont Credo is fashioned the great fortress of Ecluse, formerly facing both Switzerland and Italy, but now, since Savoy has become part of France, it guards only against Switzerland, and has, therefore, lost much of its importance. It is, however, a great fortress, thoroughly commanding the pass and all its approaches, with its batteries terraced up the hill-side, and is considered one of the chief strongholds in Europe. The railway, having got into this wild and difficult region, must get out some way, so it makes a drive right under Mont Credo, passing through a tunnel two and a half miles long, which was three years constructing, and cost one million five hundred thousand dollars. This overcomes the chief obstruction of the Jura range, but a half-dozen other tunnels are also necessary to pierce the mountain spurs, and then the train arrives at Bellegarde, the French frontier town, where the Custom-House is located.

Here the passengers and their baggage are all turned out of the train and marched into the customs office. In solemn procession, bags and bundles in hand, they proceed, in single file, through one door after another guarded by fierce-looking French soldiers, and are asked questions which they don't understand. This frontier has the reputation of being very closely watched, and probably it is. It is the only place where I have been that I was asked to show a passport. I had none, and found that it made no difference. " I am an American," was the cabalistic phrase that passed me through. They had no fear of Americans plotting for the capture of the fortress of Mont Credo. Then I moved on with the procession and laid down the travel-stained bags on the counter where the customs officers examined the baggage. In front of me was a laboring man, in a smock frock. He had a bundle slung on his back,—they carry everything tied on their backs here, even their umbrellas. It consisted of a piece of rough cloth in which a whetstone was wrapped, and a pair of aged boots. The official seized the bundle and made a speech over it, unwrapped the whetstone, held the boots up to the light, shook them, looked into them, got into a dispute and almost into a fight with the man. But nothing came out of the boots, and finally each one was chalked on the sole, to indicate that they were passed. My heart sank within me as the fierce-looking official, dressed like a field-marshal, with his sword ready to leap from the scabbard, turned from his contest with the boots to frown upon me. I was not too much scared, however, not to be able to gasp out the great word "American." He heard it, and the influence was magical. " What is this?" he asked in the politest French, taking hold of a bundle, the prominent object in which was my veteran overcoat, that has survived four winters. " American old clothes," I answered in the purest English. He chalked the bundle, and turned to a travelling-bag, which he gently pressed with his finger. I prepared for unstrapping it, but the moment I said " American dirty clothes" he deterred me, chalked the bag and all the others I had, made a polite bow, and then dived into an immense trunk, which a German alongside of me owned, and tried to get at something in the bottom. The word "American" accomplished it all, and I passed thus easily through one of the strictest Custom-Houses in Europe without unfastening a strap or exhibiting a passport. After the half-hour these ceremonies required, the journey was resumed, and the train for hours passed through the wildest scenery as the line curved in and out of the valleys and gorges of the Juras. At Culoz diverged the branch line which goes through the Mont Cenis tunnel into Italy; at Amberien, the main line which goes thence through Macon and Dijon to Paris; and then, the country quickly subsiding into a level plain, strangely contrasting with the mountainous character of the earlier journey, we coursed quickly over a prairie to the Rhone again and were at Lyons. We passed inside the fortifications, went almost entirely around the buildings, and alighted in the famous city which stands above the confluence of the Rhone and the Saone, and is the centre of the silk, satin, and velvet trades of France.

## THE LYONNAISE.

The city of Lyons gives pronounced evidence of the silk manufacture, for in the chief streets are seen the offices of the silk merchants and manufacturers, whilst the banks have signs displayed indicating that they make advances on silks; but you are disappointed in the shops. It was naturally to be expected that in this centre of the trade the shops would make attractive displays of silks, satins, and velvets, but they do not. In fact, the city, whilst having many shops, has very few large ones. The streets are, therefore, in this respect, disappointing. At the Paris Exposition you see in the combined exhibition made by the silk houses of Lyons, probably the grandest display of silks of all degrees and of silk manufactures that has ever been got together, but you see nothing of the kind in Lyons. The signs tell you the silk is here, but you see very little of it. This is caused by the nature of the trade. There are no great silk-factories. The manufacturer gives out the raw silk thread to the workman, and it is taken to the little apartment where he has his loom, and lives frequently in noisome quarters with his family, and when he has woven the piece he takes it back to the manufacturer and receives his wages. There is no such thing as a silk-factory in Lyons, such as we know a cotton- or woollen-mill at home, or Belfast knows a linen-factory. Outside of the city, and a great distance off, there are steam-mills with power-looms that make the inferior qualities of silk, but all the best goods are made on hand-looms and in the way I have indicated. This prevents seeing a silk-factory, and as the manufacturers each usually make but one quality of fabric, and sell it through commission houses, this prevents seeing any varied display of silk. Lyons has great cotton- and woollen-factories, for which it is *not* famous, and whose chimneys pour out so much smoke that a fog seems usually to lower over the city, but to make silk, for which it *is* famous, it has no factory apparent to the eye. You can go and see the single worker manipulating his loom; can, if you choose, enter his generally repulsive home, where loom, children, dogs, cats, and silk are huddled together; but this is all. Yet Lyons is the centre of an enormous trade in these fabrics, getting tribute from all the country round, receiving the raw silk thread; sending away the silk cloth; governing the silk and velvet fabrics and fashions of the world; and having the prices controlled and the trade ruled by an association of makers governing their rates by the usual discount-cards current in trade associations in America. You come to Lyons to see the silk-trade, but have to imagine it more than you can see it.

The city looks like a sort of miniature Paris, and is much smaller, probably one-eighth the size. Its buildings and building-stone resemble the Parisian construction, whilst the two rivers running parallel to each other, with their quays and bridges, are in appearance essentially Parisian. It is the chief manufacturing city of France, and the second in size and population. The Romans founded it a great while ago, and Roman remains, in the form of stone walls and broken arches, are frequent. Excepting to the westward, where the heights of Fourviere rise abruptly from the Saone, the city is flat. From these heights there is a grand view over the whole city, with the two rivers passing through it to their confluence below the town, and away off to the Jura Mountains towards the northeast, and Mont Blanc one hundred miles away to the southeast. I could distinctly see the snowy tops of Mont Blanc and its range, glistening in the sunlight. On the top of this magnificent hill a fine new church is being built to the patron saint of the city, whilst her old Church of "Notre Dame de Fourviere" stands alongside, the constant Mecca of praying devotees, who invoke her assistance, and put lighted candles all around, whilst, if cured or aided, they show their thankfulness by hanging little votive pictures or embroideries on the walls. Hundreds of candles burned around the altars, and thousands of offerings were on the walls,—some indicating safety from shipwreck, sickness, or other peril; others aid when in despair; and similar assistance. It was a strange collection, the picture, if it could, displaying the peril, whilst the embroidery told of the hope, the prayer, and the assistance. This church and the high hill on which it stands are inclosed by a fort which is a sort of citadel for the powerful defensive works surrounding the city.

The city of Lyons, though it could not show me the silk manufacture, could display some other things. It is the most radically Red Republican city of France, owing to the large numbers of silk-weavers and workmen. Here the Commune raged in 1793 even worse than in Paris, and rivers of blood ran down the Rhone from the butchered people, the frenzy finally resulting in the almost entire destruction of the city. The most Radical deputies have always been sent to the French Assembly by the Lyonnaise. When the Germans besieged Paris, and the Empire collapsed, and Gambetta went out of the beleagured city in a balloon to raise succor elsewhere, he quickly visited Lyons. Here the Prefect of the Rhone, to keep the weavers from boiling over, fixes the price of bread bi-monthly, thus controlling the bakers; and his proclamation for the first half of October now adorns the walls, declaring that ordinary bread shall be sold at bakers' shops for forty centimes the kilogramme, and in the markets for thirty-seven centimes, prices which correspond respectively to about four and three and two-fifths cents per pound. In his proclamation the price of flour is also fixed, at about forty francs per one hundred kilogrammes, which would correspond to about eight dollars per barrel. When we came into Lyons on Sunday the stores were open and the streets full of people. They were having an election for the French Assembly for a Deputy to succeed one who died. All the French elections are held on Sunday. This election resulted very much like some elections do in America,—both sides, according to their own story, won, and the day after there were universal demands for a second election, which, under certain circumstances, the French law permits. I do not know whether I understood the matter correctly, but there seem to have been four candidates. Citizen Milleron was set up by the "Central Committee of Radical Republicans." Citizen Chavanne was also set up by the same committee. (I quote their placards.) But M. Chavanne's supporters declared that there were sixty members of the committee, and that seven of these "with audacious impudence usurped the title of the committee" and set up his competitor. The third candidate was Citizen Habenack, whose placard declared he wanted to go to the Assembly to fight the Jesuits. " The Jesuits hope that you will not select Habenack," it said, "and they will then cry, 'Lyons recoils!' Lyonnaise, recoil you never! Then vote for Habenack, and war on the Jesuits." This placard was signed by the " Independent Committee of Radical Republicans." The fourth candidate was Citizen J. Castenier, also supported by an " Independent Committee of Radical Republicans," who commended him on account of his services in advancing the industrial interests of the city, and who quoted sundry very respectable people as his supporters. The election was held; Habenack, in spite of his "war on the Jesuits," and Castenier, notwithstanding his respectability, coming out at the tail, whilst neither of the others seem to have been elected. The Lyonnaise appear to know all that we do about election counting, and the streets, the day after, bristled with placards charging fraud and demanding a second election. Citizen Chavanne declared the result was returned for his opponent, when he was elected, getting five hundred and forty-seven votes to five hundred and sixteen for his opponent. Citizen Milleron declared he had five hundred and forty votes, and his opponent but five hundred and thirty-three. The counters, it seems, disagreed, and one precinct was a hot-bed of discovered fraud, showing that Lyons knows how to conduct elections as well as some other places. Yet all the election-bills close with " Vive la République!" in bold letters, and invoke the patriotism of the voter as we do at home, whilst in glowing language they speak of the "Sainted Durand,' whose death caused the vacancy about which his survivors are squabbling.

## LETTER XLVI.

### A RIDE THROUGH BURGUNDY.

PARIS, October 4.

The longest railway in France is that between Paris and Marseilles, by way of Lyons. By the fastest trains it is a ride of twenty hours, and it is the great route between England and France and all parts of the Mediterranean Sea, for Marseilles is the chief French port, and from its eligible position near the mouth of the Rhone, sends out steam-lines in all directions. Lyons is in Southern France, nearly two-thirds of the distance down to Marseilles, and the Lyonnaise partake somewhat of the ennui induced by their climate, for their business people always take a noontide rest. It would be very strange in Philadelphia, were merchants and clerks to desert their counting-rooms for two hours at mid-day, yet this is the fashion at Lyons. From about 11.30 to 1.30 it is impossible to transact business in Lyons, for during that time, which we would regard as the best part of the business day, no one can be found in his office. They are all at the cafés, taking the Frenchman's "second breakfast," gossiping, reading newspapers, playing games, or doing anything that will best kill time till they can go back again. Business is done earlier in the morning, or later in the afternoon; every one protesting against the absurdity, but every one yielding to it. Leaving Lyons in the early morning we rode for eleven hours, and were in Paris by dark. It was the fastest train on the great line, making connections farther south with the chief Oriental routes of travel, and it probably may be regarded as a representative of French fast railway travelling. Yet we can beat it in a good many ways, and on any of our leading American railways. This train, which started with much ceremony, calculated to impress the traveller with its importance, carried only first-class passengers and charged these at the rate of nearly five cents a mile. Its time-table did not require a higher rate of speed than thirty miles an hour, and this it was unable to keep up, for it got considerably behind time, owing to that well-known railroad disease—a "hot-box"; and after it had lost fifteen minutes' time, seemed incapable of gaining upon it, as our delayed trains do at home. It in no case ran over twenty miles without a stop; yet with a score of stoppages on the route,—one of them for a half-hour,— the tickets were not once looked at, and, so far as through passengers were concerned, no railway official examined them, until they were taken up on arrival in Paris. This is in strange contrast to the usual European custom of bothering the passengers for tickets every few minutes, and punching them so thoroughly that when the journey ends they look almost like a sieve.

The route from Lyons to Paris ran north, and made a perceptible change in the climate. It took us out of the warm influences of the Mediterranean into the colder region controlled by the Atlantic and North Sea. Starting in balmy air and warm breezes, before many hours overcoats and shawls had to be put on. The line runs up the Saone, then across the water-shed to the Yonne, down to the Seine and thence into Paris. Starting in the picturesque scenery of the Jura Mountains, it rushes through tunnels and around curves, and then gradually subsides to tameness, for Central France is an almost level plain, highly cultivated, but uninteresting to look at; and this was the course of the railway for hours, as the train ran through the famous province of Burgundy, about which so much has been sung and written, and over which there was in times past many a battle. This is the Frenchman's wine-garden. Here grows his claret, his beloved nectar from the region of the Côte d'Or. His best champagne, which elsewhere grows, he sends abroad, chiefly, it is said, to America, where the highest prices are obtained. But his best Burgundy the Frenchman drinks himself, and the outside world must be content with the poorer qualities. For hours we coursed along the edges of the gentle hills whereon the grapes are grown that make the claret. It was the vintage period. They were gathering the grapes and putting them in casks set on little carts. The railway gave every evidence of passing through a wine-growing country, for all the freight-trains were laden with wine-casks; all the stations were piled up with them, and nearly all the passengers carried bottles. The train would stop and the Frenchman rush into the restaurant and come back with his bottle. Mademoiselle would get aboard with a lap-dog under one arm and a bottle under the other. Every few minutes as we moved along there was the clatter of smashing glass as some passenger threw his empty bottle out of the window, and for two hundred miles that line must be at least partially ballasted with broken bottles. You could get any amount to drink, but water was very scarce.

There are about two hundred and twenty-five thousand acres of vineyards in Burgundy, the most famous being those of the Côte d'Or, of which Dijon is the centre, and the very best brands being grown near that ancient city. These best brands never leave France, for two good reasons. Their supply is limited, and the French connoisseurs will pay more for them than anybody else. Then a sea-voyage entirely spoils their bouquet. Even so short a voyage as that across the English Channel greatly damages them, and in fact they can ill bear much transportation of any kind. These fine wines are never moved excepting in bottle, and they only leave the few vineyards producing them after they have been kept some time, and they are then disposed of at auction. They are, of course, but a small proportion of the vast amount of wine that Burgundy produces, an average yield being about fifty-five million gallons, valued at ten million dollars. The Burgundians themselves know how to appreciate their famous product, for they consume about one-half of it at home, which will to some extent account for the activity among the bottles all along the line of the railway. They export the remainder, sending it to all parts of the world, and much of the "Vin ordinaire," the great French drink, is sold in Burgundy at from seven to ten cents a gallon at the vineyard, so that, even allowing for enormous retail profits, the Parisian can get his wine for ten or twelve cents a quart. The French do not want a strong wine, preferring a weak one, quantity being the object with most of them, for they rarely drink water, and must get fluid of some kind somewhere. Nature, however, adapts itself to almost anything. As the Burgundians are *not* water-drinkers, so we could travel for miles through that famous region without seeing even the smallest stream of water. Nature is not lavish of her gifts where they are not wanted.

The railway ride, otherwise than as furnishing a chance to study the wine question, is not, however, an interesting one.

It passes through Macon, where the Genevans come to go to Paris; Chalons, which has a Roman relic in the shape of a dilapidated granite column; Dijon, which sells wine; Baume, which does likewise; Tounere, which has a beautiful avenue of lime-trees; Joigny, where the Yonne is reached; Sens, with a fine Cathedral, which can be plainly seen for a long distance, though, like so many of the European churches, its towers are yet incomplete; Montereau, where the Yonne flows into the Seine, and where Napoleon I. gained his last victory; and, finally, Fontainebleau. The great forest of Fontainebleau, which contains over forty thousand acres, and is sixty-three miles in circumference, is one of the famous royal hunting-grounds of France. It is chiefly covered with heath and underwood, though it has groves of fine trees, and it is left very much in its natural state, so that it may be a roaming-place for the wild boar. Roads intersect it in all directions, and in the principal one stands the obelisk marking the spot where "the spectral black huntsman," then haunting the wood, appeared to King Henry IV. immediately before his assassination. There is a fine palace in the wood; but as a forest, the portion exhibited along the Lyons Railway does not show to great advantage, and if it is a fair specimen of the whole, the timber is not good for much. The railway runs for a long distance through the forest, and it looks like a journey through the Jersey pines to Atlantic City. The trees are small and scrawny, and the appearance is that of a miserable growth on poor land. I know many a forest of less fame near Philadelphia, that to my eyes made a much better show than this great forest of Fontainebleau. Why not empark about forty thousand acres of the Jersey pines, turn a drove of wild hogs into it, and give it a high-sounding title, and then make it the fashion for the sport-loving public to go there to chase the pigs? If this were done it would serve every useful purpose that Fontainebleau does, whilst as pleasant wine can be grown in the Jersey neighborhood as that sold here. American tourists who go thirty-five hundred miles to see this French park might also possibly be induced to go and see the other, if only the fashion were set, and the trip made sufficiently expensive. Soon after leaving Fontainebleau we crossed the Marne at its confluence with the Seine, and entering Paris, the long day's ride was over.

## LETTER XLVII.

### FROM PARIS TO LONDON.

LONDON, October 8.

As the month of October grew older we began to get warnings that it was time to leave Paris. Perpetual sunshine by no means reigns in that city. The weather became cold. Fog hung over the entire region in the mornings and rains were frequent. The piercing winds brought the leaves scurrying down from the trees, but there was not that wealth of coloring that brightens the American autumnal forest. The streets got full of mud, and, though the sun was hot enough at mid-day, the mornings and the evenings were anything but pleasant, and in fact were not as attractive as the mornings and evenings of this season at home. Thus the weather gave signal of the approach of the inclement period, which is as unpleasant at Paris as it is anywhere else, and, in spite of the glitter and show, the visitor was warned that it was time to leave. When we returned to Paris we did not take the same lodgings as on the previous visit. Mademoiselle, whose metrical system of apportioning sugar-lumps and beefsteak, at so many square inches per person, I have heretofore described, had let her apartments to some one else,—a Russian princess, she confidentially said,—and added, the next in rank to the Czar. This was told to impress us with the importance of Mademoiselle's apartments. As all Americans are kings, and gallantry is a characteristic of the race (and we could not help it), we therefore abandoned the apartments to the princess, and she is now enjoying the three or four square inches of beefsteak, and the four lumps of sugar which are the daily ration at that part of the Champs Elysées, and may possibly divide them with the Czar when he calls to see her. We got housed elsewhere in a hotel, where we were allured by the attractive words, " American Hotel," and a placard which said " English Spiked." It was a comfortable place, but the English certainly was "spiked,"—in fact, impaled, murdered,—and the conversation in that hotel during our brief stay was simply a pantomime. But we learnt enough, even by pantomime, in the hotel, to discover that the Russian princess above mentioned was an exile, who had quarrelled with her third or fourth husband, and was one out of several hundred princesses, each of whom was next in rank, etc., and the majority of whom had been put out of their own country, and had come to Paris to wait for something to turn up.

We, therefore, after a brief stay, heeding the meteorological warnings, took our last look at the Exposition, and at Notre Dame and its "gates of paradise," as the special front doors are called through which royalty only enters the great church. —a circumstance which made Victor Hugo suggest that probably the gates where ordinary people enter ought, therefore, to be called the "gates of t'other place." We also bade goodby to the Garden of Acclimatation, that attractive enclosure in the Bois de Boulogne, where Paris has its Zoological Garden, but, having eaten up most of the animals during the siege, has supplied their places as well as may be. Here is the most extraordinary collection of dogs I ever saw, embracing hundreds of all breeds and all degrees, and all barking in chorus. Here also, a fine collection of tropical birds is kept in heated apartments, including thousands of bright-colored, chirping little strangers from Africa and South America, that, as they flitted about, reminded me of the ever-changing beauties of the kaleidoscope. Here the elephants and camels carried not the children only, but grown men and women, and the bigger the rider the more anxious he seemed to get on the animal's back. Here the ostrich, harnessed to a carriage, strutted about the grounds with a load of little folks, followed by a great many more who could not get on. It is a lovely place, but the winds were playing havoc with the foliage, and giving warning that even bright Paris must succumb to approaching winter.

We got up early in the morning, long before daylight, to catch the train to London, which starts before breakfast, and, of course, from a station on the other side of the great city. This is a bad habit that railway trains have, to which I have heretofore alluded. But there was consolation in the thought that it was the quickest train between the two cities, and, as the announcement declared, went "through in nine hours" over the shortest sea-route, that by Calais and Dover. But

NOTRE DAME (WEST FRONT)

the sequel proved that railway announcements, in Europe as
in America, are liable to mistakes; the "nine hours" stretched
to eleven hours and a quarter before we arrived in London,
and the Channel passage was accompanied by all the discomforts for which it has ever been famous. How I wish some
American Bismarck of transportation would come over here
and teach these people how to conduct their travelling in a
way that is satisfactory and comfortable to the traveller! It
is amazing that on the lines connecting the two great cities of
the world things are not done better. The railway ran north
from Paris for hours through the uninteresting but highly-
cultivated plain which surrounds that city, and passed into
the historical region of Normandy. It went through Amiens,
which contains the great Cathedral of France, and the third
largest church in Europe, where they keep in state the skull
of John the Baptist, which was brought here from the East
during the Crusades. Here Peter the Hermit was born, the
preacher who inspired the Crusades. Then we passed the
battle-field of Crecy, where the use of cannon enabled the
Black Prince to defeat one hundred thousand Frenchmen,
though he had but thirty thousand English. This was over
five hundred years ago, and Albert Edward now wears the
spurs and feathers which his predecessor then won. Then
we reached the river Somme at Abbeville, got into better
scenery, and followed that river down to its mouth, at Boulogne. Here the shore of the English Channel is reached at
that famous French watering-place, where millions are being
spent to create an artificial harbor, but where the tide, twice
every day, will run down so low that it leaves almost every
floating thing high and dry. Boulogne is not so attractive as
Brighton, nor as large, but the French think a great deal of
it, and it is a strongly-fortified city as well as a watering-
place. Here Napoleon, in 1804, gathered the great army
and fleet with which he intended to invade England, but
Nelson's skill overmastered him, the stunning blow of Trafalgar
came, and the invasion, which gave John Bull more fright
than anything else threatened since the Spanish Armada, had
to be abandoned. As the railway train rushed through the
tunnelled hills the column could be seen, one hundred and
sixty-six feet high, surmounted by Napoleon's statue, erected
to mark the invasion, and which has been standing there ever

since, a token of the folly of counting chickens before they are hatched. Then, from Boulogne, the railway runs along the coast to Calais and enters the ponderous fortifications of that famous, battle-scarred town, from the ramparts of which the chalk cliffs of Dover can be distinctly seen across the Channel.

### RE-CROSSING THE CHANNEL.

The train runs out on the pier alongside the little cockle-shell steamer that is to take us across the Channel. The passengers crowd along the gangways, tugging their hand-bags and wraps. A drove of Anglo-French sailors seize the trunks, batter them about, slide them down to the steamboat deck, and give as thorough and destructive an exhibition of "baggage smashing" as can be got up in any part of America. We crowd on the steamer, the gangway being lined with French gendarmes and police agents, and undergo the last act of the constant police surveillance and espionage which dogs every stranger and half the natives in the supposed free French Republic. Our bags are looked at and every one's name and nationality demanded. It was a remarkable fact that half the English-speaking passengers were named "Smith" and "Jones," which names seemed to thoroughly satisfy the police agents, who politely thanked their givers. They were probably much more anxious about the continental nations than about the English, but the fact nevertheless disclosed the absurdity of the question. So, having passed this gauntlet, we got aboard. It was a poor little steamer, with very primitive accommodation for the passengers. They had to sit down on hard benches on a deck that had no covering, and were subject to being broiled by the sun or drenched by the rain, as the case might be. There was no comfort for any one, and as soon as the boat started, and had got fairly out in the Channel, the people began getting sick. The little craft was tossed about by the waves, and it was only a few minutes before the deck presented a pitiable sight. The seamen ran about with wash-basins, which they thrust under passengers' noses, and then held out their hands for "tips." Before the Channel had been half crossed, two-thirds the people were sick, lying on the hard benches or else on the decks. Among them the few well ones, probably to show their freedom from sickness, persisted in walking, and were tumbled pell-mell to leeward every time the boat gave a lurch. Every few minutes there thus was caused a grand scramble as some pedestrian was tumbled over a pile of invalids, and all hands, including the wash-basins, went rolling down together. Had it not been for the awful solemnity that sea-sickness inspires, the show would have been as good as the circus, but the man who would have roared with laughter at it on land, could see no fun in it on the Channel. Thus we did our crossing on the great line that promises it in ninety minutes, but does it in two hours, and we came into port a sorrowful lot, full of vexation, sadness, and complaints, inspired by the miserable ordeal. The new twin steamer, Calais-Douvres, was not on the line that day. She is prescribed as a sure preventive of sea-sickness, but they have a fashion of not running her when a bad sea is promised, the better, I suppose, to maintain her reputation. She has never yet undergone the test of very rough weather, and she is already described by travellers as a "tolerably good pitcher," many having got as thoroughly sea-sick on her as on the ordinary boats. What the Channel needs, as I have before remarked, is an effort to provide comfort for passengers who are sure to be sea-sick. Instead of endeavoring to invent preventives, the attention should be rather given to amelioration. Instead of compelling the sick passenger to lie about on the crowded, unprotected decks, he should be treated as an invalid, and given a comfortable resting-place. These people actually carry their horses across the Channel on the steamers with more attention to comfort than they give the first-class passengers; and in this all the lines are alike. It is possible on a good day and in calm weather to make the passage without sea-sickness in any of the boats; but in rough weather the Channel passage has more terrors for most people than a voyage across the Atlantic.

But we got over the Channel, and I survived, and the boat ran into still water behind the breakwater of Dover, where the white chalk cliffs of the very bold coast were dazzling in the sunlight. Then we went ashore, clambering up a narrow stairway, along which also rushed the seamen, carrying the trunks, so that the weak and unfortunate passenger, having just got out of Neptune's clutches, was in danger of having his head mashed by contact with a huge "Saratoga." Then we were seized by the railway people and sorted out for the various trains that go to the different London stations. We made a rapid run to London, the speed, scenery, and, in fact, everything being in marked contrast to the morning ride from Paris. The English railways and their appointments are much better than those of France, and they maintain higher speed and do not waste so much time at the stations. We saw Dover Castle crowning the chalk hill that overhangs the town. This hill is completely honeycombed with casemates and military storehouses, and, in fact, is a sort of small Gibraltar, where two thousand men can be kept as a garrison, and large amounts of provisions and ammunition be stored. We ran along the rich pasture-lands of this section, with their flocks of sheep and droves of cattle; passed through hill after hill, by tunnels; saw hundreds of acres of hop-poles, for the crop had but recently been gathered; and then came to the ancient town of Canterbury. The venerable Cathedral, which gives the title to the chief prelate of the English Church, showed well from the car windows, its square towers standing out against the sky. Then we crossed the Medway, and passed that "one long, dirty street," running parallel to the river, which chiefly makes the town of Chatham, best known to Americans because it gave the title to the earldom conferred on the elder Pitt. There is a dockyard and barracks here, and there occasionally are grand reviews. The Medway does not present a very brilliant appearance, being a crooked stream, running between low sand-banks, overflowed at high tide, and looking not unlike the Maurice River, in New Jersey, which stream takes more space to go a shorter distance than any other I can just now recall. Up the Medway valley the railway runs to Rochester, famous for its Cathedral and Castle, and then past Dulwich, into the maze of railways that environ London, where we trundled over the Thames and into Victoria Station. We were again in London, the world's great city, and tired enough of the eleven hours' journey not to let anything prevent seeking a much-needed rest.

## LETTER XLVIII.

### THE SOUTH KENSINGTON MUSEUM.

LONDON, October 11.

The greatest permanent institution anywhere established for the popularized exhibition of scientific and art collections, with a view to the public education, is undoubtedly the South Kensington Museum of London. It is the outgrowth of the first great World's Fair, held in London in 1851, and has increased to proportions which its projectors scarcely dreamed of. That Fair, unlike any of the subsequent ones, resulted in a profit, and this profit was made into a fund, from the proceeds of which there was subsequently purchased a large tract of land in Kensington, then away out in the country. The tract adjoined Hyde Park on the south, and the increased value of the land,—for London has since extended to and far beyond it,—coupled with the wise administration of the Fund, has enabled the Commission in charge of it not only to sell at cost a very large surface for the Museum and other public purposes, but to so lease the remainder and invest the proceeds that the Fund produces an annual income equal to the entire first cost of the ground. Thus the museum originated and its site was provided. Its buildings cover twelve acres of land at present, whilst new buildings for its libraries, etc., are going up on another tract to the westward, which is apparently more than three times as large. There are occupied and available for this great enterprise, probably seventy acres of land, and the permanent buildings already completed are of great architectural beauty, and are as thoroughly adapted to the purpose as can be devised. The Museum was opened in 1857, and has been growing for twenty-one years. The Government has already spent over six million dollars upon the buildings and the collection of curiosities, and of this nearly one million five hundred thousand dollars has been devoted to the latter object, the grants for this purpose having, for several years recently, exceeded one hundred and ten thousand dollars annually. The Museum has also been greatly enriched by private gifts, be-

24*

quests, and loans, many of its costliest gems being acquired in this way. It is organized on such an extensive scale that over three hundred persons are required to take charge of it, and here is located as the acting Director the well-known British Commissioner to the Centennial Exhibition, Colonel Sir Herbert Sandford, of whom Philadelphia has such pleasant memories, whilst A. J. R. Trendell, Esq., who was Secretary to the British Commission at Philadelphia, is also connected with the Secretariat here. Richard A. Thompson, Esq., who has been connected with the enterprise from its inception, is the Director of the Museum during the absence of Sir Francis Philip Cunliffe Owen, the Secretary of the British Commission at the Paris Exposition.

The British Government has, in what is known as the "Science and Art Department," a branch that is as yet unknown in the Government of the United States. Education is one of the matters looked after by the Government here, and upon science and art and the promotion of their instruction about one million five hundred thousand dollars of the public money is annually expended. Representation in grand international exhibitions comes under the care of this Department, over which the Duke of Richmond presides, and it also directs a large number of institutions in different parts of the kingdom, this Museum, however, being the chief. The great scope of the Museum is shown by a recapitulation of the collections embraced within its walls. These include over thirty thousand objects of ornamental art, ancient, mediæval, and modern, most of them of rarity and costliness; a similar collection, also of large extent, of reproductions of these articles in other collections, secured by electrotyping, plaster-castings, or other means; an art library of over forty-five thousand volumes, formed, like the art collections, for the especial object of art-teaching; seventeen thousand drawings, fifty-two thousand engravings, and forty-five thousand photographs, chiefly of ornamental art, also acquired for this purpose; a collection of British pictures of great merit, of which the Sheepshanks collection was the nucleus, and including six hundred and seventeen oil and twelve hundred and ninety-one water-color paintings, all being specimens of the best British masters; a fine collection of decorative sculpture of the Renaissance period, in marble, stone, and terra-cotta, including numerous specimens of the Italian glazed terra-cotta of four hundred years ago, known as Della Robbia ware; an educational library of over thirty-six thousand volumes, with several thousand specimens of scientific apparatus, models, and appliances for educational purposes; a vast aggregation of samples of building materials, and models of implements and contrivances for construction; a complete collection of the substances used for food, arranged with the object of teaching their nature and sources, and representing their chemical composition and the natural sources from which they are obtained; a collection of naval models and of the various appliances of modern warfare; the British Patent-Office exhibition of remarkable models; and besides all these, an extensive loan exhibition of great numbers of similar objects belonging to all the classes mentioned. This catalogue will give an idea of the broad scope of the South Kensington Museum. Its object is to aid in science and art teaching. For this purpose art-students are given access to its almost boundless resources, with every facility for studying and copying. A magnificent building has also been constructed on the fine new street called Exhibition Road, which runs through the grounds, in which lectures are delivered on Chemistry, Physics, and Natural History, by leading scientists. The Metropolitan Schools of Art are also attached to the Museum for special instruction in those branches, and among the latest acquisitions is a collection of furniture, cabinet-ware, and ornamental wood-work for instruction in that branch of decorative art. Three days in the week are devoted to students and three to the public, and on the latter the admission is free. The visitors number a million annually, whilst the number of students' admissions during the year is over one hundred thousand, showing how extensively this magnificent source of knowledge is availed of.

The *Ledger* would not hold the list of wonderful things and rare gems this great aggregation contains, and which it is constantly exhibiting to larger audiences by loaning for brief periods to museums elsewhere in the kingdom, this circulatory process, without detracting from the general collection, being adopted with good results. In this Museum are Raphael's famous cartoons and Michael Angelo's models; Dr. Schliemann's collection of antiquities from Troy; John Forster's collection of manuscripts, including those of many of Dickens's novels; a great number of models of ships of war and famous ocean steamers, representing almost every transatlantic line, but not including, I was sorry to see, any model of the American line; models of working steam-engines, railways, dredges docks, drawbridges, cannon, projectiles, and other weapons; the Palestine Exploration Collection; the British Arctic Expedition Collection; Watt's original models, which he constructed whilst inventing the steam-engine; two cases of ornamental snuff-boxes, and several cases of rare jewels and specimens of precious stones; a great collection of ceramics, glass, porcelain, and decorated metal-work; curious watches, rings, mosaics, miniatures, ornaments of all races, etc. There is an admirable system in the arrangement, the order of chronology being thoroughly observed in the classification, whilst the construction of the buildings is such that the objects are exhibited to the best advantage, and the buildings themselves and their ornamentation are as much for art instruction as their contents.

Such a museum, however, could only be the growth of years. It is not the British Museum, of course, for that is pre-eminently the greatest collection in the world, but as a popularized museum and instructor, South Kensington nowhere has a rival. It pleases the visitor more than any similar institution in Europe, because its objects are effectively presented, and are of a kind that suit the millions who are not able to maintain the lofty strain that some other collections require. Then its benefits are within every one's reach; it embraces the entire field of art education, and its acres of show-cases and miles of corridors contain enough to occupy a lifetime, if properly studied. It has become one of the great institutions of London, and, as it is regarded as the fountain of art education in the kingdom, it naturally furnishes the staff that represents England at the great International Exhibitions. Among the new buildings now erecting for the Museum are fine structures for its libraries and reading-rooms, which at present are very much cramped. This great enterprise has grown to the vast proportions assumed by most of London's prominent institutions, but, as it gathers continually what is valuable and rare from all parts of the world, its growth is steady, and no one can predict how enormous it may become. There is a peculiar attraction for Philadelphians in the Museum, for it displays in a very prominent place the large photograph of the Centennial Exposition made by Mr. Frederick Gutekunst, and the beautifully-engrossed copy of the resolutions passed by the City Councils thanking Her Majesty's Government for the gift to the city of St. George's House in Fairmount Park.

## LETTER XLIX.

### EAST LONDON BY GASLIGHT.

LONDON, October 14.

One half of the world, we are told, does not know how the other half live, and this is eminently true of London. The traveller, who usually sees only the West End and Centre of London, rarely learns, excepting by hearsay, that there is any such place as the East End. The resident of the West End has heard enough about it not to want to go to the East End unless he is compelled to. That section is, in fact, to most Londoners of the influential class the same as a foreign country. They go as far as the City, where their business is transacted, and they do not willingly go farther. Charles Dickens has uncovered many of the peculiarities of that extraordinary place; but Dickens is dead, and now they are known only to the police. No sensible stranger thinks of going there without a police escort, and few care to go even with it. We talk of the slums of Philadelphia and New York, but they are small compared with the slums of the great East End of London, the purlieus of Whitechapel, Spitalfields, Wapping, St. George's-in-the-East, Smithfield, Shadwell, and all that region, which has by the square mile intensified and multiplied the vice and wretchedness which, with us, is confined to a few streets and a comparatively small area. Nevertheless, curiosity sometimes overrides other considerations, and I went to see it. The authorities of the Metropolitan Police were kind enough to furnish an escort, and leaving our valuables at home, we started for the rendezvous at ten o'clock in the evening, and going away east of the Bank of England, along Aldgate High Street, and Whitechapel Road, turned from the latter into Leman Street, leading down towards the Thames, and reached the appointed place, the Leman Street Police Station, which is the police headquarters of the district, and the centre for controlling the worst region of the great area ruled by the nine thousand men on the London police force.

Here were waiting our escort, Captain Wallace, of the Central Headquarters, and Sergeant Clark, of the district, and we were first given a view of the station, cells, etc. It was Saturday night, and a brisk business was going on. Every few minutes the patrolmen brought in prisoners, mostly charged with being drunk and disorderly, fighting, and assault and battery. They were of the lowest class, and chiefly women. Along with the prisoner always came the accuser and a sympathizing crowd, whom the police drove out of the yard. Nearly all had broken heads, bleeding profusely. The patrolman, with his lantern on his belt, as soon as the prisoner was brought in, arraigned him for an immediate preliminary trial before the sergeant in charge, who decided whether there was sufficient cause to hold the prisoner for formal trial next day by the Police Magistrate. Trivial cases were thus at once dismissed. But few cases were trivial. The examination was not under oath, and consisted chiefly of a cross-fire between the accuser and the accused, the sergeant asking questions, and, with surprising skill, getting quickly at the gist of the dispute. Whilst the examination went on the police washed the broken heads, and if the wounds were serious, called in the attending physician. This was the regular course of business at the station, and the cases usually showed liquor was at the bottom of the trouble. The weapons with which wounds were inflicted were always brought along as additional testimony, and the broken-headed parties usually managed to horribly besmear themselves with blood to give weight to their testimony. In one case a father accused his son of beating the family. The father was almost stupidly drunk, whilst the son had a terrible gash over the eye, and was only less drunk than the father. The arrest was the result of a succession of fights, in which ugly wounds were inflicted all around, and the son was finally arrested to prevent a murder and locked up as a precaution. The father and son berated each other as well as their condition allowed. In another case a woman had struck a little girl with a brush-handle, and she came besmeared with blood, and her mother with her, to tell the tale. It was the usual result of a brawl in a court. The families had quarrelled all the evening, and finally blood was spilt. The mother prompted the child in her story with great volubility; the prisoner denied every word that was said, and each tried to tell of a long series of quarrels and provocations, but the sergeant had no time to hear it. The mother was careful every minute to tell her child to say "sir" to the sergeant. "Ain't you a scholar?" she said to the child. "Yes," was the answer. "Then say 'Yes, sir,' to his worship." None of them could write, and, when requested to sign the accusation on the books, they always made their marks. Thus the scene went on, the cases being summarily disposed of by the sergeant, whose object was to decide whether there was a case sufficient to be returned to the police court. Cases pressed upon him. The patrolmen came in with their prisoners faster almost than he could decide them. He was gentle, but firm, and, as I have said, showed great skill in quickly getting at the merits of each case.

In this, the worst part of London, the patrolmen have to go in couples, for one man unsupported could be easily overmastered. The rough population deal chiefly in fighting, broken heads and stabbing, with frequent cases of petty thieving. The state of affairs is such that the police effort is usually directed only to preventing serious fights, for they can do no better. To aid this purpose all the drinking-saloons, dance-houses, and amusement-places are compelled to close at midnight, and must then turn their population into the street and stop their supplies of liquor. These people may make as much noise as they please, and generally spend the greater part of the night wandering about, singing and roaring and making the streets hideous with their racket, frequently quarrelling and threatening, but so long as they do not fight they are not interfered with. There are so many thousands of them that they could at any time, if so inclined, overmaster the police, and therefore the effort is to only keep their more evil passions in check. As it was, excepting the noise, comparatively good order was maintained, and they seemed to show a wholesome respect for the police, which not only testified the wisdom of the method pursued, but was also reassuring to the six Americans (all, with one exception, from

Philadelphia), who were being escorted in their old clothes through this extraordinary region.

The tour lasted from about eleven o'clock until nearly two in the morning. We were taken first to see various dance houses and variety shows, where a promiscuous crowd, the men being chiefly sailors, were watching stage performances, or else dancing to the music of loud but discordant bands, with women whose fondness for bright colors made them dress in the most splashing costumes. Smoking and drinking went on continually, and every establishment had its bar, the bar-maids being kept busy drawing the potations, which were chiefly of malt liquors. The flags of all nations decked these establishments, as they were designed to attract the sailor, and I saw in them some of the most astonishing attempts at constructing the American flag. In the show-places the men sat with their hats on and their feet generally over the backs of the seats, and whenever a song was sung the entire audience joined in the chorus. The performers must have talked English; but they, like almost every one in this remarkable locality, used a dialect so full of slang and of uncouth pronunciation that very little of it could be understood. Tremendous noise, but good order prevailed. The moment any one attempted a disturbance he was unceremoniously hustled out. We were taken to a half-dozen of these places, some of very revolting appearance and almost stifling atmosphere. Their chief customer was the sailor, and their surroundings showed that when he was through with them there was but little chance of his having any money left. The loungers around the outside were ready to take what the harpies inside might have overlooked.

Then we were taken through various dingy, narrow streets, filled with a noisy, restless population, though it was near midnight, and, seeing frequent petty brawls and disturbances and much drunkenness, went down into a street among the docks, called Old Gravel Lane. Here, amid the warehouses, we were walked upon a drawbridge crossing a canal leading between the two sections of the London Docks. The dark and dirty water flowed beneath, and a policeman stood sentry in the fog that almost obscured the moonlight. This was the London "Bridge of Sighs," so named because that lonely place among the warehouses is the favorite resort for the most wretched and abandoned of that region to commit suicide.

It is an easy plunge over the low railing alongside the narrow footway, and the suicides were formerly so frequent that it was necessary to guard the place. A policeman is always on duty on the bridge, his beat being only its meagre length of about fifty feet. We paused a moment and then passed on. We had gone but a few steps when a noisy party came along, men and women and children. A man ahead was carrying an infant wrapped in an old shawl. A drunken woman was endeavoring to knock him down, and the crowd was excitedly following. They had been all turned out of a public-house, and the father was trying to save the innocent babe which the drunken mother in her frenzy wanted to destroy. Over the "Bridge of Sighs" went this noisy party, and the policeman there gave the needed protection.

The workhouse of St. George's-in-the-East was not far away, and we gave it a passing visit. It is a large almshouse, with a thousand permanent inmates, many of them in the hospital. Its "Casual Ward," however, was the chief attraction. Here came the tramp, and the unfortunate of both sexes, and they were taken in at any hour of the night, and given lodging and food. When received they were made to strip off their clothing and take a bath, and were then given a loaf of bread and sent to bed. Everything was clean, and, though rude, was comfortable. Recent investigations have greatly improved these workhouses. The paupers' clothing, after it is stripped from them, is bundled up and numbered, and then put in an oven, under which sulphur is burned for disinfection. Next morning they are routed out before seven o'clock, and given another loaf of bread for breakfast, after which they work three hours at sawing wood or picking oakum. They do not like the work, and it is imposed in the endeavor to break up the tramp nuisance. Eight of them at a time are set at turning a windlass which works a circular saw. This workhouse represents about the worst parish in London. Its Casual Ward was nearly filled when we looked in upon it at midnight, and the sleeping paupers lay on the rows of little beds, without pillows, which were ranged along the sides of a long room with many windows for ventilation, but the atmosphere of which was nevertheless very close, as the paupers seemed afraid of fresh air. They were a wretched lot.

Next we were taken through a long series of dark alleys

and courts with noisome houses, into a court away off from the frequented streets, at the end of which the officers knocked at the door of a little dingy house. After some time they roused the solitary inmate, a Chinaman, who groped down the narrow, winding stair, and let us in. We ascended with difficulty to his den in the upper story, a low room in which you could hardly stand upright, and lighted by a small, dirty window. The furniture consisted of two old bedsteads, with filthy bolsters set on the side against the wall. It was one of the dens of the opium-smokers, although the Chinaman had no customer at the time but himself. He reclined on the bed with his lighted lamp alongside him, and prepared the opium pellets for the Lascars and Chinamen who search him out, and for sixpence or a shilling get their beloved thimbleful of the drug, and smoke and dream away on his revolting beds. In "pidgin English" he told us his history. He had been in London forty years, and for over twenty had kept that den. He had plenty of business, and on some nights his customers consumed a half-pound of opium. He took it regularly, and his daily dose was an ounce. He could not live a day without it. He showed us the black molasses-like drug, and the little thimbles in which he sold it to his customers after heating and mixing it. He then smoked a pipe to show how it was done, and did his smoking in a way that is unknown with us. For three or four minutes he sucked the opium-smoke out of the pipe, and inhaled it all into his lungs. Then he laid the pipe down and passed an interval almost without breathing. Then he slowly exhaled great volumes of smoke, filling the room. How he could hold so much was the mystery. His movements were sluggish and his face wan and cadaverous, but his eyes were bright, and he seemed to have the most intense enjoyment of the smoke. The whole house smelled as if saturated with carbolic acid, the fumes of the opium producing an odor very much like the acid and having a similar effect in driving away vermin. "Johnny," as they called him, was perfectly harmless, but he seemed to have a wholesome dread of the police, and paid them great deference.

We were also taken to see the cheap lodging-houses of this section of London, where, at a cost of from six to eight cents, beds are let out by the night to all comers. These houses are under constant police surveillance, and some of them contain as high as three hundred beds. They all have signs announcing them to be a "Registered Lodging-House," and once or twice a week they undergo a thorough inspection, whilst twice a year a complete cleansing and whitewashing is enforced. Some take in lodgers all night; some close at 1 A.M. The lodgers are put in large dormitories and locked in. They are furnished, in the higher class houses, with a straw pillow, but in the lower class the lodger generally gets only a straw pallet and blanket, and makes a bundle of his clothes for a pillow. The down-stairs floor is the kitchen and wash-room. Here they can cook their food and wash their clothes, and sit up till they want to go to bed. The houses were all well filled. We took a survey of these houses of various classes, and were finally led into Flower-and-Dean Street, where the lowest class of these houses is found, being the resort chiefly of the most abandoned characters and thieves. We visited the "Louise and Lorne Chambers," where it was announced that "a porter would be in attendance all night," and that "all persons creating disturbance would be immediately put out without their money." Here, after one o'clock in the morning, we found a noisy crowd in the street, and some lively ones in the kitchen, who immediately informed us that they were very thirsty. There were, both inside and outside, many women carrying infants, and also children. In fact, late as it was, the streets showed frequent crowds of people roaming about, singing, quarrelling, and carousing, the majority appearing to be bareheaded women, most of them with infants. I doubt whether thousands of the poor little children of this abandoned locality ever get much shelter at night, unless their parents take them to the workhouse to find it. We examined the kitchen of this place, and then the proprietor, with a candle without a candlestick, took us up a tortuous, rickety stair to the labyrinths above, where he had hundreds of beds, most of them occupied by snoring people, who probably included some of the worst characters of London. But all were thoroughly respectful, and throughout the strange expedition no one, beyond chaffing or unintentional jostling, attempted to molest us. It was an extraordinary journey, and just before two o'clock we parted from our escort and took cabs for home. The streets were lively, for London turns night into day in the West End as well as the East End. Most of the great clubs seemed to be still open, and there were many people in the streets, aimlessly walking about, or sleeping in odd corners. Occasionally a policeman would wake up a sleeper, and giving him a sharp rubbing over the ears to effectually rouse him, compel him to "move on." But we went homeward contented with our lot in life. No lesson would better teach this content. We had left a fine dinner-table in one of London's grand houses to go and see this sight; and we came away from Whitechapel with a lesson that none will forget. Its restless population is London's problem and dread. What to do with it no one can tell. Occasionally it overflows all checks, and rages in the riots that we hear of, but in ordinary times the helmeted officer, with his mace and lantern, can control this great mass of humanity, which fills up square miles of the East End of London with probably more wretchedness and vice than is found on any other equal surface in the world.

LETTER L.

LONDON TO LIVERPOOL.

NEW YORK, October 25.

On a foggy morning, when it was difficult to see across the street until the approach of the sun drove away some of the clouds, we bade farewell to London. The cabby drove us quickly to Euston Square, for he could thread the streets whatever the weather, and we took the "Scotch Express," on the London and Northwestern Railway, to Liverpool. This is the great railway of England, and the "Scotch Express" is one of its fastest trains. We started in fog and gloom, but soon emerged into sunshine, for the fog is a peculiarity of London and the Thames Valley, and a few miles outside it entirely disappeared, and the sun came out pleasantly. We were whirling along at the rate of fifty miles an hour, whisking past stations, and through, over, and under the succession of gardens of which England seems to be almost entirely made up. We stopped twice, and in a few hours had accomplished the two hundred and two miles between London and Liverpool.

We stopped at Rugby, famous for its school and as one of the most complex railway junctions in England, whence Dickens's "Mugby Junction" is derived, and we stopped at Crewe, which seems a labyrinth of railway-shops, sidings, and storehouses. The railway has an enormous traffic, and is almost throughout its line provided with four tracks to accommodate it. Where it does not have them they are now being constructed, and the great steam-digger was seen along the line like a huge dredging-machine, scooping the earth out of the hill-side and depositing it on the gravel-cars to be hauled away. Here we were treated to frequent insights into the way of running a great English railway, and were also shown the remarkable fare-lists that English railway managers issue, which contain, in parallel columns, the rates of fare between the various stations, for first-, second-, and third-class passengers, horses and dogs, all of which are provided with accommodations on the trains. The dog is not so unceremoniously treated in England as he is with us when he travels. On the contrary, his rights are recognized. The railways provide him with special accommodations, and so do the hotels. In fact, the dogs are great travellers in Her Majesty's dominions, and they have to be taken care of; but, like everything else English, they have their well-defined position in the social scale. Therefore the English hotels hang up notices in the rooms announcing the rates for boarding dogs as well as people. "This room is five shillings," read the announcement in the Liverpool hotel, but it ominously added, "Each dog kept in this room is charged half a guinea a day." Thus the dog is a more costly boarder than his owner, because the hotel proprietor desired to force the dog-owners to put them in the place provided for them in the lower part of the hotel.

We arrived at Liverpool to find it excited about an election for City Councilmen. The politicians covered the walls and fences with placards appealing to the voters very much as we do, and I was somewhat surprised to find the great show-bills leading off with the words, "To the Electors of —— Ward, —Ladies and Gentlemen." They have got in this portion of the British Monarchy to the point that Philadelphia has not yet reached,—they enjoy female suffrage. The portion of the Liverpool inhabitants who were not engaging in the election seemed to be preparing for a migration across the Atlantic.

The arriving railway trains emptied out crowds of homeward bound Americans, and the hotels were full of them and their boxes. Fleets of steamers were leaving with full cabins, and the rush which had been eastward earlier in the season was now turned westward. We made a drop to add to the current, and found our countrymen, after roaming all over Europe, were unanimous on one thing : they preferred their own country to all others as a place to live in, and were glad to be on the homeward track again.

Reaching Liverpool we were subjected to the accident which frequently befalls ocean travellers. They make all their arrangements for the homeward journey, and having firm reliance on the certainty of the transatlantic ferry, usually go to Liverpool on the eve of their sailing day. We went thus, and found that our ship was not going. She had needed repairs, and had been docked for the purpose. But the inadequate docking facilities of Liverpool for the very large steamships of the present day is shown in the fact that, having gone into the repairing dock at the time of high spring-tides, the neap-tides had caught her, and she could not be floated out for several days. She was practically a prisoner ; she could not get out until much after her appointed day of sailing, and her passengers had to be provided elsewhere. But in the emergency the American line agents were very kind, and, through the courtesy of the Inman Steamship Company, we were transferred to their fine steamer, the City of Brussels, Captain Frederick Watkins. So, on another gloomy, foggy morning, we went down to the Prince's Landing Stage, and got on one of those strong but uncomfortable tugs that are employed to transfer passengers from the wharf to the ocean steamers. We could dimly see the vessel, with steam up, waiting for us out in mid-river. The passengers came straggling aboard the tug, and porters brought on huge trunks on their backs, and when they had piled a lighter almost full they carried in a half-dozen sacks of mails, and then we started. The tug and lighter steamed out alongside the great steamer, and in a few minutes we were off. It was just at high water, for the bar in the Mersey has to be crossed at high tide ; we passed the light-ships and buoys marking the channel there, and dimly discerning the shore through the fog, we were soon out in the Irish Sea, and steaming along the Welsh coast. All afternoon and night we kept down and across the channel, past the high, bold shore at Holyhead, and, reaching the Irish coast, we steamed along it, and in the early morning dropped anchor at Queenstown harbor entrance.

## THE COVE OF CORK AND THE BLARNEY STONE.

Fog again prevailed in the early morning, and little could be seen until the rising sun became strong enough to drive the mist away. We were lying at anchor waiting for the mails, and had to wait nearly all day. The great mails from England to America are sent from London to the steamers three times a week. They leave London every Tuesday, Thursday, and Saturday evening, and are put aboard the steamers at Queenstown on the following afternoon. The steamers have to leave Liverpool when the tide suits, hence they frequently make long waits at Queenstown, and in this case there was ample time for an excursion ashore. We, therefore, went off on the tug in the morning, and, the fog having lifted, we had a beautiful sail up through the land-locked Cove of Cork, whose green waters make one of the finest harbors in the world. The entrance is a narrow way between bold hills that are strongly fortified, and Spike Island and its attendant forts make an almost impregnable defence to this famous harbor, where over three hundred large vessels, most of them bound from America, were at anchor, having, as the mercantile phrase goes, come "to Cork for orders." Here the shipmaster, having sailed his vessel across the Atlantic, drops in as the most convenient port of call, to get orders from the shipper whither he shall go to deliver his cargo. It is one of the best and most frequented ports in Europe, and, as you sail up the Cove, Queenstown lies before you, terraced on the side of a steep hill, the growth of the recent necessities of trade. Queenstown has not much to attract the visitor, save the beauty of its situation, and he soon goes whirling up the river Lee on the railway to Cork. Here a jaunting-car rattles you around to see the sights, which the voluble driver explains with any amount of blarney, whilst beggars try to get you to part with stray coppers. Cork is not so pretentious a town as some others, but it still contains enough to make a visit pleasant. Its chief building is the new Episcopal Cathedral of St. Fin Barre, which is being built by the disestablished Irish Church, at a cost of six hundred and fifty thousand dollars, and is almost completed. This very fine church, which has been twelve years constructing, stands on a hill-top, and can be seen from afar. Its main tower is yet to be completed, and will be two hundred and sixty feet high. Cork is very proud of this church, which is one of the finest in Ireland, and much of the pride comes from the fact that its builder, once a poor boy, has been also the architect of his own fortune. I tried to find out the population of Cork, but the driver said it varied too much for him to give an accurate estimate, though it was very great indeed. I asked why it varied, and he answered, because there were so many children born that it was impossible to count them, or even baptize them. "There's many a child," he said, "that runs around Cork for a twelvemonth, without so much as having a name to bless himself with."

But a visit to Cork and its Walk of Mardyke and its pretty drives along the river Lee, is incomplete without a journey to the castle and groves of Blarney and the famous "Blarney Stone." This celebrated castle is now an ivy-covered ruin, and the "Blarney Stone" is situated in the northern angle, in an almost inaccessible position, several feet below the top. It is a broad, flat stone, set upon brackets like a cornice, and has, rudely carved in it, the inscription, "*Cormach McCarthy, fortis mi fiori fecit*, 1446." Kissing the Blarney Stone, which is, of course, the ambition of every true Irishman, is a feat of no little difficulty. To do it, he either has to be lowered down, or held, head downwards, from the top of the wall. But the Irish hereabouts have mother wit enough to get out of the difficulty. They have another stone on the Castle floor which they say has all the virtues of the real one, and is much easier to kiss. It is quite possible that this is true, but whether it be so or not, the veritable "Blarney Stone" is so hard to get at that it ought to do some good for the venturesome man who may try to reach it. The old song says:

"There is a stone there, whoever kisses,
Oh, he niver misses to grow eloquint;
'Tis he may clamber to a lady's chamber,
Or become a mimber of swate Parliamint.
A clever spouter he'll sure turn out, or
An out-an-outer to be lit alone.
Don't hope to hinder him or to bewilder him;
Shure he's a pilgrim from the Blarney Stone."

And now, having paid devotion to the famous "Blarney Stone," what better could I do than to immediately start for America? We at once left for Queenstown to join the steamer. The mails arrived in the afternoon, and with them the stray passengers. They all came down to the tender at the Queenstown wharf, followed by a crowd of peddlers and mendicants, who scented profit from afar. There were the itinerant venders of Irish lace, bog-oak jewelry, and the shillelahs, made of the "rale ould Limerick blackthorn, which it is an honor to your worship to carry home wid ye to Ameriky." The mails, nearly four tons of them, were carried aboard on men's backs, and thrown down on the deck of the tender, and the gang-plank was hauled in, and the whistle blew, but still we did not start. A passenger was on the wharf chaffering with an ancient Irish dame, who had come all the way from Limerick to sell shillelahs. He wanted the price reduced; she would not reduce, for "it wad dishonor that noble stick not to charge a fair price for it;" and the great transatlantic mail was waiting, including a ponderous despatch bag for the Secretary of State, until the bargain was concluded. But the old lady would not yield, and the mail probably would have been waiting until now, had not an officer brought the passenger aboard—without the shillelah. The tender steamed out through the fleet of vessels, past Spike Island and its forts and penal settlement, and between the two great forts that guard the harbor entrance,—Rocky Island, with its excavated caverns and chambers that hold many thousand barrels of gunpowder, and Haulbowline Island, with its great water-tank hewn out of the solid rock,—and the tender finally came alongside the steamer. The mails were carried aboard and thrown down into the hold. Then the steamer started, and, the tug parting company, the pilot was taken off, and the journey began along the Irish coast and out into the Atlantic. We rapidly sailed along the bold Irish shore, gradually moving farther and farther away from its great headlands, and, when dark night had come, we passed Fastnet Light far to the north of us. The great light, perched on its isolated rock, revolving and quickly flashing far across the sea, and the more distant and more slowly-revolving light on Calf Rock, were the last we saw of Ireland. Before long both were left far behind us, the steamer had taken her bearings for a long stretch across the ocean, and

N*

day after day the transatlantic voyage continued, with little to see but sea and sky, clouds and rain, fog and storm, as the vessel rocked and rolled, but pushed steadily onward.

## HOMEWARD BOUND.

Day after day the monotonous voyage continued; the passengers nearly all sea-sick at the beginning, for a heavy head sea stirred up the waves and entirely demoralized every one's internal arrangements; but gradually growing better, until on Sunday, October 20, almost all were able to appear at divine service, conducted in the main saloon, by the captain. But the relief was only temporary, for another storm struck us, and again the cabin was demoralized and the people were unhappy. The steamer rolled and pitched for two days as a heavy head sea retarded her voyage, and when every one's sides were aching and all wished they had never ventured on the ocean, the sun reappeared and the sea became comparatively calm again. The joy at returning ease was shown by an impromptu concert on the evening of Wednesday, October 23, and after an attractive entertainment, in which one of the ship's stewards, an elocutionist and comic vocalist of great power, carried off the chief honors, we went to bed feeling happy. But the happiness was of short duration. Just as Thursday morning came another gale struck us, which I afterwards learned had been sent us direct from Philadelphia. The ship rolled fearfully. Everything seemed to be running down-hill. You were knocked about in the little state-rooms; the crockery was rolled off the tables, and the sea-sickness was renewed. The 24th of October, with the gale constantly increasing in intensity, as the water swept over the decks and the steamer was tossed about, will long be remembered by as miserable a party of passengers as ever crossed the Atlantic. All day and half the night it continued, and one huge wave brought aboard a large horse-mackerel, which was duly seized by the stewards. But the stout engine continued its unwearying task and drove us through the storm, and the gale at midnight moderated and the weather cleared. In the early morning of October 25 we took aboard the pilot off Nantucket, and he reported terrible weather, and then the sun coming out cheerfully, and the sea being calmed, the passengers once more were happy, as they crowded out on the last day to look for land. And the land came,—first Long Island, then Sandy Hook, and entering the harbor, the voyage ended. The great engine, which had turned the screw a half-million times, stopped. The stokers, who had poured three tons of coal in every hour, and the engineers who had also every hour dropped on the journals two gallons of olive-oil, had a rest. The passengers were rid of sea-sickness, and one of the worst voyages across the ocean was brought to a close with every one heartily glad to be again in America.

A brief delay at quarantine whilst the port physician satisfied himself that sea-sickness had been the only epidemic on board (his inspection being chiefly made through the bottom of a tumbler kindly loaned him by the ship's doctor, who did likewise) was followed by a sail through the Narrows to the pier on North River. Myriads of steam-whistles greeted us from all the craft we passed. The noise was deafening, for they recognized a ship that all had feared would be wrecked. Then, by the aid of several tugs and a steamboat, the great steamer was gradually coaxed into her dock. It was night when we were landed, and a crowd of stevedores came aboard to carry off the baggage. " Is this New York ?" asked one of our English passengers. He was told it was. " Why, it looks very much like Ireland," he continued, as the regiment of Hibernians noisily wrestled with the trunks. Bidding good-by to the captain, and bestowing our last shillings on the stewards, we went ashore and there saw Captain Burton and his squad of Custom-House officers drawn up in martial array across the wharf. The hearts of seventy-two cabin passengers sank within them. It is all very well to say " I am an American" to the unsophisticated Custom-House officers in Europe, and thus slip through the tariffs over there, but the American official of that ilk knows his fellow-countrymen too well to be thus bamboozled. How those passengers who had been trailing their new dresses over the decks all through the voyage, to make them look old and dirty, trembled for the result !*

---

* During the voyage this dread of the Custom-House examination was the chief subject of conversation, especially among the ladies. Nearly all had bought new clothing, and they appeared on deck in the worst weather in the most costly costumes and ornaments, so as to be able to tell the Custom-House officer at New York they had worn them. A young and handsome widow among the passengers brought over two

The trunks were all brought out and put upon the wharf, and Captain Burton detailed his officers to examine them. The ladies, with great ability, explained how very few things they had, and how very old they were, and how awfully anxious they were to catch the next train. People who never knew how to strap trunks before were adepts at it as soon as the officer's back was turned. On all sides there was a disgorging of small sums of money for duties, and at last the chalk-marks were put on. Never before had chalk seemed so delightful, and half the passengers went out with themselves all chalked in their eagerness to get their boxes away. The examination was careful, quick, and kindly done; and, in my case, the shabby condition in which I had got, added to the fact, so well known to Custom-House officers, that in newspaper circles honesty and poverty usually go hand-in-hand, got me through the ordeal pleasantly. "There is no duty on old clothes," said the official, as he chalked my overcoat; "but I advise you to get a new one as soon as possible." The chalk-marks on, there was another Hibernian irruption, which seized the baggage and took it off the wharf. Then, as we emerged, it seemed as if Bedlam had broken loose, as the horde of hackmen tried to seize us and our goods. Such howling, screaming, and tugging I never heard or saw in any part of Europe. The fellows who were not trying to get possession of us were endeavoring to drive their wagons over us. The foreign passengers whose first view of America was thus opened, were sure that the red Indians had made a raid into New York. But we survived it, though we got out of New York as soon as possible, and were soon rushing over the Pennsylvania Railroad, homeward bound, finding it as complete a railway as the best one abroad.

On this tour, which has now ended, I was accompanied by my wife and two children, and also by a lady and gentleman

---

meerschaum pipes as presents. She was afraid the officials would not pass them unless they had been smoked, and a young gentleman on board gallantly offered to do it. But, unfortunately, sea-sickness dogged him so closely that he never could muster sufficient courage to begin the task. Several times daily he explained this to the lady as they unsteadily walked the deck together; and finally, though not courageous enough to smoke the pipes, he did get bold enough to make her a proposal of marriage.

of Philadelphia, so that throughout the journey it was a party of six. On the Continent we were also accompanied by a Philadelphia lady who is a resident of Paris. The children, a boy of ten years and a girl of six, were chiefly engaged throughout the journey in swindling untutored European landlords, who contracted to board them for half price, but when they saw how much the children could eat, wished they hadn't. This party went through Europe like a disciplined army. Each one had a regular duty to perform. One person did all the paying, and the others thus saved unending gratuities. Every evening the journey of the next day was mapped out. We took no trunks when on the wing, but, instead, had a number of stout linen bags made, in which clothing was carried in convenient parcels, bound by shawl straps. Each person had certain parcels to carry and look after. When a train arrived at the station, in a moment our procession started out to coach or omnibus with bags in hand, but one person doing the inquiring or talking and the others following their leader. We were a large enough party to strike the porters and hackmen with awe and the landlords with respect. Everywhere we met kind treatment, and in the rare cases where incivility was attempted, it was met with stern rebuke in the good old American language, no matter what might be the tongue the offender spoke. This language, as I have before remarked, carries the strongest weight in Europe. They may not understand what is said, but they know the dialect, and also know that it means business. Thus I end the record of this holiday tour,—hastily and imperfectly written to jot down impressions as they came; written sometimes on rushing railway cars or tossing steamers, sometimes by the roadside, sometimes at midnight by the uncertain light of the solitary candle the European landlord furnished at a high price in the apartment of his guest; but written always in good spirit, and with the intention of recording an honest American impression, be it never so hasty, of scenes as they occurred. I hope it may have revived in some, pleasant memories of former homes or bygone visits; and that it may have given to others an idea of what opportunity may have thus far prevented their seeing. But whilst the impressions given of European grandeur, beauty, strength, and power may be great, indeed, still stronger is the impression made that no country in Europe is as suitable a *home* for the American as the United States. He goes abroad gladly; he satiates with sight-seeing, and he comes home with a zest for American comforts, institutions, habits, and ideas that he never felt before. This is the strongest lesson an European tour teaches, and whilst we may look on at the sights and glories of the Old World, a brief experience convinces that they are not to be exchanged for the more sober, yet more comfortable, realities of the New World. With this as the most strongly-fixed impression of all made by the visit, I close the Holiday Tour.

# INDEX.

Aar River, 229, 239.
Abbeville, 277.
Abelard and Heloise, tomb, 156.
Absenteeism in Ireland, 45.
Acclimatation Garden, 276.
Agriculture, English, 128, 134.
Aix-la-Chapelle, 191.
Aix-la-Chapelle Cathedral, 191.
Alexandra Palace, 119.
Allan, Bridge of, 66.
Alma Bridge, 159.
Alnwick Castle, 75.
Alpine negotiation, 256.
Alpine scenery, 218.
Alpnach, 220, 228.
Amberien, 267.
American-French, 143, 146, 165, 170, 176.
American Minister, 117.
American Steamship Line, 14, 76.
Amiens Cathedral, 277.
André's tomb, 97.
Antrim, Earl of, 50.
Aquarium, Brighton, 132.
Arch of Triumph, 142, 151, 157, 170, 176, 181.
Ardoyne, 48.
Argyle, Duke of, 61.
Arpenaz Cascade, 250.
Arth, 224.
Arthur's Seat, 67, 72.
Arve River, 249, 258.
Ascensions of Mont Blanc, 252.
Aubonne, 244.
Avenue Bois de Boulogne, 181.
Avenue of the Opera, 176.
Avon River, 90.

Bacharach, 201.
Baden-Baden, 208.

Baden Castle, 211.
Baggage, 127.
Baggage smashing, 278.
Ballachulish, 63.
Balloon, 173.
Bank of England, 108.
Bank of Ireland, 38.
Bannockburn, 66.
Barberine Cascade, 259.
Barbers, French, 169.
Basle, 217, 223.
Baume, 274.
Bears, 231, 236.
Beds, 203, 234.
Beer, 208, 211.
Belfast, 45.
Belgium, 185.
Bellegarde, 266.
Benmore, 62.
Ben Nevis, 65.
Berne, 236.
Berwick-upon-Tweed, 74.
Billingsgate, 106, 115.
Bingen, 202.
Black Forest, 211.
Blanc, Mont, 244, 252.
Blarney Stone, 296.
Bog-oak jewelry, 297.
Bois du Boulogne, 141, 180.
Bonn, 196.
Bonnivard, 245, 264.
Boppard, 200.
Boulogne, 277.
Boyne River, 42.
Bread prices, 269.
Breadalbane, Earl of, 62, 65.
Breakfasts, French, 169, 171.
Bridal parties, Parisian, 180.
Bridge of Sighs, London, 288.
Brienz Lake, 229, 232.

Brighton, 129.
Britanuia Tubular Bridge, 34.
British Channel Squadron, 22.
British Museum, 119.
Browhead Signal Station, 24.
Brown stout, 39.
Broxsburne House, 75.
Brunig Pass, 228.
Brunswick, Duke of, 247.
Brussels, 186.
Brussels Cathedral, 188.
Bull, Cow, and Calf, 23.
Burgundy, 272.
Burton, Captain, 299.
Bute, Marquis of, 61.
Butter without salt, 77, 169.
Byron, 197, 244.

Cabs, 127, 144, 182.
Caithness, Earl of, 73.
Calais, 277.
Calais-Douvres, steamer, 135, 279.
Calf-Rock Light, 23, 297.
Calvin, John, 184, 247.
Cambrai, 185.
Canterbury Cathedral, 280.
Cantyre peninsula, 62.
Cape Henlopen, 9.
Cape May, 9, 10.
Carberry Hill, 75.
Cardross Castle, 61.
Cat Castle, 200.
Cemetery, French, 152.
Chain Pier, Brighton, 131.
Chalons, 274.
Chamois, 231.
Chamounix, 250, 251.
Champs Elysées, 141, 142, 152, 174, 176.
Chancy, 265.
Channel crossing, 134, 278.
Channel passages, 135.
Chantilly, 184.
Charens, 244.
Charlemagne, 191.
Charlemagne relics, 191.
Chatham, 280.
Chatham's, Earl, tomb, 96, 97.
Chatsworth, 86.
Chaucer's tomb, 96
Chester, 29.
Chester Castle, 30.
Chester Cathedral, 31.
Chester Town Hall, 30.

Chevet, 176.
Childs, George W., 97.
Childwall Abbey, 28.
Chillon Castle, 245, 264.
Chimney-pots, 27, 58, 247.
City of Brussels, steamer, 294.
Claret wine, 272.
Cleopatra's Needle, 107.
Clock, Strasburg, 216.
Clyde River, 55, 60.
Coal-fields, 185.
Coblentz, 198.
Coilantogle Ford, 66.
Coleridge, Chief Justice, 31.
Coleridge, S. T., 194.
Cologne, 192, 195.
Cologne Cathedral, 192, 194, 196.
Cologne water, 192.
Communists, 151, 155, 157.
Compiègne, 184.
Concert gardens, 176.
Condé, Prince of, 184.
Congress, Swiss, 238.
Conway Castle, 35.
Coppet, 244.
Cork, 295.
Corliss engine, 47, 162.
Coronation chair, 98.
Côte d'Or, 272.
Courbevoie, 151.
Cove of Cork, 24, 295.
Cowper memorial window, 97.
Craigneish Loch, 62.
Crecy, battle-field, 277.
Credo, Mont, 265.
Crewe, 293.
Crinan Canal, 62.
Crystal Palace, 88, 119.
Culoz, 267.
Custom-Houses, 140, 185, 190, 217, 266, 290.

Darlington, 76.
Darnley, Lord, 70, 73.
Dean Cemetery, 72.
Dee River, 29.
Dent de Morcles, 263.
Dent du Midi, 242, 263.
Derwent River, 84.
De Staël, Madame, 244.
Devonshire, Duke of, 86.
Dickens's manuscripts, 283.
Dieppe, 133, 137.
Dijon, 274.

## INDEX.

Dinners, French, 175.
Divine service at sea, 20, 298.
Dixon, John, 107.
Dogs, 187, 276, 293.
Donegal, Marquis of, 45.
Donkeys, 27, 41, 83, 253.
Dover, 279.
Dover Castle, 280.
Drachenfels, 196.
Dredging-machines, 56, 60.
Drexel, Harjes & Co., 172.
Drinking-water, 125.
Drogheda, 42.
Dublin, 37.
Dudley, Earl of, 65.
Dulwich, 280.
Dumbarton Castle, 60.
Dunbar Castle, 75.
Dunluce Castle, 52.
Dunolly Castle, 62.
Dunstaffnage Castle, 63.
Durham Castle, 76.
Durham Cathedral, 76.

Early trains, 183.
East London, 115, 285.
Eaton Hall, 32.
Eau Noire, 259.
Ecluse, Fortress, 265.
Edinburgh, 66.
Edinburgh Castle, 67, 69.
Education, Council Committee on, 119.
Edward the Confessor's tomb, 97, 98.
Ehrenbreitstein, 198.
Elections in Liverpool, 293.
Elections in Lyons, 269.
Electric light, 22, 112, 142, 176.
Emperor Fountain, 89.
Emperor of Brazil, 50.
English Channel, 129, 137.
English pronunciation, 80, 81, 288.
Equipages, Parisian, 181.
Esk River, 73.
Espionage, French, 278.
Ethiopia, steamer, 60.
Etive Glen, 65.
Etive Loch, 63.
Evain, 245.
Exclusiveness, English, 126.
Exposition of 1878, 147, 157.

Falkenberg, 201.

Falkirk, 66.
Farina, Jean Maria, 192.
Fashions, Paris, 167.
Fastnet Light, 24, 297.
Favorite Palace, 211.
Fête of St. Cloud, 177.
Filter, Alpine, 242.
Fin McCool, 51.
Fire-engines, 132.
Fire Monument, London, 106
Firth of Clyde, 55, 61.
Firth of Forth, 74.
Five-Fathom Bank, 9.
Flax, 187.
Fluelen, 221.
Fontainebleau, 274.
Food in England, 123.
Food in Paris, 145, 148.
Forclaz Mountain, 260.
Fountains at Versailles, 148.
Four Cantons Lake, 220.
Fourviere, 268.
French State carriages, 150.
Freyburg, 241.
Funerals, English, 27.
Funerals, French, 153.
Furstenberg Castle, 201.
Fyne, Loch, 62.

Gaming, 209, 245.
Gateacre, 28.
Gee, Sir William, 79.
Geneva, 245, 264.
Geneva Lake, 242.
Giant's Causeway, 48.
Gibbon, 212, 244.
Giessbach Falls, 229.
Gifford Gate, 75.
Glaciers, 242.
Glasgow, 58.
Glasgow Cathedral, 58.
Glencoe, 63.
Glyn & Co., 109.
Goat-wagons, 131.
Gog and Magog, 105.
Goitre, 262.
Grand Mulets, 252.
Great St. Bernard Pass, 262.
Greenock, 55, 56, 61.
Grosvenor Park, 33.
Guildhall, 105.
Guinness's Brewery, Dublin, 39.
Guinness, Sir Benjamin Lee, 39.
Gutekunst, F., 285.

/ INDEX.

Gutenberg, 202.
Guy of Warwick, 91.
Haddon Hall, 84.
Halle, 186, 187.
Ham, Fortress, 184.
Hartington, Marquis of, 86.
Hathaway, Anne, 93.
Haulbowline Island, 297.
Hawkshaw, Sir John, 104.
Heidelberg, 205.
Heidelberg Castle, 205.
Heidelberg University, 205.
Heimberg, 201.
Henry VII.'s tomb, 97.
Herald reading-room, 172.
Heralds' College, London, 106.
Herbert memorial window, 97.
Herbesthal, 190.
Highlands of Scotland, 62.
Hobgoblin Hall, 75.
Holborn Viaduct, 100.
Holy Ghost Church, 207.
Holyhead, 35, 295.
Holyrood, 70, 71.
Holy Trinity Church, Stratford, 93.
Hookes, Nicholas, 35.
Hotels, Alpine, 234.
Hotels, English, 122.
Hotels, German, 203.
Hotspur's tomb, 79.
Houndsditch, 115.
Howth, 37, 41.
Hugo, Victor, 276.
Hyde Park, 121.

Ice-cream, 123, 213.
Industrial Museum, Glasgow, 59.
Interlacken, 233.
Invalides, 151.
Ireland, 37.
Ireland's Eye, 42.
Irish coast, 23.
Irish mail-train, 33.
Irish Sea, 294.

Jaunting-cars, 37, 47, 295.
Jeffrey, Lord, 68, 72.
Jena Bridge, 159.
Jennings estate, 109.
Joan of Arc, 184.
Johannisberg Castle, 202.
Joigny, 274.

Jungfrau, 224, 235, 260.
Jura Mountains, 265, 272.
Jura Sound, 62.

Katzanellenbogen, Counts of, 199.
Kehl, 214.
Kelvingrove Park, 59.
Kenilworth, 91.
Kew Gardens, 120.
Kingstown, 37.
Kinsale Head, 24.
Knights of Liberty, 179.
Knox, John, 58, 68, 71, 247.
Königstuhl, 199, 207.
Kussnach, 220.
Kyles of Bute, 61.

La Batiaz Castle, 261.
La Harpe, General, 244.
Lace-making, 186.
Lager beer, 192.
Lahn River, 199.
Lahneck, 199.
Lamberton Kirk, 75.
Lasswade, 73.
Lausanne, 242, 244, 245.
Leamington, 89.
Lee River, 295.
Leicester's tomb, 92.
Length of ocean voyages, 18.
Leven, Loch, 63.
Liebenfels, 199.
Liege, 190.
Liffey River, 37.
Linen manufacture, 47.
Linlithgow, 66.
Lion of Lucerne, 220.
Liverpool, 25, 293.
Liverpool Docks, 25, 294.
Lloyds, 105.
London, 94, 280.
London Bridge, 101.
London cheap lodging-houses, 291.
London Docks, 288.
Long Island, 299.
Lorch, 201.
Lore stone, 74.
Lorne, Marquis of, 61.
Louise and Lorne Chambers, 291.
Lucerne, 219.
Lucerne, Lake, 220.
Lungren Lake, 228.
Lurelio Rock, 200.
Lyons, 267.

McCormick, Richard C., 163.
MacDonald Clan massacre, 63.
Mellwain, Rev. Dr., 46.
Macon, 274.
Main River, 202.
Manners, Lord John, 84.
Mannheim, 207.
Mansion House, 105.
Marck, William de la, 190.
Marksburg, 199.
Marne River, 274.
Martigny, 261.
Mary, Queen of Scots, 59, 68, 69, 75.
Mary, Queen of Scots, tomb, 97.
Mauberge, 185.
Mauvais Pas, 258.
Mayence, 202.
Mayence Cathedral, 204.
Medway River, 280.
Meals in England, 124.
Menage River, 249.
Mer de Glace, 255, 258.
Mersey River, 25, 294.
Meuse River, 190.
Monk, the, 235.
Mons, 185.
Mons Meg, 70, 186.
Montereau, 274.
Montets, 258.
Montmartre, 151, 170.
Montreux, 244.
Mont St. Valerien, 151, 170, 177.
Morat Lake, battle, 241.
Morges, 244.
Morrison, Captain Henry, 9, 19.
Moselle River, 198.
Mosquitoes, 226.
Mountain names, 248.
Mouse Tower, 202.
Multangular Tower, York, 80.
Murray, Lindley, 80.
Museum, British, 119.
Museum, Brussels, 188.
Musical boxes, 246.

Nahe River, 201.
Nantucket, 298.
Nassau, Duke of, mummy, 217.
Neckar River, 207.
Necropolis, Glasgow, 58.
New Haven, 133, 136.
Newcastle-upon-Tyne, 75.
Newington, 73.
Newry, 44.

Newton's tomb, 97.
Normandy, 277.
North Allerton, 76.
Northumberland, Duke of, 75.
Notre Dame Cathedral, 152, 276.
Notre Dame de Fourviere Church, 269.
Noyes, General E. F., 117, 170.
Noyon, 184.
Nyon, 244.

Oban, 62.
Oberlin's tomb, 216.
Oberwesel, 200.
Octopus, 132.
Octroi, 148.
Odenwald, 205.
Office hours in Scotland, 58.
Offling, William, 30.
Ohio, steamer, 7, 19.
Old Clothes Market, 115.
Old red sandstone, 203.
Olten, 218.
Omnibus, 151, 170, 182.
Oos River, 208.
Opium smoking, 290.
Orchy Glen, 65.
Ouchy, 244, 245.
Ouse River, 77.
Overcrowding in Paris, 182.
Owen, Sir F. Philip C., 282.

Palace of Justice, Brussels, 187.
Palais Royal, 176.
Paris, 140.
Paris by night, 175.
Parisian homes, 144.
Pâtés de fois gras, 217.
Paxton, Sir Joseph, 88.
Peacock Inn, 84.
Peak of Derbyshire, 87.
Peat, 44.
Pennsylvania Railroad, 18, 300
Pentland Hills, 67.
Père la Chaise, 153.
Perkeo, 206.
Peter the Hermit, 277.
Pfalz, 201.
Phil's Buildings, 115.
Phœnix Park, 40.
Pilatus, Mount, 219, 222.
Pissevache Falls, 262.
Place de la Concorde, 176.
Police, London, 286.

## INDEX.

Port Rush, 48
Prangins, 244.
'Prentice pillar, Rosslin Chapel, 73.
Preston Pans, 75.
Printing-House Square, 111.
Providence House, Chester, 30.
Pullman palace-cars, 76, 126, 165.

Quarantine, New York, 299.
Queen's Park, Glasgow, 59.
Queenstown, 24, 295.

Railway conductors, 189.
Railway, Rigi, 222, 224.
Railways, Baden, 208, 213.
Railways, English, 280, 292.
Railways, French, 271, 276.
Railways, Swiss, 239, 263.
Raphael's cartoons, 283.
Raspail's tomb, 155.
Reading Railroad locomotive, 165.
Recreation in London, 119.
Regalia of Scotland, 69.
Republic, steamboat, 7.
Reuss River, 219.
Rheinfels, 200.
Rheingau, 202.
Rheinstein, 201.
Rhine River, 189, 195.
Rhine wines, 197.
Rhone River, 242, 245, 231, 264.
Richmond, Duke of, 282.
Rigi, Mont, 219, 222.
Rizzio, David, 70.
Roberts' Head, 24.
Roche's Point, 24.
Rochester, 280.
Rockville, 74.
Rocky Island, 297.
Rolandseck Castle, 197.
Rolle, 244.
Rosslin Chapel, 73.
Rothesay, Duke of, 61.
Rotten Row, 121.
Rousseau, 244.
Rousseau's Island, 245.
Rowsley, 83.
Roxburgh, Duke of, 75.
Rubens, Peter Paul, 188
Rudesheim, 202.
Rugby, 293.
Rutland, Duke of, 84.

Salisbury Craigs, 67.

Sambre River, 185.
Sandford, Sir Herbert, 282.
Sandstone, 203.
Sandy Hook, 299.
Saone River, 268.
Sarine River, 241.
Sarnen Lake, 228.
Savoy, 244, 249.
Saxe's monument, 216.
St. Bernard dogs, 259.
St. Bernard Pass, 262.
St. Cloud, 151, 177.
St. Fin Barre, Cathedral, 295.
St. George's Church, Belfast, 46.
St. George's Hall, Liverpool, 27.
St. George's-in-the-East, 280.
St. Giles' Cathedral, 71.
St. Gothard Pass, 221.
St. John Baptist Church, Chester, 32.
St. Margaret's Chapel, 70.
St. Mary's Church, Conway, 35.
St. Mary's Church, Warwick, 92.
St. Patrick's Cathedral, Dublin, 39.
St. Paul's Cathedral, 95.
St. Quentin, 184.
St. Thomas' Church, Strasburg, 216.
St. Ursula, 193.
St. Ursula Church, 193.
St. Ursula Convent, 197.
St. Waudra Church, 186.
St. Zoar, 200.
Scarborough, 81.
Scheldt River, 184.
Schliemann's antiquities, 283.
Schomberg Castle, 201.
Schools in Wales, 36.
Scone, stone of, 63, 98.
Scott, Sir Walter, 59, 66, 68, 69, 74, 87, 190.
Sea-bathing, 82, 129.
Sea-horses, 133.
Sea of Ice, 255, 258.
Sea-sickness, 10, 278, 298.
Seine River, 151, 170, 177, 184, 274.
Sempach Lake, 218.
Seus, 201.
Seven Sisters, 201.
Shakspeare, 92.
Shakspeare Memorial, 93.
Shantytown, Paris, 160.
Sheepshanks collection, 282.
Shillelahs, 297.

Ship-building, 57.
Siebenbierge, 196.
Siegfried, 197.
Silk manufacture, 267.
Silver Needle Mountain, 258.
Simplon, 262.
Smith, Mrs. Amanda, 21.
Smithfield, 106, 115.
Soldiers, British, 43.
Soldiers, Swiss, 238.
Somme River, 277.
Sooneck, 201.
South Kensington Museum, 119, 281.
Spa, 190.
Spielhorn, 224.
Spike Island, 295, 297.
Stage-bill, old, 78.
Stahlick Castle, 201.
Stanley, Lady Augusta's tomb, 99.
Steam-digger, 293.
Steamship inspection, 20.
Stephenson, Robert, 34.
Stirling Castle, 66.
Stores in Paris, 167.
Strasburg, 214.
Strasburg Cathedral, 215.
Stratford-on-Avon, 92.
Street railways, 26, 58, 119, 182.
Sunday at sea, 20, 298.
Sunday in Baden-Baden, 208.
Sunday in Belfast, 46.
Sunday in London, 94.
Sunday in Lyons, 269.
Sunday in Paris, 147.
Swindles at Giant's Causeway, 54.
Sybilla Augusta, 212.

Tantallan Castle, 75.
Tavernier, 244.
Taxation in London, 113.
Taxation on equipage, 122.
Taylor, Bayard, 117.
Tell, William, 221, 231.
Tell's Chapel, 221.
Tête Noire, 259.
Theatre Becker, 179.
Theatre Guignolet, 175.
Theatres, puppet, 174.
Thiers, Adolphe, 152.
Thiers' tomb, 154.
Thompson, Richard A., 282.
Thornton, John, 79.
Thorwaldsen, 202, 220.

Three Kings of Cologne, 194.
Thun Lake, 233, 239.
Tidal gauges, 8.
Times office, London, 111.
Tipping, 88, 92, 235.
Tombs, French, 154.
Tonnere, 274.
Transatlantic mails, 295.
Transatlantic traffic, 15.
Trendell, A. J. R., 282.
Trianons, 150.
Trient Gorge, 260, 263.
Trocadero Palace, 151, 159.
Tuileries, 173.
Tumbrils, 170.
Tun, Heidelberg, 206.
Tweed River, 75.
Tweeddale, Marquis of, 75.
Tyndrum, 65.
Tyne River, 75.
Tyrconnel, Lady, 43.

Underground Railway, 100, 115.
Uri, 220.

Valois, 244.
Vauban, 185.
Vaud, 244.
Vegetables in England, 123.
Vegetables in Paris, 145.
Vernon, Dorothy, 85.
Versailles, 149.
Verviers, 190.
Vevay, 244.
Victoria Embankment, 101.
Victoria Regia, 89, 120.
Virgins' bones, 192.
Visnau, 224.
Voltaire, 242, 244.
Vouache, Mont, 265.

Wacht am Rhein, 198.
Wales, 34.
Walter, John, 112.
Warwick Castle, 90.
Warwick, Earl of, 91.
Washerwomen, 238, 246.
Water of Leith, 68.
Waterloo, 188.
Watkins, Captain Frederick, 294.
Waverley Memorial, 68.
Wear River, 76.
Wellington's tomb, 96.
Welsh, John, 117.

Westminster Abbey, 96.
Westminster, Duke of, 32.
Wetterhorn, 224, 235.
Whitechapel, 285.
Wilson, Erasmus, 107.
Winkelreid, Arnold, 218.
Wisper River, 201.
Wood-carving, 229, 232.
Wolf's Crag, 75.
Wye River, 84.

Yonne River, 274.
York, 77.
York Castle, 78.
York Minster, 78.

Zahringen, Berthold, 236, 241.
Zoological Garden, London, 119.
Zoological Garden, Paris, 276.
Zug Lake, 224.
Zurich, 221, 223.

THE END.

www.ingramcontent.com/pod-product-compliance
Lightning Source LLC
Chambersburg PA
CBHW030306240426
43673CB00040B/1075